THE SHORT STORY AND PHOTOGRAPHY
1880's–1980's

THE

SHORT STORY

AND

PHOTOGRAPHY

1880's–1980's

A CRITICAL ANTHOLOGY

Edited by Jane M. Rabb

Foreword by Eugenia Parry

UNIVERSITY OF NEW MEXICO PRESS

ALBUQUERQUE

For my friends — some near, others far, all dear

"Friendship is a sheltering tree."

SAMUEL TAYLOR COLERIDGE

Copyright © 1998 by the University of New Mexico Press
All rights reserved.
FIRST EDITION

Library of Congress Cataloging-in-Publication Data
The short story and photography, 1880's–1980's ; a critical anthology /
edited by Jane M. Rabb. — 1st ed.
p. cm.
Includes bibliographical references.
ISBN 0-8263-1871-1 (pbk. : alk. paper)
1. Short stories. 2. Photography—Fiction. 3. Literature and
photography. 4. Photography in literature. 1. Rabb, Jane M.
(Jane Marjorie).
PN6120.95.P42S56 1998
808.83'108356—dc21   97-40355
                                                              CIP

CONTENTS

PREFACE

This anthology is, in some ways, the inevitable offspring of my larger one, *Literature and Photography: Interactions, 1840–1990* (1995). Some of the stories presented here were deemed too long to include in that collection, especially when other equally fine, representative, and shorter examples were available by the same artists (such as Faulkner or Updike) or were the work of writers (Daphne Du Maurier or Bing Xin) who were not otherwise as involved with photography as those selected. Still other stories I hadn't yet discovered, especially those suggested by Thomas Barrow, Marsha Bryant, and David Mattison (thanks to Elsa Dorfman), who himself once considered publishing a collection and generously shared his titles.

But even if the parent anthology never existed, this collection of short stories involving photography in some interesting and significant way would claim our attention for multiple reasons. It is also gratifying to know that it will help bridge the genre gap remaining since Alan Trachtenberg's and Vicki Goldberg's collections of essays on photography by often eminent writers and Mark Melnicove's anthology of poems that involve photography—which will be joined by one being compiled by Trudy Wilner Stack and Eleanor Wilner.[1] Naturally I hope that these short stories will engage the general reader as well as specialists and students in literature or photography.

This collection roughly spans a century, concluding with stories from the early 1980's. Since then, the number of short stories involving photography, especially those written by women, has dramatically increased. One can look forward to other collections of more contemporary short fiction involving photographs or photographers, such as the recent one by Barry Munger;[2] and perhaps news or journalistic photography, a subject still rarely treated, will feature more prominently as our evolving media require even more visual materials. These stories, like many of their predecessors, are usually listed in the *Short Story Index* (New York: H. W. Wilson, 1951 and annually thereafter), which David Mattison first called to my attention.

The short story was a literary form long before photography's birth in 1839. Interestingly, "the bastard stepchild of literature," as Raymond Carver once called the short story,[3] was only recognized as a serious genre with its own traditions and rules around the same time. Surely it is relevant that many of these nineteenth-century masters who elevated short fiction were fascinated by Daguerre's new invention, some even becoming serious photographers themselves. For example, credit for the short story's reinvention during the 1830's and 1840's is generally given to Edgar Allan Poe, who was among the earliest writers enthusiastic about photography.[4] Short fiction, previously devoted to a sequence of actions, subsequently focused—somewhat like a camera lens—on a single effect, a "slice of life," or the psychology of one or more characters.[5] At the turn of the century, many of the writers who excelled in this genre continued to be those with a serious interest in photography such as Arthur Conan Doyle, himself a passionate amateur photographer; his brother-in-law E. W. Hornung, whose fiction suggests his own engagement with the camera; and Thomas Hardy, who often used real or imagined pictures in his fiction and poetry. Even Thomas Mann, who displayed no interest in photography at the time of writing the story included here, later fell under its spell. All helped to make short fiction as respectable as the novel and (aside from the young Mann) photography more respectable as a sister art.[6]

During the twentieth century, the short story also became popular among some of the most stimulating and worldly European and Latin American writers. Many of those who kept reinvigorating the genre also brought a keen interest in photography. Italo Calvino (born in Cuba, raised in Italy, and later resident in Paris) and Eugène Ionesco (raised in Romania before moving to Paris) used photography in a significant way mainly in their stories reprinted here. But Julio Cortázar (born in Brussels and raised in Argentina before moving to Paris) published his own photographs while experimenting with narrative perspectives; and the more traditional French writer Michel Tournier has contributed as much to photography as to literature.[7]

In this century's final quarter, many writers continue to regard the form as more suitable to depict aspects of their ever-fragmenting age than longer fiction, which requires more coherence. (Many artists and their audiences value a photograph over a movie for the same reason.) Carver, for example, was "hooked on writing short stories," doubtless because they best suited his minimalist narratives.[8] The same genre still provides a suitable vehicle for the intense domestic dramas and polished style of John Updike, who has long appreciated its ability to provide "a glimpse into another country, an occasion for surprise, an excuse for wisdom, and an argument for charity."[9] Others, like Cynthia Ozick, have secured more recognition for their short stories, which more succinctly dramatize complex ideas, than for their other writing.

Some maintain that ours is a golden age of the short story.[10] Certainly the same period has also been relatively "golden" for photography. Both art forms have secured aesthetic respectability while treading roughly parallel paths from objective narrative to idiosyncratic statement (and for some shared reasons). It would be asking too much of our stories to represent adequately the complex histories of both kinds of art. Of our authors included here, only Cortázar, Updike, and Tournier have taken the camera seriously enough to accompany some of their writing with their own photographs—and then only sporadically. And none of our selections appears to have been inspired by any notable photograph. But the stories do suggest some of the ways that significant literary figures have presented aspects of photography over a century and a half, which doubtless reflected— and may have influenced—their audiences' perceptions of it.

These fictions also suggest some of the complexity and variety of the writer's focus—and hence the audience responses. For example, Hornung, Calvino, Du Maurier, Cortázar, Carver, Tournier, and Ozick explore both photographers and their pictures. Doyle, Hardy, Mann, Faulkner, Bing Xin, and Ionesco place the photograph at the center of their plots— whether mysteries, romances, tragedies, or hybrids—while Updike and Ozick are far more interested in exploring the psychology of the photographer and his subjects. The stories of Kipling and Davenport employ past and present beliefs about the camera, albeit very differently. The resulting associations with photography range widely, including the sentimental (Hornung, Bing Xin, Doyle, Updike), the tawdry (Mann), the obsessive (Calvino), the tragic (Hardy, Faulkner), the sinister (Ionesco, Cortázar, Carver), and even the fatal (Kipling, Du Maurier, Tournier, Ozick). For most of these writers, photography, supposedly the most realistic of the arts, turns out to be among the most ambiguous.

The capacity of photography for both documentary reality and moral and psychological ambiguity may explain why so many of our stories involve mysteries. Doyle creates what became the classic form of the detective mystery, though the one included here proves to be the only one Sherlock Holmes cannot solve. Faulkner, Ionesco, and Cortázar provide no detectives to make sense of their complicated narratives; their readers must figure out for themselves, sometimes helped by the description of the photographs, just what is happening. Some of our earlier authors, such as Hornung, Hardy, Mann, and Du Maurier, and even some later ones like Tournier here do compose linear plots with conclusive endings—whether happy or tragic—which many now consider "old-fashioned." But more contemporary writers apparently prefer shifting perspectives and inconclusive endings, which reflect the profound moral and ethical uncertainties rampant throughout the world since—and partly owing to—the birth of photography.

NOTES

1. See Vicki Goldberg, ed., *Photography in Print: Writings from 1816 to the Present* (New York: Touchstone/Simon & Schuster, 1981), reprinted without photographs (Albuquerque: University of New Mexico Press, 1989); Alan Trachtenberg, ed., *Classic Essays on Photography* (New Haven, Conn.: Leete's Island Books, 1980); and Mark Melnicove, ed., *Poets on Photography* (So. Harpswell, Me.: Dog Ear Press, 1981). The working title of the collection being compiled by Trudy Wilner Stack, the curator of the Center for Creative Photography at the University of Arizona in Tucson, and her mother, Eleanor Wilner, a poet and a recent MacArthur Fellow, is *Here and Never: Poets on Photography*.

2. See Barry Munger, ed., *Caught in the Act: The Photographer in Contemporary Fiction* ([New York]: Timken Publishers [1996]), whose collection of ten short stories includes the ones appearing here by Calvino, Cortázar, and Ozick.

3. Carver, quoted in Robert Pope and Lisa McElhinny, "Raymond Carver Speaking" (1982) in *Conversations with Raymond Carver*, edited by Marshall Bruce Gentry and William L. Stull (Jackson: University Press of Mississippi, 1990), p. 11.

4. See Jane M. Rabb, ed., *Literature and Photography, Interactions 1840–1990* (Albuquerque: University of New Mexico Press, 1995), pp. 3-5.

5. See William Carlos Williams, *A Beginning on the Short Story [Notes]* (Yonkers, N.Y.: Alicat Bookshop Press, 1950), pp. 1, 7, 16, and Peter Prescott, ed., Introduction to *The Norton Book of American Short Stories* (New York: Norton, 1988), p. 13.

6. See Rabb, *Literature and Photography*, pp. 206-7, 226-31, and 238-42, and Walter Allan, *The Short Story in English* (Oxford: Clarendon Press/Oxford University Press, 1981), p. 76.

7. See Rabb, *Literature and Photography*, pp. 461-65.

8. Carver, "On Where I'm Calling From," *No Heroics Please* (New York: Vintage, 1992), p. 121.

9. Updike, "The Short Story Today," Introduction to *The Best American Short Stories* (Boston: Houghton Mifflin, 1984), reprinted in Robert M. Luscher, *John Updike: A Study of the Short Fiction* (New York: Wayne [1993]), p. 182.

10. For example, Carver, in *No Heroics Please*, p. 171, declared there was a "real renaissance in the short story going on" before his death in 1988, and Prescott, in his Introduction to *The Norton Book of American Short Stories*, p. 19, suggests that the present period may well be the genre's "golden age."

I'VE GOT YOU NOW

Eugenia Parry

How many people, after deciding to commit suicide,
have been satisfied with tearing up their photograph!

JULES RENARD[1]

Fiction writing about photographs can be sinister and strange. In this collection camera pictures turn up. Like a worrisome mole on the skin, a bad-news telegram, a vicious letter unsent. Somebody's evidence, they're weapons. Tear up a photograph of yourself and you can believe you're as good as dead, Renard noted in his journal. He understood the power of photographs to make us believe the impossible, how they become magical insurance against future calumnies, useful for extracting gold ransoms. When Conan Doyle announces, "She threatens to send the photograph," it's a mallet to the head. Call in the authorities. Hire a detective.[2]

"He took with him Judith's picture in a metal case that closed like a book and locked with a key," Faulkner observes. No one complained about the loss. The purloined keepsake is an emblem of family knots. Have ghost for you, a photograph might whisper. One look. The blood drains from your face. You double-lock the doors. But the intruder is already inside the house.

An Ionesco character displays snapshots of "a colonel" to entrap the curious so he can drown them in a fountain. Dozens of victims. Deplorable, of course. But the agent of this perfidy, puny and ill-shaven in a shabby overcoat, stands like a camera staring "with his one eye" which has "the same steely glitter" as the blade in his hand. What use are pistols "against the boundless energy of that absolute cruelty?"

Photography's archaic truths have the power to ruin lives in ways more alarming than maniacal stabbing or drowning. Misread pictures can make fools of people who, by turn, find others to torture. Hardy has a father

xiii

decide his child resembles the dead poet in a photograph his "imaginative" wife kept among her treasures. "What sly animals women are!" The would-be cuckold clings to his confusion. Addressing his alien offspring, he howls: "Get away, you poor little brat! You are nothing to me!"

Misreadings and willed ignorance enhance the clouded atmosphere of photographic stories. Most fiction writers don't care about getting the history of photography right. Like Ozick, they may love "anything brown and brittle and old and decaying at the edges." As for history, she exclaims, "What an annoyance that so blatant a thing as picture-taking is considered worth applying a history to!" Mentioning real photographers, Tournier concocts surrealistic repartee:

"Brassaï, why the umbrella?"

"It's an obsession. It came over me the day I gave up smoking."

Davenport contrives the invention of the medium in some impossible city where Indians troop in for their portraits, thinking it was "the only interesting thing the white man had come up with in all these years." He invents the back of van Gogh's red head photographed in black and white, contemplates the one hundred freckles on the artist's cheeks, reported by a classmate, "who survived to a great age." He imagines historians of photography dropping everything to devote the rest of their lives to "getting a clear picture of the Loch Ness Monster." The creature appears with "a long wet nose and lifted lip, an expressionless reptilian eye, and a gleaming flipper." Its image is published upside down with the caption: "Archduke Franz Ferdinand arriving in Sarajevo for a visit of state."

The chaos resulting from the wonderfully literal is chilling when writers contemplate photographic optics and chemistry. Spurious nineteenth-century science claimed not only that the eye was a camera but that the human retina was a light-sensitive plate which retained for hours after death the last thing a person saw. Kipling sets this fascination in apoplectic heat with lonely military men in India. "There are very many places in the East where it is not good or kind to let your acquaintances drop out of sight even for one short week."

Dropping "out of sight" is the crux. "No darkroom trickery [is] equivalent to the elastic tolerance of our eyes," observes Updike. The corpse's eye is a dead-letter describing the indelible aggressor. But who? "Powers of darkness me molest!" Kipling cries. The retina has only to be peeled off in the dissection theater and examined under magnification to learn the truth.[3]

Other writers dispense with the camera box in order to reconfigure photographic procedures into a narcissistic philosophy of the grotesque. Tournier's character called Veronica, for the saint whose veil touched the face of the Man of Sorrows and forever carried his image on it, practices "*Dermatography*" on her boyfriend. After dipping him in corrosive chemicals she has him lie on light-sensitive paper which permanently fixes his form. Hector's lesions "resembled the professional skin diseases to be found in tanners, dry-salters, and engravers." Veronica ends up quite literally "having his hide."

Hector is a modern version of Hornung's classic "spoilt negative," a comedy of camera blunders which annoy a pretty girl but aid her love-struck suitor in his proposal of marriage. When the suitor, a photographic fashionable, double-exposes the adored idol with an image of a cow, "from the shapely head protruded two great horns—from the feet hung an unmistakable tail." Such foibles don't stop at levity. They lead straight to hallucination.

What Hornung called the "dirty tricks" of photographic alchemy Mann parades as immoral jokes. He has a self-righteous student stare in a shop window at a reproduction that has changed a painted Madonna into a photographic she-devil with "smoldering, dark-rimmed eyes" and "riddlingly smiling lips, . . . vice itself . . . —naked sensuality." The young man begs for its removal and is thought a prig. Prayer is useless in exorcising for him the ghastly contradiction.

Scrambling the facts, shadow play reveals what is "spiritistically" in back of every mind, as if it too were a negative plate, addled, plagued by accidents, barbs, and crossed meanings. But some writers turn the camera itself into a distortion of a monstrous clicking machine, guided by obsessives whose only goal is to cover the entire world with facsimiles. "One trick of the trade is a lot of takes," says Updike's guileless snapshooter. Calvino explores this taking as a philosophy of having and half-knowing. Photograph each fraction of a second, blade of grass, brick, journal page, grain of sand, ocean wave, beautiful woman—every tooth in the head of every beautiful woman. "You have stolen my image twenty-two thousand two-hundred-and-thirty-nine times," Calvino's heroine protests. Why not? Don't stop. "Everything . . . not photographed is lost, as if it had never existed." Then photograph the photographs to see what the already unreliable looks like.[4]

A snapshot—"I look so ridiculous!"—will be used to sum up love between Bing Xin's spinster and her female charge that ten years of life together failed to convey. Such pictures are necessarily incomplete. It's the source of their power to evoke what doesn't appear—ancient Chinese cities, courtyards, and rose trellises, which cause the woman to long to return to her adopted homeland. The picture was "photogenic" in surpassing the real object, not by showing its beauty but by creating it.

The world made photographically beautiful is rarely interesting to writers of photographic stories. Camera handlers are burglars of the visible, examiners of private dissatisfactions. To underscore the fact, many characters are drawn with ugly deformities. Updike gives even the *son* of a photographer a club foot. As for the camera artists themselves, Du Maurier creates a small, self-effacing Italian with a special orthopedic shoe and a limp. He wears an ugly grey coat. His eyes have a rapturous expression. He is called Mr. Paul. The sound of his name suggests the dark velvet cloth shrouding the instrument which fairly suffocates his sitter. The idle Marquise, flattered by his pictures, surrenders to his spell. She has to push him off a cliff to get rid of him.

Or consider Carver's photographer without any hands, using two metal hooks attached to his wrists to work a nasty old Polaroid lashed to his chest. Recording his subject, who climbs onto a roof and throws stones, won't be enough. The photographer must listen to the man's miserable confession. Through the cascade of stones and revelations comes the story.

To some writers, photographers are interchangeable with marginal investigators. The profession of Conan Doyle's freak-hero Sherlock Holmes consists of collecting fragment-clues and attaching them, uncannily, to motives. He is "the most perfect reasoning machine . . . the world has seen." Holmes has a melancholy intelligence. He sneers at love and plays the violin. His confidence is an attack—"You may see, but you do not observe." Cocaine sharpens his nerve: "A gentleman walks into my rooms smelling of iodoform, with a black mark of nitrate of silver on his right forefinger, and a bulge on the side of his top hat to show where he has secreted his stethoscope, I must be dull indeed if I do not pronounce him to be an active member of the medical profession."

"Perhaps true total photography . . . is a pile of fragments of private things, against the creased background of massacres and coronations," Cortázar ponders. Of these private fragments, Updike fixes on a mauled rabbit, dragged in by the cat, which inspires a photographer to record everything surrounding this brutal, natural event. After an entire day using his camera the snapshooter discovers he believes again in the virtues of family life. "The day of the dying rabbit . . . preserved us all."

"I kept her because she was dead," Ozick says of a photograph. She was "a rapturous hint on the other side of art. . . . Still I had her . . . because someone had once looked through the bunghole of a box and clicked off a lever.

. . . What happened then was here now. I had it in the pocket of my blouse."

Many writers compare photography to the short story as the extraction of a few simple truths "worth the trouble to stay and watch," as Cortázar puts it. Like taking photographs, writing requires the "duty to be attentive . . . waiting for everything to happen," shaping actions within a clear frame. Taking photographs is "an activity in which one should start becoming an adept very early . . . , teach it to children since it requires discipline, aesthetic education, a good eye. . . . I'm not talking about waylaying the lie like any old reporter," observes Cortázar's photographer, who feels compelled to give words to what led him to make his pictures. "I have to write. One of us all has to write if this is going to get told."

NOTES

1. Entry from November 1888. *The Journal of Jules Renard*, edited and translated by Louise Brogan and Elizabeth Roget (New York: George Braziller, 1964), p. 21.

2. "Handcarved Coffins, A Non-Fiction Account of an American Crime," in *Music for Chameleons: New Writing by Truman Capote* (New York: Random House, 1980), pp. 67–146, could not be included here since it reports an actual story, but it shares the dread of certain fictional renderings that place photographs at the center of a narrative. A murderer, never caught for killing ten people in a small western state, announces his victims' upcoming death by sending them a miniature hand-carved coffin, "undecorated . . . beautifully made" with a photograph of themselves inside," —a casual, candid snapshot. . . . It was not a posed picture; one sensed that the subjects were unaware that they were being photographed" (p. 69).

3. For a French scientific study systematically disproving the claims of Dr. Bourion, who believed in this phenomenon of persistent images and described it in a paper before the Société de Médecine Légale de Paris on December 13, 1869, see M. Vernois, "Applications de la Photographie à la Médecine Légale, Rapport sur une Communication de M. Le Docteur Bourion," in the *Bulletin de la Société de Médecine Légale de Paris* (Paris: J.-B. Baillière et Fils, 1869), t. 1, pp. 401–13. In the laboratory Vernois murdered, by poison or strangulation, some seventeen dogs and cats, holding before their eyes, during the agony of death, various objects, a ring, baton, bunch of keys, or pince-nez. On the surface of the victims' retinas "nothing" appeared, only "bizarre shadow forms" which one could only dream "imitated, more or less well, the appearance of men, animals, or plants" (p. 405). Vernois illustrates several retinas in two photographic reproductions. Kipling's story "At the End of the Passage," 1890, included here, precedes *L'Oeil du Mort*, a novel by Jules Claretie, who in 1897 was still attracted to the fantastic side of Dr. Bourion's claims, which appeared to all as careless science, if not wonderful fiction, not to mention the methods of his scientific detractors.

4. This is Italo Calvino's view in "The Adventures of a Photographer," 1955, included here. A story of comparable obsession is J. Michael Yates's "an inquest into the disappearance and possible death of (the late) Sono Nis, photographer," in *Man in the glass octopus* (Vancouver: Sono Nis Press, 1968), pp. 77–109. The hero X-rays himself so thoroughly that he is rendered sterile and threatened by death. Copying each existent photograph of himself and then continuously photographing and re-photographing all the photographs in his albums, then all the pages of his journal, then buying another Rollei camera to photograph himself loading and unloading the Rollei, "suggests the very paradigm of the consciousness he seeks" (p. 92). I am grateful to Siegfried Halus for making this story known to me.

A SPOILT NEGATIVE

1888

Hornung (1866–1921) combined his talent for writing, his interest in social conditions and crime, and his passion for cricket in his best-known stories, which featured a gentleman robber, Raffles, and his equally well born friend, Bunny. The amoral pair, admired by Graham Greene and analyzed by George Orwell, has been viewed as a kind of inversion of Sherlock Holmes and Dr. Watson, the heroes of the famous detective stories by Sir Arthur Conan Doyle.[1] Hornung met Doyle, then a doctor and an avid amateur photographer, when both were contributing to various London newspapers and journals in the early 1890's. They became friends, and then relatives, when Hornung married Doyle's sister Constance in 1893. This early story suggests that Hornung may have shared some of Doyle's photographic interests, though they are evident only occasionally elsewhere in his life and fiction, where they usually introduce romantic central characters.[2] He supplies a far more detailed account of late Victorian photographic equipment and processes in this lighthearted love story than did the fiction of his more knowledgeable future brother-in-law. Hornung's later mystery novel, The Camera Fiend *(1911), features a villain obsessed with spirit photography, an obsession Doyle also shared.[3]*

1. See Greene's play *The Return of A. J. Raffles* (London: Bodley Head; New York: Simon & Schuster, 1975), loosely based on Hornung's characters, and Orwell's essay "Raffles and Miss Blandish," *Horizon* 10, no. 58 (October 1944): 232–44, reprinted in *The Collected Essays, Journalism and Letters of George Orwell*, edited by Sonia Orwell and Ian Angus (London: Secker & Warburg, 1969), pp. 212–24. See also Friedrich Depken, *Sherlock Holmes, Raffles, and Their Prototypes* [1914], translated by Jay Finlay Christ ([Chicago]: Fanlight House, 1949), and Evan M. Wilson, "Sherlock Holmes and A. J. Raffles," *Baker Street Journal* 34, no. 3 (September 1984): 155–58, who dis-

cuss the antecedents and similarities of Doyle's Victorian detective and Hornung's Edwardian criminal.

2. Richard Lancelyn Green first called this story and the author's relationship to Doyle to the editor's attention. For other instances of Hornung's use of photography in his fiction, see *A Bride from the Bush* (New York: Scribner's, 1897), pp. 14–15, 226–28; *No Hero* (New York: Scribner's, 1903), pp. 8–9, 13, 15, 200; and *The Thousandth Woman* (Indianapolis: Bobbs-Merrill, 1913), pp. 14, 53, 62, 197–99.

3. In *The Camera Fiend* (New York: Scribner's, 1911), which Andrew Cahan called to the editor's attention, the villain fits a stereoscopic camera with a gun as well as film to catch human souls at the moment of their physical deaths, which he has caused. For more on Doyle's interest in spirit photography, see the preface to his story below and Rabb, *Literature and Photography*, pp. 226–31. One wonders to what extent Hornung's attitude might have affected his relationship with Doyle, whose evolving interest in spiritualism he found "absurd and insulting to the dead," according to Richard Lancelyn Green in a letter to the editor of June 15, 1994. Julian Symons, *Portrait of an Artist: Conan Doyle* (London: Whizzard Press/Deutsch, 1979), pp. 116, reports that Doyle "communicated" with his dead brother-in-law, who, though a skeptic in life, reportedly said, "I am so glad to be here, Arthur, this is wonderful." Green asserts that Hornung "would have been appalled by the spurious communications which Doyle claimed came from him."

A SPOILT NEGATIVE

Dick Auburn was an artist: not a painter, nor a sculptor, nor a musician, nor, indeed, a devotee at the shrine of any Fine Art—yet an artist. He could draw no more than a baby; his genius was anything but histrionic; he was not even a man of letters—but he was an artist. On the other hand, he was no house-painter nor designer of ornamental friezes. Indeed, in his own opinion and in that of a few enthusiasts as bigoted as himself, Dick's Art *was* a Fine Art, and he wrote his Art with a capital—a length to which your most eminent decorator scarcely goes. Though confessedly an amateur at his craft, Dick was as conscientiously painstaking as the most earnest-minded professional, besides being the technical equal and the artistic superior of most professionals. When at work he was an artist first and a man afterwards: he was only once known to allow human infirmity to interfere with the mechanism of his Art. But since that one recorded slip made an episode in his life, I take it that the events connected therewith are the legitimate and indisputable property of the faithful historian.

Besides being an artist, Dick Auburn was also—in a secondary kind of way—a jolly, genial, good-looking, and perfectly eligible young fellow. He was blessed with a mercurial temperament, a gay humour (when untrammelled by artistic anxieties), and an independent income. Worldly possession, indeed, alone deterred him from enlisting in professional ranks, and led him into a determination to follow Art for its own sake, in sublime confidence that such a course must bring its own reward. When at work Dick wore professorial spectacles: at all other times he sported a smart-looking single eye-glass. The change thus wrought in his appearance was typical of the contrast between the light-hearted young blade and the anxious, care-ridden travailer in Art—a contrast which nobody who spent a day in Dick's company could fail to remark.

Every art demands an apprenticeship: Dick Auburn's Art was no exception to this rule. The first stage in Dick's apprenticeship was embodied in a course of lessons (thrown in with the necessary "plant") at a certain Palace of Art in Regent Street. The second stage entailed lonely hours spent in a cellar remote from solar beams, whence issued smells and vapours the most vile. Dick himself would follow these nasal invaders from the under-world, looking pale and careworn, and wearing on his hands the stains—not, indeed, of blood, but of some virulent chemical compound far less easy to expunge. The third and last of the elementary stages brought forth slanders in portraiture on all Dick's relations and many of his friends, not to speak of elliptical libels on such architectural accommodation as the neighbourhood afforded. But Dick rose superior to the very frank discouragement of coldly critical relatives and the sickening chill born of reiterated failure. In six months, thanks to stubborn effort and pliable purse, he became not only an ambitious but a highly accomplished amateur photographer.

But to come to Dick Auburn's one photographic blunder—for he persists that it is the only mistake of a gross kind he ever made, during the whole of his artistic experience: at any rate it is the only one of which (to speak very literally) positive evidence has been preserved.—There stands on the Middlesex side, somewhere between Richmond and Hampton Court, quite the most charming villa, for its size, that can be found anywhere on either bank of the Thames. It is built of red brick and is a modern version of Gothic architecture, with quaint little points and acute angles: it is surrounded by majestic cedars, which in the sleepy noontide are synonyms for shade and shelter and rest: a lawn of close-cropped, velvety grass slopes gently from the French windows to the river's brim, picked out with brilliant flower-beds: and the villa and its grounds are the property of Major Irvine, Dick's uncle, who spends there each summer, surrounded by a small but festive party of young people.

Thither in August came our artist, with camera, lens, tripod, and the hundred and one accessories which make up a photographer's impedimenta. He had been at "his dirty tricks" (as Jack Irvine delighted in stigmatising the artistic processes) for a year by this time, and could take a more or less instantaneous picture with more than tolerable precision and certainty; and he had determined to immortalise in his album every weir, lock, reach, and island of Father Thames ere September drove him north again. But though the amateur loves best bold landscape effects for his lens, fate and his familiar friends so rule it that groups—portrait groups—almost invariably obtain an undesirable precedence. For in the matter of groups it does seem that the amateur photographer's lot is—to use the mildest phrase—a thankless one. He either flatters his friends, and achieves thereby a certain ephemeral popularity—which is, at best, cheap; or he does *not* flatter them, in which case he is covered with unmerited odium—under any circumstances extremely nasty.

Dick hated taking groups. When he had hooded himself in the velvet focussing-cloth, and wore the professorial spectacles and the preoccupied, artistic air—when he stood, watch in hand, waiting to take the cap off the lens—it irked him not a little that Jack Irvine must needs seize the opportunity to play the common buffoon. It is well known that no nerves are so easily excited as the collective risible nerves of a group posed before the camera; under such circumstances any idiot can evoke roars of laughter from a group of usually sane persons, and that with the most contemptible apology for a joke. Poor Dick would join feebly in the laugh that stayed his hand on the very brink of "exposure," but it jarred terribly upon his artistic temper. Though none could be more frivolous than he—when photography was not in question—he felt frivolity on such occasions to be not only out of place but a degradation to both Art and artist. He would have dearly loved to tell Jack, in good nervous English, what he thought of him; but the presence of the girls precluded even that spice of satisfaction, and it seemed too trifling a matter to mention in cold blood afterwards, over their pipes. Dick excused himself from the uncongenial task on every plea: in the first place, his lens was only a landscape-lens, he said, and not well adapted to any other kind of photography; in the second place, groups were the most difficult things out, even with a proper lens. But no: groups only, and plenty of them, were insisted on, and by dint of coercion obtained. Groups at tennis, groups at tea, groups in the boat, fancy-dress groups, groups *en tableau*, groups at every hour and in every costume. If the party chanced to be dull, or tired, or from other causes unequal to the task of amusing each other, Dick was called upon to administer his infallible panacea—somebody, of course, coming down with a handsome suggestion for a new and original pose.

On the other hand Dick objected less to taking single portraits. To take a single portrait he would "lead his victim" (as that ass Jack said) "to a lonely place," where, however, after the most elaborate selection and arrangement of light, shade, background, and pose, a successful negative— if not a satisfactory portrait; who is ever satisfied with his portrait?—was generally obtained.

But one there was whom Dick's artistic soul coveted—as a model; one who turned a deaf ear to the voice of his solicitations, charmed he never so wisely. And that was his cousin May's schoolfellow, Elsie Keswicke. She was the worst offender in every group: she was an intolerable tease during the progress of the important after-processes of developing, printing, and toning; and it was she alone who dared to clap a tiny pink palm over the aperture of the lens while he was focussing, causing thereby total eclipse of the inverted image on the ground glass. Of course, she systematically "came out" as badly as possible—that was but a part of her policy of exasperation. And yet it is a solemn fact that, from the very first, Dick would have exchanged his complete apparatus for the gratification of obtaining one good negative of Elsie Keswicke. True, the artistic ambition which first led his aspirations in this direction began, after a week or two, to be gradually pushed from its position of chief motor by an even stronger influence. But Dick was unaware of this merely psychological detail: he only knew that he desired above all other things to photograph Elsie Keswicke.

One fine morning—somehow they were *all* fine mornings that August, when Dick would have liked nothing better than a little wet weather, bringing with it respite from purgatorial hack-photography—a venerable-looking gentleman waited on Dick with an anxious yet insinuating smile, and a request couched in deferential terms. Name was Partridge. Had been an acquaintance and neighbour of the Major's those nineteen years. Was an old colonist; also a fancier and breeder of cattle—quite a hobby with him, that. Had heard the young gentleman took wonderful photographs. Would he—as a favour, and if it was not asking *too* much, and taking *too* great a liberty—would he mind taking just one picture of a remarkably beautiful Alderney cow and calf? If the young gentleman would do an old fellow such a kindness—though, to be sure, it would prove a picture worth having—would he come over then and there, as they (cow and calf) had just been sold and were about to be taken away?

Now Dick had not the smallest inclination to add to his collection a study of an Alderney cow and calf. But there was just this in it; he would rather take a whole herd of cows, and calves, than another group; and whispered suggestions for another group were already afloat in the morning air. So he assented to the cattle-fancier's request, and went at once to get the apparatus. As he fitted his camera into the leather sling-case, he could not help regarding the inoffensive Honduras and brass and leather with an expression of gloomy mistrust. A morbid feeling came over him that after all it was the destiny of himself and that mahogany thing to rise to nothing better than perpetuators of grotesque buffoonery. To-day, certainly, it was bovine beauty for a change; but what was there in that to satisfy ambition—to even mitigate disgust at the whole thing?

"So Dick has gone over to old Partridge's, and left word he won't be back for some time," said Jack. "The old sinner! That was such a stunning idea we had for a photo up at Hampton Court—wasn't it, May?"

"Rather!" returned May. "I wonder what the maze man would have thought of it—of course we would have had him in it! But we must insist on it another day. However, there is no reason why we shouldn't row up there as we had planned, even if we don't have a photograph. Eh, Jack?"

"None whatever. It will serve old Dick right for leaving us in the lurch. You coming, Nell?"

"Me!" cried Nell the youngest; "should think I am. Did anyone ever know *me* refuse a row?"

"Then there's Elsie," Jack continued. "She's over here in the hammock. Of course you'll come, Elsie?—River—Hampton Court—now."

Elsie opened her hazel eyes just wide enough to distinguish Jack's blazer through the network of her long dark lashes. "Of course nothing of the kind! Dear me, how we do take things for granted this morning! You know very well I have a headache, and that the sun makes anyone's headache worse. I don't intend to stir from this hammock or leave this dear old cedar for *hours*."

Jack went over and told May, adding *sotto voce* that he didn't believe a word about the headache. May declared she would not dream of going on the river and leaving Elsie all alone behind. Whereupon Miss Keswicke vowed that if she (May) dared to stay at home, she (Miss Keswicke) would go straight to bed, and that was all about it. And as the latter young lady was known to possess a quite alarming "will of her own," May at last gave in, reluctantly and almost tearfully, and left her friend to the shade of the grand old cedar and the lotos-like luxury of the hammock.

Half an hour later back came Dick from old Partridge's, and deposited the camera-case and telescopic tripod on the lawn. Then he complacently filled and lit a pipe, and made up his mind to develop the negative he had just taken in a thoroughly scientific manner, now that he was sure of peace for an hour or two. He went into the house, and presently returned with a heavy, unwieldy tripod, which plainly belonged to no camera. This he set up with care before bringing out a curious square box, which he fixed to the triangle at the top of the tripod by means of a screw and nut. Dick next put his hand through a small square opening which had the appearance of a miniature window, undid a couple of bolts within, and lifted off bodily one of the sides of the box. He then took up a roll of dark yellow cloth and shook it out displaying a piece of the size of a large travelling-rug, with a square opening three feet wide in the centre. The edges of the opening in the cloth he fastened with spring clamps to the edges of the open side of the box, from the top of which it hung like a curtain over the open side. Dick now inserted a ruby-coloured glass slide in the small window-like opening; and finally he held up the curtain, thrust head and shoulders into the box, wrapped the curtain closely round his body, and satisfied himself that not a ray of white light penetrated within. For this was what Dick called his "dark-tent"—the product of his own ingenuity of design and skill in carpentry. It fell short in convenience of the dark-room attached to his laboratory at home; it bore no sort of comparison with the very portable tents which the trade advertises; but it answered its purpose in shedding none other than a lurid light upon the occult alchemy of that veritable wizard, the photographer, whose deeds are in truth the deeds of darkness. Moreover, this somewhat clumsy contrivance possessed one advantage which Dick believed to be unique, and which certainly is not possessed by any photographic dark-tent yet placed before the public.

Dick had made all ready for the important process technically known as "development"; he had carried scales and weights, graduated measures, and stoppered bottles from the house, and had placed them, together with ebonite trays and a jug of water, in readiness in the tent; he had even set some queer, crystalline stuff to dissolve in a tray half filled with water, and it was just as he was going to take from the camera-case the dark slide containing the embryo negative of Mr. Partridge's cow and calf, that his eye caught a glimpse of delicate pink on the farther side of the old cedar at the other end of the lawn. He paused for a moment, stooping over the case; then, scarcely raising the upper portion of his body, he crept towards the tree with a feline stealth of which he would have stoutly denied he was capable—unless, indeed, some sprite had seethed him in his own craft and presented the photographer with his own instantaneous likeness, literally taken in the act! As he drew near the cedar he described a wide circle, and at last drew breath behind a propitious laurel some ten paces from the tree. And then it was that a dream of loveliness broke upon the artist's eyes!

There, in a light hammock of network—there, all plastic curves and softened outline, lay his coveted model, asleep! She lay robed in palest pink that seemed to his kindled fancy, against the deep shades of the tree, like the first wan streak of dawn over treeless plains. The gold-brown hair that crowned her pale, fair face showed like amber filigree against one white hand beneath her head; the other hand hung lightly over the hammock's side. Long lashes fringed each cool cheek beneath the closed eyelids; red lips, just parted in a smile that had been checked by slumber in its dawning, displayed one gleaming flake of white between.

Indefinite ideas took still more indefinite shape in Dick's brain. Swiftly and incoherently he thought of the Dryads in their wooded bowers; of "beautiful brow'd Ænone" amid the vales and vines of Ida; of the Fairy Queen on her bank of wild thyme; Wood-nymph, river-nymph, Fairy Queen—all faded into meagre mediocrity beside the inexpressible loveliness here. This was no exquisite vision, no conjured fancy, but an enchanting reality that a man's eye—an artist's eye—ah! the hour he had yearned for had come at last! A moment longer the man knelt chained to the spot; the next, the artist stole back across the lawn as noiselessly as he had approached.

Now I do not say that Elsie had never been asleep at all (to hint half as much would be to destroy Dick's most cherished illusion), but this much is certain: no sooner had Dick slunk fairly away than the hazel eyes half opened, and the smooth face rippled over with silent mirth. Nevertheless, when, three minutes later, he sneaked back to the shelter of the kindly laurel, there seemed to him no greater change in the pose and expression of his slumbering wood-nymph than takes place in sculptured marble. He little knew that the wood-nymph was now, at any rate, acutely conscious of all that was taking place, and had determined on a subtly sweet revenge.

He placed the tripod just behind the bush, with the camera at such a height that the lens peeped inconspicuously over the dark green leaves. How his heart beat as he plunged his head beneath the velvet cloth! And then—was there ever so divine an image on focussing-glass before? Was there ever before such good reason to sit down and weep because the tints on the ground glass could not, in this era of half-fledged science, be transmitted to the negative? The image was inverted by refraction, of course, but to the practised eye that mattered nothing; besides (as Jack flippantly observed when Dick made a clean breast of the whole affair to him), it couldn't have mattered in any case, seeing that Dick himself at the time didn't know whether he was standing on his head or on his heels.

The focussing was over, the cap was in readiness on the lens; Dick drew from beneath his coat, very gingerly, a shallow mahogany arrangement containing one sensitive dry-plate on each side, completely protected from the light by tightly-fitting slides. One plate had already done duty at Mr. Partridge's; the other was destined—ha! did she move? Dick slid in the mahogany arrangement, quickly but carefully drew out the inner slide, thus exposing the plate to the lens, took off the cap for half a second, and—the photograph was taken!

He crept in stealthy triumph from the scene of the deed, taking everything with him, and feeling like a successful burglar escaping with his swag. At last, at last! The yearned-for photograph had been taken at last! All that remained to be done was to develop the negative (he would do it at once in the tent), and to print the picture that should never, never fade (that must be done secretly).

Dick was on the point of finally thrusting head, shoulders, and arms into the black box, and swathing his body in the hanging cloth and thus effecting an ostrich-like concealment of his upper man, when a light footstep behind him sent his heart into his mouth, and caused him to start and turn like a thief at bay. And as he found himself face to face with Elsie Keswicke, he not only felt but looked like the guiltiest wretch unhanged!

Elsie greeted him with a chill little smile, half severity, half self-restraint, as if she wanted to laugh very badly indeed. A gleam of merriment—though he was not in a condition to perceive it—lurked in her hazel eyes as she said scornfully:

"Up to your 'dirty tricks' again—eh, Mr. Auburn?"

"Well, I—I—" stammered Dick—"I've been taking a photo; that's all. But—but I thought you were on the river, Miss Keswicke?"

"*Did* you!" replied Miss Keswicke, and there was something in her tone which sent Dick's heart down from his mouth into his tennis-shoes.

An awkward pause followed, during which Dick played nervously with a corner of the curtain.

"Tell me what you have been taking," said Elsie presently in a friendly, interested tone, which at any other time would have launched Dick into an exultant, enthusiastic exposition.

"Oh, you know, I've been taking a cow—an Alderney cow—oh, and a calf too, by-the-by—for a friend of—"

"Ah!" interrupted Miss Keswicke chillingly. "But you have been taking a photograph just now! The camera didn't come from Mr. Partridge's *on its legs*, you know," pointing to the tripod; "moreover, I can see the dark slide in it still. What is the photo of—or perhaps I should say *whom* have you taken?"

What a fool he had been not to put away the camera at once! Here was direct evidence that a photograph was newly taken—she might want to see the negative next! Dick shifted nervously from one foot to the other, and then she understood him to reply, though he mumbled the words rather indistinctly:

"It's a view."

"Really you are very vague! I can see you don't want to be bothered with me, so I shall go. And it is the last time ever I shall show curiosity about your odious, contemptible Art, as you call it. Be quite sure of that."

She managed the tone of pique with such elocutionary perfection, and finished so near to a whimper as she turned away, that it was more than poor Dick could stand. He sprang forward, and, with a sudden access of reckless foolhardiness, took her hand in his.

"Don't go," he cried excitedly; "please don't go, Miss Keswicke! Stop and see me develop these negatives. I want you to see them particularly— I do indeed."

Elsie withdrew her hand; but she looked unresentingly and with an assumed frankness straight into Dick's honest, spectacled eyes—for they did wear an honest expression now that he had determined to have the worst out. A wicked triumph thrilled the girl's heart. She breathed the first sweet incense of Revenge already!

"I can't see you develop through that horrid red glass," she answered, pouting.

"But suppose I fix the thing up so that you *can* see—will you let me show you how to develop a negative then?"

"I may," dubiously.

"Then hold on a minute!" And he dashed eagerly into the house.

When he was out of sight and hearing, Elsie laughed gaily to herself. Here was promise of quite a delightful little game of cross-purposes! Dick had photographed her while (as he thought) she was unconscious; and now he was going to develop the negative before her eyes, doubtless intending it as a huge surprise, if not actually to lead up to—well, never mind to what. For her part, she had resolved to let him know that it was no surprise: to smash his negative—nip in the bud the sequel he had in view— and leave him heaped with contumely and utterly annihilated! So much for her scheme of just vengeance. But Elsie had yet another end in view— an end she would scarcely have owned to herself; and that was, to find out whether Dick really cared for her—whether, after all, it was not simply his so-called Art that he was in love with! In either case he should find himself only very much the worse off for the mean advantage he had dared to take!

Dick came back carrying a dark yellow curtain with a square hole in the middle, exactly like that which already formed a part of the "dark-tent." Without a word he took off the side of the black box opposite to the already open side, and fastened the second curtain in precisely the same manner as the first: so that there was a clear passage through the box but for the curtains which fell over each open side.

"There! That's my own patent," said Dick, with jealous pride, "my very own! I made it up at home, so that Flo (that's my sister) could help in the developing when we went trips with the camera, just as she did in the permanent dark-room at home. It's the only double-dark-tent in the world!— You'll be Flo, while I develop these two negatives, won't you? It will only take a minute or two; and, you know, you almost promised just now."

Elsie looked up at the windows: the Major had gone up to town for the day, and not a soul appeared to be about. The church clock in the village was striking twelve: May and Nell and Jack would not be back from Hampton Court for at least an hour. Where was the harm—when it was all for Revenge?

"Yes," she said, half defiantly, "I'll be Flo for a minute or two."

Not a ray of white light came in from without. A warm ruby glow suffused everything in the "tent," bathing faces and hands in deep crimson, as though they had been dipped in liquid sunset. It was well that it was so, for it became of no consequence whether Elsie blushed or paled. And after all, it was rather an embarrassing position—to be alone with Dick Auburn in this little hole, *tête-à-tête* across three feet of deal! But it was only for a minute—and for Revenge!

"Be quick," she said to Dick; "I shall be stifled if I stay many seconds. Then I shall have to wriggle out, and the light will come in and spoil everything."

"Now promise me that you will do nothing of the kind, that you will not spoil my negatives—or I shan't take 'em out of the slide at all," said the photographer firmly.

"Very well—I promise," said Elsie. In her heart she was mortified that Dick should contemplate her possible flight only as so much damage to his wretched plates; she set her teeth and inwardly vowed to smash the negative—so soon as it should be nicely finished—into atoms!

Dick looked lingeringly at the bewitching crimson face before him. He would have preferred talking with his wood-nymph to manipulating dry-plates; saying a certain something—which must out at all hazards during the next ten minutes—to plunging his fingers into his beloved chemicals.

"Go on," said Elsie inexorably.

Dick took up a bottle, poured an ounce into a graduated measure, and added an equal quantity from another bottle.

"This is the developer," he began didactically. "It contains pyrogallic acid, ammonia, bromide of—"

"Oh, never mind the names of the chemicals. Let me see the plate."

The artist opened the dark-slide, and drew out a piece of glass coated on one side with a thin film. In the red glow it looked like a slice of ruby marble.

"Why, Mr. Auburn," cried Elsie, surprised out of herself, "where's the photograph?"

"It don't make its appearance until I charm it with this philter," said Dick, laying the plate in an ebonite oblong tray, and pouring over it the solution he had just mixed. "You will see something on the plate directly," he continued, rocking the tray so that the fluid spread in even waves over the sensitive film.

"Which photograph is this?"

"The cow, I think. I can't say for certain. But—but please, don't speak to me for a minute or two, Elsie," said Dick in his artist's anxious tone, bending the professorial spectacles close to the exciting tray, insensible alike to ammonia fumes and to the fact that he had called Elsie by her Christian name for the first time in his life.

"Only one more question then—how long will it be before we see anything on the plate?"

"Half an hour—that is, I mean half a minute," Dick replied abstractedly. But even as he spoke he felt a shudder of dread pass down his spinal column like lightning down a conductor!

The cogent solution had immersed the plate already for half a minute, but not the faintest suspicion of outline or detail appeared. A minute—a minute and a half—two minutes passed, in terrible suspense for Dick: still nothing was to be seen on the virgin pink of the film. Dick mixed a fresh developing solution, and applied it after pouring off the old one. Still no sign of incipient development. Something might have gone wrong with either plate or chemicals—but there was a more probable and a much more serious hypothesis. After about five minutes Elsie spoke:

"I thought you had taken a photograph? If you have, you have utterly failed, for once in a way. I don't think you can be much of a photographer after all. Now try the other one."

"Oh! Elsie, I dare not."

"Dare not! Why dare not?"

"Because—because it is of—"

"Of what?"

"Of you!"

Elsie's eyes flashed indignation at the unhappy photographer.

"So," she began, "you dared to tell me it was a view—"

"A *view* and *of you* sound so abominably alike, you see. I answered you honestly enough, only you misunderstood me." Dick made an ineffectual attempt to turn it off lightly.

"Of me! Yes, I have known it all along! Then develop it at once, Mr. Auburn—it is the least you can do after such an astounding impertinence!" Her voice was cold and hard, as if she meant every word she uttered; and her eyes gleamed cruelly, like fiery coals in the crimson glow.

"Oh, blessed ruby light, granting colour to Dick's bloodless cheeks!

"Dearest—" he began, in an agony, trying to catch her hand in his.

She snatched her hand away, but looked him full in the face. "How *dare* you? You think you'll drive me from the tent by insulting me! But I stir not an inch until you have developed the other plate. Begin this instant."

Dick looked at her helplessly. Ah, if she could only know what she was about to bring down on them both! Dick saw certain shipwreck staring him in the face. Yet she drove him relentlessly onward!

"Begin at once," she repeated mercilessly.

There was no help for it. Dick bent over the slide and took out the other plate with shaking hand; his forehead was bathed in perspiration; his heart rapped loudly, as if seeking exit from his miserable carcase. And as he bent fumbling with the plate, Elsie smiled a wicked little smile of triumph. Yet her smile quickly ended in a puzzled expression; for—it suddenly struck her—why should he be so afraid of letting her see the negative? But the answer came almost as spontaneously: of course, he divined her intention of smashing the plate, and was heart-broken at the prospect of losing his ill-gotten sun-picture! Poor fellow—poor Dick! There was really some little tiny reason to pity him after all—and he had called her "dearest," too. But he should not have taken a mean advantage!

Dick laid the plate in the solution, and began rocking the tray mechanically. He knew that the worst would come in a few seconds now, and he determined to be cool at the last.

"So you dared to take me while I was asleep, did you?" said Miss Keswicke tauntingly. "Ah, here I come, face and dress first, black as coals, of course, and the hammock—Great Heavens! what have you dared—?" A natural aposiopesis ended the scream to which her voice had risen, for her breath was fairly taken away!

But Dick went on mechanically rocking the ebonite tray. For it was no worse than he had foreseen, and he might as well go through with it like a Briton. So he allowed every detail to be fully brought out—indeed, he had never exercised greater technical care with a negative in his life. He tried to forget that each detail in this one was a nail in the coffin of his new-born, yet darling, hopes! But he dared not look up, and it was as well that he was not over-bold. Elsie stood speechless, quivering with passion—a veritable Pythoness!

Most conspicuous on the plate, indeed, were Elsie's form and face—black as ink, of course, with the usual reversal of the lights. But from the shapely head protruded two great horns—from the feet hung an unmistakable tail—she was plainly supported on four cloven hoofs—her hand rested on the back of what appeared to be an ill-shapen black dog! Reader, have you ever witnessed dissolving views? And have you noted their appearance at the moment of dissolution, when the canvas is shared equally by the coming and the parting guest—when you see, maybe, Sir Christopher Wren's colossal face working its way through the dome of St. Paul's? The effect of Dick's unlucky negative was precisely the same as the effect of that view when dome and face were in mid conflict. The result was a literal and compact rendering of Beauty and the Beast. The enthusiast had committed the prime blunder in photography—he had taken two photographs on one plate!

"Monster!" Elsie managed to gasp at length. "Brute!"

"I couldn't help it," murmured Dick ruefully, and hardly truthfully, seeing that assuredly nobody else could have helped it.

"Couldn't help it" repeated Elsie in a low tone of withering scorn. "I wouldn't add falsehood to outrage, if I were you! Why not confess at once that you have played me a low, vulgar trick—a trick that no *gentleman* could play?"

"It wasn't a trick, it was an accident," said Dick doggedly.

"And I suppose it was by accident that you persuaded me to degrade myself by putting my head into this box, just to see myself made a f-fool of! Oh! it is the worst thing I ever heard of in my life!"

"You insisted I should develop it, when you saw I didn't want to," groaned the unlucky Dick. "Next thing," he thought, "I suppose she'll cry, and after that—why after that it's all *u, p.*"

"I meant to break the horrid thing in any case," continued Elsie, with a breaking voice; "but I shan't now. Oh dear, no. I shall keep it to show all the world what a—what an *apology for a gentleman* you are!" She seized the fatal piece of glass as she finished speaking; but a moment later it slipped from her nerveless fingers back into the ebonite tray, and she burst into a torrent of passionate sobs.

"Oh! Elsie," cried Dick, eagerly seizing both her hands, "can't you see it was all a confounded mistake?"

"N-n-o-o—it wasn't—you did it on purpose."

"I swear I did not!"

But Elsie struggled to free her hands from his grasp, and it was not in Dick to retain them by force. So he withdrew one of his hands, seized a measure full of filthy-looking yellow solution, raised it to his lips, and said solemnly:

"Elsie, if you persist in leaving me before I can say what I've meant all along to say, I'll drain every drop of this—this deadly poison!"

Then he put down the measure. Then, somehow, his hands relinquished hers altogether, and rested for a moment like epaulets on her soft red shoulders. Then, somehow, he leant forward and drew her to him over the three feet of glass and chemicals. Then—oh, blessed ruby light! What matters a blushing cheek in your crimson glow?

"Yes, darling," said Dick, as they packed away the apparatus. "We'll preserve the negative for ever and ever. It shall go down to posterity as an unbroken record!"

"Oh, Dick, I never heard you make a joke before!"

"How could I crack jokes when I was in love—"

"With your Art!"

"No, my Elsie, with you! And yet—oh! it was a shocking blunder!" added the artist with a sigh.

And when Jack asked how the "dirty tricks" had been getting on, Dick replied that "he had spoilt a negative." And so indeed he had—in more senses than one.

AT THE END OF THE PASSAGE

1890

Kipling (1865–1936) was born in Bombay and educated in England. After work-ing as a journalist in India from 1882 to 1889, he returned to England in 1890 as an acclaimed writer. His Indian experiences continued to inspire many of his finest early poems and short stories, such as this enigmatic classic about external threats to the human condition, which here prove fatal. Henry James heralded it as a "perfect little piece" whose "vivid picture" of place and atmosphere held far greater communicative value than a complex plot or characterization; Ernest Hemingway credited it as an influence on his own famous spare style; and, more than sixty years after its first appearance, Somerset Maugham judged it among Kipling's best work.[1] In the tale's problematic ending, Kipling draws on his own terrifying experience with optical delusions when exhausted but also on Eastern fears of the imperialist Western camera. He also dramatizes a contemporary be-lief that the human eye resembled a camera with film and that the retina of the dead retained the last image it viewed (such as, for example, the murderer poised to strike).[2] This quasi-supernatural idea was often used by writers of mysteries and other literary forms at the turn of the century,[3] but Kipling's story is doubt-less its most enduring embodiment.

1. See Henry James, Introduction to Kipling, *Mine Own People* (New York: Lovell, 1891), pp. vii–xxvi, esp. p. xxv; Elliott L. Gilbert, *The Good Kipling: Studies in the Short Story* ([Athens]: Ohio University Press [1970]), p. 42; and *Maugham's Choice of Kipling's Best* (Garden City, N.Y.: Doubleday, 1953). Bill Jay called this story and its interesting photographic conception to the editor's attention.

2. See Lord Birkenhead, *Rudyard Kipling* (New York: Random House, 1978), p. 25, who also notes that the story reflects the author's own mood of exhaustion at the time. See also Nancy Martha West, *Soft Murder by the Camera Eye: Photographic Fears*

and the Victorian Writer (Ann Arbor, Mich.: UMI Research Press, 1994), pp. 158–73; and Bill Jay, "Images in the Eyes of the Dead," *British Journal of Photography* 128 (January 30, 1981): 124–27, 132–35. See also Doyle, n. 4, below.

3. See Jay, cited above. In his discussion, Jay also notes that Kipling was inspired to write the stage version of his famous *Jungle Book* by the photographer H. H. Hay Cameron, a son of the Victorian photographer Julia Margaret Cameron; his mother's reputation was later revived by her grandniece Virginia Woolf in her introduction to Mrs. Cameron's *Victorian Photographs of Famous Men and Fair Women* (London: Hogarth Press; New York: Harcourt, Brace, 1926).

AT THE END OF THE PASSAGE

The sky is lead, and our faces are red,
And the Gates of Hell are opened and riven,
And the winds of Hell are loosened and driven,
And the dust flies up in the face of Heaven,
And the clouds come down in a fiery sheet,
Heavy to raise and hard to be borne.
And the soul of man is turned from his meat,
Turned from the trifles for which he has striven,
Sick in his body, and heavy-hearted,
And his soul flies up like the dust in the street,
Breaks from his flesh and is gone and departed
Like the blasts that they blow on the cholera-horn.

HIMALAYAN.

Four men, each entitled to "life, liberty, and the pursuit of happiness," sat at a table playing whist. The thermometer marked—for them—one hundred and one degrees of heat. The room was darkened till it was only just possible to distinguish the pips of the cards and the very white faces of the players. A tattered, rotten punkah of whitewashed calico was puddling the hot air and whining dolefully at each stroke. Outside lay gloom of a November day in London. There was neither sky, sun, nor horizon,—nothing but a brown-purple haze of heat. It was as though the earth was dying of apoplexy.

From time to time clouds of tawny dust rose from the ground without wind or warning, flung themselves tableclothwise among the tops of the parched trees, and came down again. Then a whirling dust-devil would scutter across the plain for a couple of miles, break, and fall outward, though there was nothing to check its flight save a long low line of piled railway-sleepers white with the dust, a cluster of huts made of mud, condemned rails, and canvas, and the one squat four-roomed bungalow that belonged to the assistant engineer in charge of a section of the Gaudhari State line then under construction.

The four, stripped to the thinnest of sleeping-suits, played whist crossly, with wranglings as to leads and returns. It was not the best kind of whist, but they had taken some trouble to arrive at it. Mottram of the Indian Survey had ridden thirty and railed one hundred miles from his lonely post in the desert since the night before; Lowndes of the Civil Service, on special duty in the Political Department, had come as far to escape for an instant the miserable intrigues of an impoverished Native State whose king alternately fawned and blustered for more money from the pitiful revenues contributed by hard-wrung peasants and despairing camel-breeders; Spurstow, the doctor of the line, had left a cholera-stricken camp of coolies to look at itself for forty-eight hours while he associated with white men once more. Hummil, the assistant engineer, was the host. He stood fast and received his friends thus every Sunday if they could come in. When one of them failed to appear, he would send a telegram to his last address, in order that he might know whether the defaulter were dead or alive. There are very many places in the East where it is not good or kind to let your acquaintances drop out of sight even for one short week.

The players were not conscious of any special regard for each other. They squabbled whenever they met; but they ardently desired to meet, as men without water desire to drink. They were lonely folk who understood the dread meaning of loneliness. They were all under thirty years of age,—which is too soon for any man to possess that knowledge.

"Pilsener?" said Spurstow, after the second rubber, mopping his forehead.

"Beer's out, I'm sorry to say, and there's hardly enough soda-water for to-night," said Hummil.

"What filthy bad management!" Spurstow snarled.

"Can't help it. I've written and wired; but the trains don't come through regularly yet. Last week the ice ran out,—as Lowndes knows."

"Glad I didn't come. I could ha' sent you some if I had known, though. Phew! it's too hot to go on playing bumble-puppy." This with a savage scowl at Lowndes, who only laughed. He was a hardened offender.

Mottram rose from the table and looked out of a chink in the shutters.

"What a sweet day!" said he.

The company yawned all together and betook themselves to an aimless investigation of all Hummil's possessions,—guns, tattered novels, saddlery, spurs, and the like. They had fingered them a score of times before, but there was really nothing else to do.

"Got anything fresh?" said Lowndes.

"Last week's *Gazette of India*, and a cutting from a Home paper. My father sent it out. It's rather amusing."

"One of those vestrymen that call 'emselves M.P.'s again, is it?" said Spurstow, who read his newspapers when he could get them.

"Yes. Listen to this. It's to your address, Lowndes. The man was making a speech to his constituents, and he piled it on. Here's a sample: 'And I assert unhesitatingly that the Civil Service in India is the preserve—the pet preserve—of the aristocracy of England. What does the democracy—what do the masses—get from that country, which we have step by step fraudulently annexed? I answer, nothing whatever. It is farmed with a single eye to their own interests by the scions of the aristocracy. They take good care to maintain their lavish scale of incomes, to avoid or stifle any inquiries into the nature and conduct of their administration, while they themselves force the unhappy peasant to pay with the sweat of his brow for all the luxuries in which they are lapped.' " Hummil waved the cutting above his head. "'Ear! 'ear!" said his audience.

Then Lowndes, meditatively: "I'd give—I'd give three months' pay to have that gentleman spend one month with me and see how the free and independent native prince works things. Old Timbersides'—this was his flippant title for an honoured and decorated feudatory prince—'has been wearing my life out this week past for money. By Jove, his latest performance was to send me one of his women as a bribe!"

"Good for you! Did you accept it?" said Mottram.

"No. I rather wish I had, now. She was a pretty little person, and she yarned away to me about the horrible destitution among the king's womenfolk. The darlings haven't had any new clothes for nearly a month, and the old man wants to buy a new drag from Calcutta,—solid silver railings and silver lamps, and trifles of that kind. I've tried to make him understand that he has played the deuce with the revenues for the last twenty years and must go slow. He can't see it."

"But he has the ancestral treasure-vaults to draw on. There must be three millions at least in jewels and coin under his palace," said Hummil.

"Catch a native king disturbing the family treasure! The priests forbid it except as the last resort. Old Timbersides has added something like a quarter of a million to the deposit in his reign."

"Where the mischief does it all come from?" said Mottram.

"The country. The state of the people is enough to make you sick. I've known the tax-men wait by a milch-camel till the foal was born and then hurry off the mother for arrears. And what can I do? I can't get the Court clerks to give me any accounts; I can't raise anything more than a fat smile from the commander-in-chief when I find out the troops are three months in arrears; and old Timbersides begins to weep when I speak to him. He has taken to the King's Peg heavily,—liqueur brandy for whisky, and Heid-sieck for soda-water."

"That's what the Rao of Jubela took to. Even a native can't last long at that," said Spurstow. "He'll go out."

"And a good thing, too. Then I suppose we'll have a council of regency, and a tutor for the young prince, and hand him back his kingdom with ten years' accumulations."

"Whereupon that young prince, having been taught all the vices of the English, will play ducks and drakes with the money and undo ten years' work in eighteen months. I've seen that business before," said Spurstow. "I should tackle the king with light hand if I were you, Lowndes. They'll hate you quite enough under any circumstances."

"That's all very well. The man who looks on can talk about the light hand; but you can't clean a pig-stye with a pen dipped in rose-water. I know my risks; but nothing has happened yet. My servant's an old Pathan, and he cooks for me. They are hardly likely to bribe him, and I don't accept food from my true friends, as they call themselves. Oh, but it's weary work! I'd sooner be with you, Spurstow. There's shooting near your camp."

"Would you? I don't think it. About fifteen deaths a day don't incite a man to shoot anything but himself. And the worst of it is that the poor devils look at you as though you ought to save them. Lord knows, I've tried everything. My last attempt was empirical, but it pulled an old man through. He was brought to me apparently past hope, and I gave him gin and Worcester sauce with cayenne. It cured him; but I don't recommend it."

"How do the cases run generally?" said Hummil.

"Very simply indeed, Chlorodyne, opium pill, chlorodyne, collapse, nitre, bricks to the feet, and then—the burning-ghat. The last seems to be the only thing that stops the trouble. It's black cholera, you know. Poor devils! But, I will say, little Bunsee Lal, my apothecary, works like a demon. I've recommended him for promotion if he comes through it all alive."

"And what are your chances, old man?" said Mottram.

"Don't know; don't care much; but I've sent the letter in. What are you doing with yourself generally?"

"Sitting under a table in the tent and spitting on the sextant to keep it cool," said the man of the Survey. "Washing my eyes to avoid ophthalmia, which I shall certainly get, and trying to make a sub-surveyor understand that an error of five degrees in an angle isn't quite so small as it looks. I'm altogether alone, y'know, and shall be till the end of the hot weather."

"Hummil's the lucky man," said Lowndes, flinging himself into a long chair. "He has an actual roof—torn as to the ceiling-cloth, but still a roof—over his head. He sees one train daily. He can get beer and soda-water and ice 'em when God is good. He has books, pictures,'—they were torn from the *Graphic*,—' and the society of the excellent sub-contractor Jevins, besides the pleasure of receiving us weekly."

Hummil smiled grimly. "Yes, I'm the lucky man, I suppose. Jevins is luckier."

"How? Not—"

"Yes. Went out. Last Monday."

"By his own hand?" said Spurstow quickly, hinting the suspicion that was in everybody's mind. There was no cholera near Hummil's section. Even fever gives a man at least a week's grace, and sudden death generally implied self-slaughter.

"I judge no man this weather," said Hummil. "He had a touch of the sun, I fancy; for last week, after you fellows had left, he came into the veranda and told me that he was going home to see his wife, in Market Street, Liverpool, that evening.

"I got the apothecary in to look at him, and we tried to make him lie down. After an hour or two he rubbed his eyes and said he believed he had had a fit,—hoped he hadn't said anything rude. Jevins had a great idea of bettering himself socially. He was very like Chucks in his language."

"Well?"

"Then he went to his own bungalow and began cleaning a rifle. He told the servant that he was going to shoot buck in the morning. Naturally he fumbled with the trigger, and shot himself through the head—accidentally. The apothecary sent in a report to my chief, and Jevins is buried somewhere out there. I'd have wired to you, Spurstow, if you could have done anything."

"You're a queer chap," said Mottram. "If you'd killed the man yourself you couldn't have been more quiet about the business."

"Good Lord! what does it matter?" said Hummil calmly. "I've got to do a lot of his overseeing work in addition to my own. I'm the only person that suffers. Jevins is out of it,—by pure accident, of course, but out of it. The apothecary was going to write a long screed on suicide. Trust a Babu to drive when he gets the chance."

"Why didn't you let it go in as suicide?" said Lowndes.

"No direct proof. A man hasn't many privileges in this country, but he might at least be allowed to mishandle his own rifle. Besides, some day I may need a man to smother up an accident to myself. Life and let live. Die and let die."

"You take a pill," said Spurstow, who had been watching Hummil's white face narrowly. "Take a pill, and don't be an ass. That sort of talk is skittles. Anyhow suicide is shirking your work. If I were Job ten times over, I should be so interested in what was going to happen next that I'd stay on and watch."

"Ah! I've lost that curiosity," said Hummil.

"Liver out of order?" said Lowndes feelingly.

"No. Can't sleep. That's worse."

"By Jove, it is!" said Mottram. "I'm that way every now and then, and the fit has to wear itself out. What do you take for it?"

"Nothing. What's the use? I haven't had ten minutes' sleep since Friday morning."

"Poor chap! Spurstow, you ought to attend to this," said Mottram. "Now you mention it, your eyes *are* rather gummy and swollen."

Spurstow, still watching Hummil, laughed lightly. "I'll patch him up, later on. Is it too hot, do you think, to go for a ride?"

"Where to?" said Lowndes wearily. "We shall have to go away at eight, and there'll be riding enough for us then. I hate a horse when I have to use him as a necessity. Oh, heavens! what is there to do?"

"Begin whist again, at chick points ["a chick" is supposed to be eight shillings] and a gold mohur on the rub," said Spurstow promptly.

"Poker. A month's pay all round for the pool,—no limit,—and fifty-rupee raises. Somebody would be broken before we got up," said Lowndes.

"Can't say that it would give me any pleasure to break any man in this company," said Mottram. "There isn't enough excitement in it, and it's foolish." He crossed over to the worn and battered little camp-piano,—wreckage of a married household that had once held the bungalow,—and opened the case.

"It's used up long ago," said Hummil. "The servants have picked it to pieces."

The piano was indeed hopelessly out of order, but Mottram managed to bring the rebellious notes into a sort of agreement, and there rose from the ragged keyboard something that might once have been the ghost of a popular music-hall song. The men in the long chairs turned with evident interest as Mottram banged the more lustily.

"That's good!" said Lowndes. "By Jove! the last time I heard that song was in '79, or thereabouts, just before I came out."

"Ah!" said Spurstow with pride, "I was Home in '80." And he mentioned a song of the streets popular at that date.

Mottram executed it roughly. Lowndes criticised and volunteered emendations. Mottram dashed into another ditty, not of the music-hall character, and made as if to rise.

"Sit down," said Hummil. "I didn't know that you had any music in your composition. Go on playing until you can't think of anything more. I'll have that piano tuned up before you come again. Play something festive."

Very simple indeed were the tunes to which Mottram's art and the limitations of the piano could give effect, but the men listened with pleasure, and in the pauses talked all together of what they had seen or heard when they were last at Home. A dense dust-storm sprung up outside, and swept roaring over the house, enveloping it in the choking darkness of midnight, but Mottram continued unheeding, and the crazy tinkle reached the ears of the listeners above the flapping of the tattered ceiling-cloth.

In the silence after the storm he glided from the more directly personal songs of Scotland, half humming them as he played, into the Evening Hymn.

"Sunday," said he, nodding his had.

"Go on. Don't apologise for it," said Spurstow.

Hummil laughed long and riotously. "Play it, by all means. You're full of surprises to-day. I didn't know you had such a gift of finished sarcasm. How does that thing go?"

Mottram took up the tune.

"Too slow by half. You miss the note of gratitude," said Hummil. "It ought to go to the 'Grasshopper's Polka,' — this way." and he chanted, *prestissimo*, —

> *"Glory to thee, my God, this night,*
> *For all the blessings of the light.*

"That shows we really feel our blessings. How does it go on? —

> *"If in the night I sleepless lie,*
> *My soul with sacred thoughts supply;*
> *May no ill dreams disturb my rest, —*

"Quicker, Mottram! —

"Or powers of darkness me molest!

"Bah! what an old hypocrite you are!"

"Don't be an ass," said Lowndes. "You are at full liberty to make fun of anything else you like, but leave that hymn alone. It's associated in my mind with the most sacred recollections—"

"Summer evenings in the country,—stained-glass window,—light going out, and you and she jamming your heads together over one hymn-book," said Mottram.

"Yes, and a fat old cockchafer hitting you in the eye when you walked home. Smell of hay, and a moon as big as a band-box sitting on the top of a haycock; bats,—roses,—milk and midges," said Lowndes.

"Also mothers. I can just recollect my mother singing me to sleep with that when I was a little chap," said Spurstow.

The darkness had fallen on the room. They could hear Hummil squirming in his chair.

"Consequently," said he testily, "you sing it when you are seven fathom deep in Hell! It's an insult to the intelligence of the Deity to pretend we're anything but tortured rebels."

"Take *two* pills," said Spurstow; "that's tortured liver."

"The usually placid Hummil is in a vile bad temper. I'm sorry for his coolies to-morrow," said Lowndes, as the servants brought in the lights and prepared the table for dinner.

As they were settling into their places about the miserable goat-chops and the smoked tapioca pudding, Spurstow took occasion to whisper to Mottram, "Well done, David!"

"Look after Saul, then," was the reply.

"What are you two whispering about?" said Hummil suspiciously.

"Only saying that you are a damned poor host. This fowl can't be cut," returned Spurstow with a sweet smile. "Call this a dinner?"

"I can't help it. You don't expect a banquet, do you?"

Throughout that meal Hummil contrived laboriously to insult directly and pointedly all his guests in succession, and at each insult Spurstow kicked the aggrieved persons under the table; but he dared not exchange a glance of intelligence with either of them. Hummil's face was white and pinched, while his eyes were unnaturally large. No man dreamed for a moment of resenting his savage personalities, but as soon as the meal was over they made haste to get away.

"Don't go. You're just getting amusing, you fellows. I hope I haven't said anything that annoyed you. You're such touchy devils." Then, changing the note into one of almost abject entreaty, Hummil added, "I say, you surely aren't going?"

"In the language of the blessed Jorrocks, where I dines I sleeps," said Spurstow. "I want to have a look at your coolies to-morrow, if you don't mind. You can give me a place to lie down in, I suppose?"

The others pleaded the urgency of their several duties next day, and saddling up, departed together, Hummil begging them to come next Sunday. As they jogged off, Lowndes unbosomed himself to Mottram:—

". . . And I never felt so like kicking a man at his own table in my life. He said I cheated at whist, and reminded me I was in debt! Told you you were as good as a liar to your face! You aren't half indignant enough over it."

"Not I," said Mottram. "Poor devil! Did you ever know old Hummy behave like that before or within a hundred miles of it?"

"That's no excuse. Spurstow was hacking my shin all the time, so I kept a hand on myself. Else I should have—"

"No, you wouldn't. You'd have done as Hummy did about Jevins; judge no man this weather. By Jove! the buckle of my bridle is hot in my hand! Trot out a bit, and 'ware rat-holes."

Ten minutes' trotting jerked out of Lowndes one very sage remark when he pulled up, sweating from every pore:—

"Good thing Spurstow's with him to-night."

"Ye-es. Good man, Spurstow. Our roads turn here. See you again next Sunday, if the sun doesn't bowl me over."

"S'pose so, unless old Timbersides' Finance Minister manages to dress some of my food. Good-night, and—God bless you!"

"What's wrong now?"

"Oh, nothing." Lowndes gathered up his whip, and, as he flicked Mottram's mare on the flank, added, "You're not a bad little chap,—that's all." And the mare bolted half a mile across the sand, on the word.

In the assistant engineer's bungalow Spurstow and Hummil smoked the pipe of silence together, each narrowly watching the other. The capacity of a bachelor's establishment is as elastic as its arrangements are simple. A servant cleared away the dining-room table, brought in a couple of rude native bedsteads made of tape strung on a light wood frame, flung a square of cool Calcutta matting over each, set them side by side, pinned two towels to the punkah so that their fringes should just sweep clear of the sleeper's nose and mouth, and announced that the couches were ready.

The men flung themselves down, ordering the punkah-coolies by all the powers of Hell to pull. Every door and window was shut, for the outside air was that of an oven. The atmosphere within was only 104°, as the thermometer bore witness, and heavy with the foul smell of badly trimmed kerosene lamps; and this stench, combined with that of native tobacco, baked brick, and dried earth, sends the heart of many a strong man down to his boots, for it is the smell of the Great Indian Empire when she turns herself for six months into a house of torment. Spurstow packed his pillows craftily so that he reclined rather than lay, his head at a safe elevation above his feet. It is not good to sleep on a low pillow in the hot weather if you happen to be of thick-necked build, for you may pass with lively snores and gugglings from natural sleep into the deep slumber of heat-apoplexy.

"Pack your pillows," said the doctor sharply, as he saw Hummil preparing to lie down at full length.

The night-light was trimmed; the shadow of the punkah wavered across the room, and the "*flick*" of the punkah-towel and the soft whine of the rope through the wall-hole followed it. Then the punkah flagged, almost ceased. The sweat poured from Spurstow's brow. Should he go out and harangue the coolie? It started forward again with a savage jerk, and a pin came out of the towels. When this was replaced, a tomtom in the coolie-lines began to beat with the steady throb of a swollen artery inside some brain-fevered skull. Spurstow turned on his side and swore gently. There was no movement on Hummil's part. The man had composed himself as rigidly as a corpse, his hands clinched at his sides. The respiration was too hurried for any suspicion of sleep. Spurstow looked at the set face. The jaws were clinched, and there was a pucker round the quivering eyelids.

"He's holding himself as tightly as ever he can," thought Spurstow. "What in the world is the matter with him?—Hummil!"

"Yes," in a thick constrained voice.

"Can't you get to sleep?"

"No."

"Head hot? Throat feeling bulgy? or how?"

"Neither, thanks. I don't sleep much, you know."

"Feel pretty bad?"

Pretty bad, thanks. There is a tomtom outside, isn't there? I thought it was my head at first. . . . Oh, Spurstow, for pity's sake give me something that will put me asleep,—sound asleep,—if it's only for six hours!" He sprang up, trembling from head to foot. "I haven't been able to sleep naturally for days, and I can't stand it!—I can't stand it!"

"Poor old chap!"

"That's no use. Give me something to make me sleep. I tell you I'm nearly mad. I don't know what I say half my time. For three weeks I've had to think and spell out every word that has come through my lips before I dared say it. Isn't that enough to drive a man mad? I can't see things correctly now, and I've lost my sense of touch. My skin aches—my skin aches! Make me sleep. Oh, Spurstow, for the love of God make me sleep sound. It isn't enough merely to let me dream. Let me sleep!"

"All right, old man, all right. Go slow; you aren't half as bad as you think."

The flood-gates of reserve once broken, Hummil was clinging to him like a frightened child. "You're pinching my arm to pieces."

"I'll break your neck if you don't do something for me. No, I didn't mean that. Don't be angry, old fellow." He wiped the sweat off himself as he fought to regain composure. "I'm a bit restless and off my oats, and perhaps you could recommend some sort of sleeping mixture,—bromide of potassium."

"Bromide of skittles! Why didn't you tell me this before? Let go of my arm, and I'll see if there's anything in my cigarette-case to suit your complaint." Spurstow hunted among his day-clothes, turned up the lamp, opened a little silver cigarette-case, and advanced on the expectant Hummil with the daintiest of fairy squirts.

"The last appeal of civilisation," said he, "and a thing I hate to use. Hold out your arm. Well, your sleeplessness hasn't ruined your muscle; and what a thick hide it is! Might as well inject a buffalo subcutaneously. Now in a few minutes the morphia will begin working. Lie down and wait."

A smile of unalloyed and idiotic delight began to creep over Hummil's face. "I think," he whispered,—"I think I'm going off now. Gad! it's positively heavenly! Spurstow, you must give me that case to keep; you—" The voice ceased as the head fell back.

"Not for a good deal," said Spurstow to the unconscious form. "And now, my friend, sleeplessness of your kind being very apt to relax the moral fibre in little matters of life and death, I'll just take the liberty of spiking your guns."

He paddled into Hummil's saddle-room in his bare feet and uncased a twelve-bore rifle, an express, and a revolver. Of the first he unscrewed the nipples and hid them in the bottom of a saddlery-case; of the second he abstracted the liver, kicking it behind a big wardrobe. The third he merely opened, and knocked the doll-head bolt of the grip up with the heel of a riding-boot.

"That's settled," he said, as he shook the sweat off his hands. "These little precautions will at least give you time to turn. You have too much sympathy with gun-room accidents."

And as he rose from his knees, the thick muffled voice of Hummil cried in the doorway, "You fool!"

Such tones they use who speak in the lucid intervals of delirium to their friends a little before they die.

Spurstow started, dropping the pistol. Hummil stood in the doorway, rocking with helpless laughter.

"That was awf'ly good of you, I'm sure," he said, very slowly, feeling for his words. "I don't intend to go out by my own hand at present. I say, Spurstow, that stuff won't work. What shall I do? What shall I do?" And panic terror stood in his eyes.

"Lie down and give it a chance. Lie down at once."

"I daren't. It will only take me half-way again, and I shan't be able to get away this time. Do you know, it was all I could do to come out just now? Generally I am as quick as lightning; but you had clogged my feet. I was nearly caught."

"Oh yes, I understand. Go and lie down."

"No, it isn't delirium; but it was an awfully mean trick to play on me. Do you know I might have died?"

As a sponge rubs a slate clean, so some power unknown to Spurstow had wiped out of Hummil's face all that stamped it for the face of a man, and he stood at the doorway in the expression of his lost innocence. He had slept back into terrified childhood.

"Is he going to die on the spot?" thought Spurstow. Then, aloud, "All right, my son. Come back to bed, and tell me all about it. You couldn't sleep; but what was all the rest of the nonsense?"

"A place, — a place down there," said Hummil, with simple sincerity. The drug was acting on him by waves, and he was flung from the fear of a strong man to the fright of a child as his nerves gathered sense or were dulled.

"Good God! I've been afraid of it for months past, Spurstow. It has made every night hell to me; and yet I'm not conscious of having done anything wrong."

"Be still, and I'll give you another dose. We'll stop your nightmares, you unutterable idiot!"

"Yes, but you must give me so much that I can't get away. You must make me quite sleepy, — not just a little sleepy. It's so hard to run then."

"I know it; I know it. I've felt it myself. The symptoms are exactly as you describe."

"Oh, don't laugh at me, confound you! Before this awful sleeplessness came to me I've tried to rest on my elbow and put a spur in the bed to sting me when I fell back. Look!"

"By Jove! the man has been rowelled like a horse! Ridden by the nightmare with a vengeance! And we all thought him sensible enough. Heaven send us understanding! You like to talk, don't you?"

"Yes, sometimes. Not when I'm frightened. *Then* I want to run. Don't you?"

"Always. Before I give you your second dose try to tell me exactly what your trouble is."

Hummil spoke in broken whispers for nearly ten minutes, whilst Spurstow looked into the pupils of his eyes and passed his hand before them once or twice.

At the end of the narrative the silver cigarette-case was produced, and the last words that Hummil said as he fell back for the second time were, "Put me to sleep; for if I'm caught I die,—I die!"

"Yes, yes; we all do that sooner or later,—thank Heaven who has set a term to our miseries," said Spurstow, settling the cushions under the head. "It occurs to me that unless I drink something I shall go out before my time. I've stopped sweating, and—I wear a seventeen-inch collar." He brewed himself scalding hot tea, which is an excellent remedy against heat-apoplexy if you take three or four cups of it in time. Then he watched the sleeper.

"A blind face that cries and can't wipe its eyes, a blind face that chases him down corridors! H'm! Decidedly, Hummil ought to go on leave as soon as possible; and, sane or otherwise, he undoubtedly did rowel himself most cruelly. Well, Heaven sent us understanding!"

At mid-day Hummil rose, with an evil taste in his mouth, but an unclouded eye and a joyful heart.

"I was pretty bad last night, wasn't I?" said he.

"I have seen healthier men. You must have had a touch of the sun. Look here: if I write you a swingeing medical certificate, will you apply for leave on the spot?"

"No."

"Why not? You want it."

"Yes, but I can hold on till the weather's a little cooler."

"Why should you, if you can get relieved on the spot?"

"Burkett is the only man who could be sent; and he's a born fool."

"Oh, never mind about the line. You aren't so important as all that. Wire for leave, if necessary."

Hummil looked very uncomfortable.

"I can hold on till the Rains," he said evasively.

"You can't. Wire to headquarters for Burkett."

"I won't. If you want to know why, particularly, Burkett is married, and his wife's just had a kid, and she's up at Simla, in the cool, and Burkett has a very nice billet that takes him into Simla from Saturday to Monday. That little woman isn't at all well. If Burkett was transferred she'd try to follow him. If she left the baby behind she'd fret herself to death. If she came,— and Burkett's one of those selfish little beasts who are always talking about a wife's place being with her husband,—she'd die. It's murder to bring a woman here just now. Burkett hasn't the physique of a rat. If he came here he'd go out; and I know she hasn't any money, and I'm pretty sure she'd go out too. I'm salted in a sort of way, and I'm not married. Wait till the Rains, and then Burkett can get thin down here. I'll do him heaps of good."

"Do you mean to say that you intend to face—what you have faced, till the Rains break?"

"Oh, it won't be so bad, now you've shown me a way out of it. I can always wire to you. Besides, now I've once got into the way of sleeping, it'll be all right. Anyhow, I shan't put in for leave. That's the long and the short of it."

"My great Scott! I thought all that sort of thing was dead and done with."

"Bosh! You'd do the same yourself. I feel a new man, thanks to that cigarette-case. You're going over to camp now, aren't you?"

"Yes; but I'll try to look you up every other day, if I can."

"I'm not bad enough for that. I don't want you to bother. Give the coolies gin and ketchup."

"Then you feel all right?"

"Fit to fight for my life, but not to stand out in the sun talking to you. Go alone, old man, and bless you!"

Hummil turned on his heel to face the echoing desolation of his bungalow, and the first thing he saw standing in the veranda was the figure of himself. He had met a similar apparition once before, when he was suffering from overwork and the strain of the hot weather.

"This is bad,—already," he said, rubbing his eyes. "If the thing slides away from me all in one piece, like a ghost, I shall know it is only my eyes and stomach that are out of order. If it walks—my head is going."

He approached the figure, which naturally kept at an unvarying distance from him, as is the use of all spectres that are born of overwork. It slid through the house and dissolved into swimming specks within the eyeball as soon as it reached the burning light of the garden. Hummil went about his business till even. When he came in to dinner he found himself sitting at the table. The vision rose and walked out hastily. Except that it cast no shadow it was in all respects real.

No living man knows what that week held for Hummil. An increase of the epidemic kept Spurstow in camp among the coolies, and all he could do was to telegraph to Mottram, bidding him go to the bungalow and sleep there. But Mottram was forty miles away from the nearest telegraph, and knew nothing of anything save the needs of the Survey till he met, early on Sunday morning, Lowndes and Spurstow heading towards Hummil's for the weekly gathering.

"Hope the poor chap's in a better temper," said the former, swinging himself off his horse at the door. "I suppose he isn't up yet."

"I'll just have a look at him," said the doctor. "If he's asleep there's no need to wake him."

And an instant later, by the tone of Spurstow's voice calling upon them to enter, the men knew what had happened. There was no need to wake him.

The punkah was still being pulled over the bed, but Hummil had departed this life at least three hours.

The body lay on its back, hands clinched by the side, as Spurstow had seen it lying seven nights previously. In the staring eyes was written terror beyond the expression of any pen.

Mottram, who had entered behind Lowndes, bent over the dead and touched the forehead lightly with his lips. "Oh, you lucky, lucky devil!" he whispered.

But Lowndes had seen the eyes, and withdrew shuddering to the other side of the room.

"Poor chap! poor old chap! And the last time I met him I was angry. Spurstow, we should have watched him. Has he — ?"

Deftly Spurstow continued his investigations, ending by a search round the room.

"No, he hasn't," he snapped. "There's no trace of anything. Call the servants."

They came, eight or ten of them, whispering and peering over each other's shoulders.

"When did your Sahib go to bed?" said Spurstow.

"At eleven or ten, we think," said Hummil's personal servant.

"He was well then? But how should you know?"

"He was not ill, as far as our comprehension extended. But he had slept very little for three nights. This I know, because I saw him walking much, and specially in the heart of the night."

As Spurstow was arranging the sheet, a big straight-necked hunting-spur trembled on the ground. The doctor groaned. The personal servant peeped at the body.

"What do you think, Chuma?" said Spurstow, catching the look on the dark face.

"Heaven-born, in my poor opinion, this that was my master has descended into the Dark Places, and there has been caught because he was not able to escape with sufficient speed. We have the spur for evidence that he fought with Fear. Thus have I seen men of my race do with thorns when a spell was laid upon them to overtake them in their sleeping hours and they dared not sleep."

"Chuma, you're a mud-head. Go out and prepare seals to be set on the Sahib's property."

"God has made the Heaven-born. God has made me. Who are we, to inquire into the dispensations of God? I will bid the other servants hold aloof while you are reckoning the tale of the Sahib's property. They are all thieves, and would steal."

"As far as I can make out, he died from—oh, anything; stoppage of the heart's action, heat-apoplexy, or some other visitation," said Spurstow to his companions. "We must make an inventory of his effects, and so on."

"He was scared to death," insisted Lowndes. "Look at those eyes! For pity's sake don't let him be buried with them open!"

"Whatever it was, he's clear of all the trouble now," said Mottram softly.

Spurstow was peering into the open eyes.

"Come here," said he. "Can you see anything there?"

"I can't face it!" whimpered Lowndes. "Cover up the face! Is there any fear on earth that can turn a man into that likeness? It's ghastly. Oh, Spurstow, cover it up!"

"No fear—on earth," said Spurstow. Mottram leaned over his shoulder and looked intently.

"I see nothing except some grey blurs in the pupil. There can be nothing there, you know."

"Even so. Well, let's think. It'll take half a day to knock up any sort of coffin; and he must have died at midnight. Lowndes, old man, go out and tell the coolies to break ground next to Jevin's grave. Mottram, go round the house with Chuma and see that the seals are put on things. Send a couple of men to me here, and I'll arrange."

The strong-armed servants when they returned to their own kind told a strange story of the Doctor Sahib vainly trying to call their master back to life by magic arts,—to wit, the holding of a little green box that clicked to each of the dead man's eyes, and of a bewildered muttering on the part of the Doctor Sahib, who took the little green box away with him.

The resonant hammering of a coffin-lid is no pleasant thing to hear, but those who have experience maintain that much more terrible is the soft swish of the bed-linen, the reeving and unreeving of the bed-tapes, when he who has fallen by the roadside is apparelled for burial, sinking gradually as the tapes are tied over, till the swaddled shape touches the floor and there is no protest against the indignity of hasty disposal.

At the last moment Lowndes was seized with scruples of conscience. "Ought you to read the service, — from beginning to end?" said he to Spurstow.

"I intend to. You're my senior as a Civilian. You can take it if you like."

"I didn't mean that for a moment. I only thought if we could get a chaplain from somewhere, — I'm willing to ride anywhere, — and give poor Hummil a better chance. That's all."

"Bosh!" said Spurstow, as he framed his lips to the tremendous words that stand at the head of the burial service.

After breakfast they smoked a pipe in silence to the memory of the dead. Then Spurstow said absently: —

" 'Tisn't in medical science."

"What?"

"Things in a dead man's eye."

"For goodness' sake leave that horror alone!" said Lowndes. "I've seen a native die of pure fright when a tiger chivied him. I know what killed Hummil."

"The deuce you do! I'm going to try to see." And the doctor retreated into the bath-room with a Kodak camera. After a few minutes there was the sound of something being hammered to pieces, and he emerged, very white indeed.

"Have you got a picture?" said Mottram. "What does the thing look like?"

"It was impossible, of course. You needn't look, Mottram. I've torn up the films. There was nothing there. It was impossible."

"That," said Lowndes, very distinctly, watching the shaking hand striving to relight the pipe, "is a damned lie."

Mottram laughed uneasily. "Spurstow's right," he said. "We're all in such a state now that we'd believe anything. For pity's sake let's try to be rational."

There was no further speech for a long time. The hot wind whistled without, and the dry trees sobbed. Presently the daily train, winking brass, burnished steel, and spouting steam, pulled up panting in the intense glare. "We'd better go on on that," said Spurstow. "Go back to work. I've written my certificate. We can't do any more good here, and work'll keep our wits together. Come on."

No one moved. It is not pleasant to face railway journeys at mid-day in

June. Spurstow gathered up his hat and whip, and, turning in the door-way, said: —

> *"There may be Heaven, — there must be Hell.*
> *Meantime, there is our life here. We-ell?"*

Neither Mottram nor Lowndes had any answer to the question.

A SCANDAL IN BOHEMIA

1891

Doyle (1859–1930), a young doctor with literary aspirations, probably became an avid amateur photographer around 1881. From then until his marriage in 1885, he also frequently contributed articles about his camera excursions in England and abroad to the British Journal of Photography, *the world's oldest photographic magazine (1854).*[1] *"A Scandal in Bohemia" was the second detective story—and the first to feature Sherlock Holmes—that Doyle wrote for the new* Strand Magazine, *and the only one whose plot centered around a photograph. He later listed it among his dozen best stories because it "opened the path for the others" and contained "more female interest than is usual."*[2] *Its instant success emboldened the author to give up his medical practice and sell his instruments, using the proceeds to buy new camera equipment. Oddly, Doyle thereafter rarely referred to photography in his detective fiction, though Holmes is unusually knowledgeable about chemistry.*[3] *He mainly photographed family members and friends, especially after his knighthood in 1902, when he traveled abroad extensively.*[4] *However, the loss of both his son and his brother in 1919 intensified Doyle's interest in "spirit" photographs, in which manipulated images—usually of the dead—appeared. He avidly defended the credibility of such pictures, using those he collected as "evidence" in his popular lectures and writings as well as displays in a museum attached to the Psychic Bookshop he established in 1925.*[5] *Such activities impaired Doyle's own credibility but not that of his popular detective stories, which relied so heavily on objective evidence and logical analysis.*

1. See the editors' introduction to Doyle's *Essays on Photography*, edited by John Michael Gibson and Richard Lancelyn Green (London: Secker & Warburg [1982]), pp. viii–xxi; and West, *Soft Murder by the Camera Eye*, pp. 172–73. See also the illus-

trations based on Doyle's Swiss photographs in D. G. Thomson, "Tobogganing and Ski-Running," *Pearson's Magazine* (December 1897): 696–704, and his faked ones for *The Lost World* (London: Hodder and Stoughton, 1912), discussed in Gibson and Green's introduction to *Essays*, p. xviii, and in John Carr, *The Life of Sir Arthur Conan Doyle* (New York: Harper, 1979), pp. 258–59. The whereabouts of most of Doyle's photographs are not known.

2. See Doyle's list and assessment quoted in Doyle, *Sherlock Holmes: The Main Stories with Contemporary Critical Essays*, edited by John A. Hodgson (New York: Bedford Books/St. Martin's Press, [1994]), pp. 435–36. See also S[usan] E. Sweeney, "Purloined Letters: Poe, Doyle, Nabokov," *Russian Literature Triquarterly* 24 (1991): 213–37, who notes the parallels between Doyle's story here and Poe's story "The Purloined Letter" (1844), as well as Nabokov's debts to both Poe and Doyle in *The Real Life of Sebastian Knight* (1941), reportedly his first fiction composed in English. All three writers were involved with photography, though in different ways, as noted in Rabb, *Literature and Photography*, pp. 3–5, 74–79, and 243–44. See also William D. Jenkins, "We Were Both in the Photographs: I. Adler and Adah I.," *Baker Street Journal: An Irregular Quarterly of Sherlockiana* 36, no. 1 (March 1986): 6–16, who persuasively notes the parallels between the story's heroine and Adah Isaacs Menken, the famous actress-adventuress who was one of the first to use photographs to enhance her celebrity; some, however, caused problems as Dumas *père*, one of her lovers, discovered—also noted in Rabb, *Literature and Photography*, p. 79, n. 5.

3. Photography provides a cover for the villain in Doyle's "The Red-headed League," *Strand* 2 (August 1891): 190–204; is a hobby of the villain in "The Adventure of the Copper Beeches," *Strand* 2 (June 1892): 613–28; and helps solve the mysterious death in "The Adventure of the Lion's Mane," *Strand* 72 (December 1926): 539–50, all reprinted in *The Complete Sherlock Holmes* (New York: Doubleday, [1960]), and widely elsewhere. See also Allen H. Butler, "A Speculation: Did Holmes Have Photo-Processing Capabilities at the Villa?," *Baker Street Journal* 40, no. 3 (September 1990): 159–60.

4. See, for example, Doyle's photograph of Rudyard Kipling's house in Vermont (with a small, barely discernible figure that might be his even more celebrated host), reproduced in Rabb, *Literature and Photography*, p. 227.

5. Doyle's relevant spiritualist works (all published in London by Hodder and Stoughton and in New York by George H. Doran unless otherwise indicated) include: *The Lost World* (1912), pp. 11, 35–37, 160, 219–21; *The Vital Message* (1919), pp. 156–61; *The Wanderings of a Spiritualist* (1921); *The Case for Spirit Photography* (London: Hutchinson, 1922); *The Coming of the Fairies* (1922; rev. ed., London: Psychic Press, 1928); "Spirit Photography," *The History of Spiritualism* (London: Cassell, 1926), vol. 2, pp. 123–48; "The Combermere Photograph," *Quarterly Transactions of the British College of Psychic Science* 5 (October 1926): 190–92. See also Geoffrey Crawley, "That Astounding Affair of the Cottingley Fairies," *British Journal of Photography* (December 24, 1982–April 8, 1983).

A SCANDAL IN BOHEMIA

I

To Sherlock Holmes she is always *the* woman. I have seldom heard him mention her under any other name. In his eyes she eclipses and predominates the whole of her sex. It was not that he felt any emotion akin to love for Irene Adler. All emotions, and that one particularly, were abhorrent to his cold, precise, but admirably balanced mind. He was, I take it, the most perfect reasoning and observing machine that the world has seen: but, as a lover, he would have placed himself in a false position. He never spoke of the softer passions, save with a gibe and a sneer. They were admirable things for the observer—excellent for drawing the veil from men's motives and actions. But for the trained reasoner to admit such intrusions into his own delicate and finely adjusted temperament was to introduce a distracting factor which might throw a doubt upon all his mental results. Grit in a sensitive instrument, or a crack in one of his own high-power lenses, would not be more disturbing than a strong emotion in a nature such as his. And yet there was but one woman to him, and that woman was the late Irene Adler, of dubious and questionable memory.

I had seen little of Holmes lately. My marriage had drifted us away from each other. My own complete happiness, and the home-centered interests which rise up around the man who first finds himself master of his own establishment, were sufficient to absorb all my attention; while Holmes, who loathed every form of society with his whole Bohemian soul, remained in our lodgings in Baker Street, buried among his old books, and alternating from week to week between cocaine and ambition, the drowsiness of the drug, and the fierce energy of his own keen nature. He was still, as ever, deeply attracted by the study of crime, and occupied his immense faculties and extraordinary powers of observation in following out those clues, and clearing up those mysteries, which had been abandoned as hopeless by the official police. From time to time I heard some vague account of his doings: of his summons to Odessa in the case of the Trepoff murder, of his clearing up of the singular tragedy of the Atkinson brothers at Trincomalee, and finally of the mission which he had accomplished so delicately and successfully for the reigning family of Holland. Beyond these signs of his activity, however, which I merely shared with all the readers of the daily press, I knew little of my former friend and companion.

One night—it was on the 20th of March, 1888—I was returning from a journey to a patient (for I had now returned to civil practice), when my way led me through Baker Street. As I passed the well-remembered door, which must always be associated in my mind with my wooing, and with the dark incidents of the Study in Scarlet, I was seized with a keen desire to see Holmes again, and to know how he was employing his extraordinary powers. His rooms were brilliantly lit, and, even as I looked up, I saw his tall spare figure pass twice in a dark silhouette against the blind. He was pacing the room swiftly, eagerly, with his head sunk upon his chest, and his hands clasped behind him. To me, who knew his every mood and habit, his attitude and manner told their own story. He was at work again. He had risen out of his drug-created dreams, and was hot upon the scent of some new problem. I rang the bell, and was shown up to the chamber which had formerly been in part my own.

His manner was not effusive. It seldom was; but he was glad, I think, to see me. With hardly a word spoken, but with a kindly eye, he waved me to an arm-chair, threw across his case of cigars, and indicated a spirit case and a gasogene in the corner. Then he stood before the fire, and looked me over in his singular introspective fashion.

"Wedlock suits you," he remarked. "I think, Watson, that you have put on seven and a half pounds since I saw you."

"Seven," I answered.

"Indeed, I should have thought a little more. Just a trifle more, I fancy, Watson. And in practice again, I observe. You did not tell me that you intended to go into harness."

"Then, how do you know?"

"I see it, I deduce it. How do I know that you have been getting yourself very wet lately, and that you have a most clumsy and careless servant girl?"

"My dear Holmes," said I, "this is too much. You would certainly have been burned had you lived a few centuries ago. It is true that I had a country walk on Thursday and came home in a dreadful mess; but, as I have changed my clothes, I can't imagine how you deduce it. As to Mary Jane, she is incorrigible, and my wife has given her notice; but there again I fail to see how you work it out."

He chuckled to himself and rubbed his long nervous hands together.

"It is simplicity itself," said he; "my eyes tell me that on the inside of your left shoe, just where the firelight strikes it, the leather is scored by six almost parallel cuts. Obviously they have been caused by some one who has very carelessly scraped round the edges of the sole in order to remove crusted mud from it. Hence, you see, my double deduction that you had been out in vile weather, and that you had a particularly malignant boot-slitting specimen of the London slavey. As to your practice, if a gentleman walks into my rooms smelling of iodoform, with a black mark of nitrate of silver upon his right forefinger, and a bulge on the side of his top hat to show where he has secreted his stethoscope, I must be dull indeed if I do not pronounce him to be an active member of the medical profession."

I could not help laughing at the ease with which he explained his process of deduction. "When I hear you give your reasons," I remarked, "the thing always appears to me to be so ridiculously simple that I could easily do it myself, though at each successive instance of your reasoning I am baffled, until you explain your process. And yet I believe that my eyes are as good as yours."

"Quite so," he answered, lighting a cigarette, and throwing himself down into an arm-chair. "You see, but you do not observe. The distinction is clear. For example, you have frequently seen the steps which lead up from the hall to this room."

"Frequently."

"How often?"

"Well, some hundreds of times."

"Then how many are there?"

"How many! I don't know."

"Quite so! You have not observed. And yet you have seen. That is just my point. Now, I know that there are seventeen steps, because I have both seen and observed. By the way, since you are interested in these little problems, and since you are good enough to chronicle one or two of my triflings experiences, you may be interested in this." He threw over a sheet of thick pink-tinted note-paper which had been lying open upon the table. "It came by the last post," said he. "Read it aloud."

The note was undated, and without either signature or address.

"There will call upon you to-night, at a quarter to eight o'clock," it said, "a gentleman who desires to consult you upon a matter of the very deepest moment. Your recent services to one of the Royal Houses of Europe have shown that you are one who may safely be trusted with matters which are of an importance which can hardly be exaggerated. This account of you we have from all quarters received. Be in your chamber then at that hour, and do not take it amiss if your visitor wear a mask."

"This is indeed a mystery," I remarked. "What do you imagine that it means?"

"I have no data yet. It is a capital mistake to theorise before one has data. Insensibly one begins to twist facts to suit theories, instead of theories to suit facts. But the note itself. What do you deduce from it?"

I carefully examined the writing, and the paper upon which it was written.

"The man who wrote it was presumably well-to-do," I remarked, endeavouring to imitate my companion's processes. "Such paper could not be bought under half a crown a packet. It is peculiarly strong and stiff."

"Peculiar—that is the very word," said Holmes. "It is not an English paper at all. Hold it up to the light."

I did so, and saw a large *E* with a small *g*, a *P*, and a large *G* with a small *t* woven into the texture of the paper.

"What do you make of that?" asked Holmes.

"The name of the maker, no doubt; or his monogram, rather."

"Not at all. The *G* with the small *t* stands for 'Gesellschaft,' which is the German for 'Company.' It is a customary contraction like our 'Co.' *P*, of course, stands for 'Papier.' Now for the *Eg*. Let us glance at our Continental Gazetteer." He took down a heavy brown volume from his shelves. "Eglow, Eglonitz—here we are, Egria. It is in a German-speaking country—in Bohemia, not far from Carlsbad. 'Remarkable as being the scene of the death of Wallenstein, and for its numerous glass factories and paper mills.' Ha, ha, my boy, what do you make of that?" His eyes sparkled, and he sent up a great blue triumphant cloud from his cigarette.

"The paper was made in Bohemia," I said.

"Precisely. And the man who wrote the note is a German. Do you note the peculiar construction of the sentence—'This account of you we have from all quarters received.' A Frenchman or Russian could not have written that. It is the German who is so uncourteous to his verbs. It only remains, therefore, to discover what is wanted by this German who writes upon Bohemian paper, and prefers wearing a mask to showing his face. And here he comes, if I am not mistaken, to resolve all our doubts."

As he spoke there was the sharp sound of horses' hoofs and grating wheels against the kerb, followed by a sharp pull at the bell. Holmes whistled.

"A pair by the sound," said he. "Yes," he continued, glancing out of the window. "A nice little brougham and a pair of beauties. A hundred and fifty guineas apiece. There's money in this case, Watson, if there is nothing else."

"I think that I had better go, Holmes."

"Not a bit, Doctor. Stay where you are. I am lost without my Boswell. And this promises to be interesting. It would be a pity to miss it."

"But your client—"

"Never mind him. I may want your help, and so may he. Here he comes. Sit down in that arm-chair, Doctor, and give us your best attention."

A slow and heavy step, which had been heard upon the stairs and in the passage, paused immediately outside the door. Then there was a loud and authoritative tap.

"Come in!" said Holmes.

A man entered who could hardly have been less than six feet six inches in height, with the chest and limbs of a Hercules. His dress was rich with a richness which would, in England, be looked upon as akin to bad taste. Heavy bands of astrakhan were slashed across the sleeves and fronts of his double-breasted coat, while the deep blue cloak which was thrown over his shoulders was lined with flame-coloured silk, and secured at the neck with a brooch which consisted of a single flaming beryl. Boots which extended half-way up his calves, and which were trimmed at the tops with rich brown fur, completed the impression of barbaric opulence which was suggested by his whole appearance. He carried a broad-brimmed hat in his hand, while he wore across the upper part of his face, extending down past the cheek-bones, a black vizard mask, which he had apparently adjusted that very moment, for his hand was still raised to it as he entered. From the lower part of the face he appeared to be a man of strong character, with a thick, hanging lip, and a long straight chin, suggestive of resolution pushed to the length of obstinacy.

"You had my note?" he asked, with a deep, harsh voice and a strongly marked German accent. "I told you that I would call." He looked from one to the other of us, as if uncertain which to address.

"Pray take a seat," said Holmes. "This is my friend and colleague, Dr. Watson, who is occasionally good enough to help me in my cases. Whom have I the honour to address?"

"You may address me as the Count von Kramm, a Bohemian nobleman. I understand that this gentleman, your friend, is a man of honour and discretion, whom I may trust with a matter of the most extreme importance. If not, I should much prefer to communicate with you alone."

I rose to go, but Holmes caught me by the wrist and pushed me back into my chair. "It is both, or none," said he. "You may say before this gentleman anything which you may say to me."

The Count shrugged his broad shoulders. "Then I must begin," said he, "by binding you both to absolute secrecy for two years, at the end of that time the matter will be of no importance. At present it is not too much to say that it is of such weight that it may have an influence upon European history."

"I promise," said Holmes.

"And I."

"You will excuse this mask," continued our strange visitor. "The august person who employs me wishes his agent to be unknown to you, and I may confess at once that the title by which I have just called myself is not exactly my own."

"I was aware of it," said Holmes dryly.

"The circumstances are of great delicacy, and every precaution has to be taken to quench what might grow to be an immense scandal and seriously compromise one of the reigning families of Europe. To speak plainly, the matter implicates the great House of Ormstein, hereditary Kings of Bohemia."

"I was also aware of that," murmured Holmes, settling himself down in his arm-chair and closing his eyes.

Our visitor glanced with some apparent surprise at the languid, lounging figure of the man who had been no doubt depicted to him as the most incisive reasoner, and most energetic agent in Europe. Holmes slowly reopened his eyes, and looked impatiently at his gigantic client.

"If your Majesty would condescend to state your case," he remarked, "I should be better able to advise you."

The man sprang from his chair, and paced up and down the room in uncontrollable agitation. Then, with a gesture of desperation, he tore the mask from his face and hurled it upon the ground. "You are right," he cried, "I am the King. Why should I attempt to conceal it?"

"Why, indeed?" murmured Holmes. "Your Majesty had not spoken before I was aware that I was addressing Wilhelm Gottsreich Sigismond von Ormstein, Grand Duke of Cassel-Falstein, and hereditary King of Bohemia."

"But you can understand," said our strange visitor, sitting down once more and passing his hand over his high, white forehead, "you can understand that I am not accustomed to doing such business in my own person. Yet the matter was so delicate that I could not confide it to an agent without putting myself in his power. I have come incognito from Prague for the purpose of consulting you."

"Then, pray consult," said Holmes, shutting his eyes once more.

"The facts are briefly these: Some five years ago, during a lengthy visit to Warsaw, I made the acquaintance of the well-known adventuress Irene Adler. The name is no doubt familiar to you."

"Kindly look her up in my index, Doctor," murmured Holmes, without opening his eyes. For many years he had adopted a system of docketing all paragraphs concerning men and things, so that it was difficult to name a subject or a person on which he could not at once furnish information. In this case I found her biography sandwiched in between that of a Hebrew Rabbi and that of a staff-commander who had written a monograph upon the deep-sea fishes.

"Let me see," said Holmes. "Hum! Born in New Jersey in the year 1858. Contralto—hum! La Scala, hum! Prima donna Imperial Opera of Warsaw—Yes! Retired from operative stage—ha! Living in London—quite so! Your Majesty, as I understand, became entangled with this young person, wrote her some compromising letters, and is now desirous of getting those letters back."

"Precisely so. But how—"

"Was there a secret marriage?"

"None."

"No legal papers or certificates?"

"None."

"Then I fail to follow Your Majesty. If this young person should produce her letters for blackmailing or other purposes, how is she to prove their authenticity?"

"There is the writing."

"Pooh, pooh! Forgery."

"My private note-paper."

"Stolen."

"My own seal."

"Imitated."

"My photograph."

"Bought."

"We were both in the photograph."

"Oh, dear! That is very bad! Your Majesty has indeed committed an indiscretion."

"I was mad—insane."

"You have compromised yourself seriously."

"I was only Crown Prince then. I was young. I am but thirty now."

"It must be recovered."

"We have tried and failed."

"Your Majesty must pay. It must be bought."

"She will not sell."

"Stolen, then."

"Five attempts have been made. Twice burglars in my pay ransacked her house. Once we diverted her luggage when she travelled. Twice she has been waylaid. There has been no result."

"No sign of it?"

"Absolutely none."

Holmes laughed. "It is quite a pretty little problem," said he.

"But a very serious one to me," returned the King, reproachfully.

"Very, indeed. And what does she propose to do with the photograph?"

"To ruin me."

"But how?"

"I am about to be married."

"So I have heard."

"To Clotilde Lothman von Saxe-Meningen, second daughter of the King of Scandinavia. You may know the strict principles of her family. She is herself the very soul of delicacy. A shadow of a doubt as to my conduct would bring the matter to an end."

"And Irene Adler?"

"Threatens to send them the photograph. And she will do it. I know that she will do it. You do not know her, but she has a soul of steel. She has the face of the most beautiful of women, and the mind of the most resolute of men. Rather than I should marry another woman, there are no lengths to which she would not go—none."

"You are sure that she has not sent it yet?"

"I am sure."

"And why?"

"Because she has said that she would send it on the day when the betrothal was publicly proclaimed. That will be next Monday."

"Oh, then, we have three days yet," said Holmes, with a yawn. "That is very fortunate, as I have one or two matters of importance to look into just at present. Your Majesty will, of course, stay in London for the present?"

"Certainly. You will find me at the Langham, under the name of the Count von Kramm."

"Then I shall drop you a line to let you know how we progress."

"Pray do so. I shall be all anxiety."

"Then, as to money?"

"You have *carte blanche*."

"Absolutely?"

"I tell you that I would give one of the provinces of my kingdom to have that photograph."

"And for present expenses?"

The King took a heavy chamois leather bag from under his cloak, and laid it on the table.

"There are three hundred pounds in gold, and seven hundred in notes," he said.

Holmes scribbled a receipt upon a sheet of his notebook, and handed it to him.

"And mademoiselle's address?" he asked.

"Is Briony Lodge, Serpentine Avenue, St. John's Wood."

Holmes took a note of it. "One other question," said he. "Was the photograph a cabinet?"

"It was."

"Then, good night, Your Majesty, and I trust that we shall soon have some good news for you. And good night, Watson," he added, as the wheels of the Royal brougham rolled down the street. "If you will be good enough to call to-morrow afternoon, at three o'clock, I should like to chat this little matter over with you."

I I

At three o'clock precisely I was at Baker Street, but Holmes had not yet returned. The landlady informed me that he had left the house shortly after eight o'clock in the morning. I sat down beside the fire, however, with the intention of awaiting him, however long he might be. I was already deeply interested in his inquiry, for, though it was surrounded by none of the grim and strange features which were associated with the two crimes which I have elsewhere recorded, still, the nature of the case and the exalted station of his client gave it a character of its own. Indeed, apart from the nature of the investigation which my friend had on hand, there was something in his masterly grasp of a situation, and his keen, incisive reasoning, which made it a pleasure to me to study his system of work, and to follow the quick, subtle methods by which he disentangled the most inextricable mysteries. So accustomed was I to his invariable success that the very possibility of his failing had ceased to enter into my head.

It was close upon four before the door opened, and a drunken-looking groom, ill-kempt and side-whiskered with an inflamed face and disreputable clothes, walked into the room. Accustomed as I was to my friend's amazing powers in the use of disguises, I had to look three times before I was certain that it was indeed he. With a nod he vanished into the bedroom, whence he emerged in five minutes tweed-suited and respectable, as of old. Putting his hands into his pockets, he stretched out his legs in front of the fire, and laughed heartily for some minutes.

"Well, really!" he cried, and then he choked; and laughed again until he was obliged to lie back, limp and helpless, in the chair.

"What is it?"

"It's quite too funny. I am sure you could never guess how I employed my morning, or what I ended by doing."

"I can't imagine. I suppose that you have been watching the habits, and perhaps the house, of Miss Irene Adler."

"Quite so, but the sequel was rather unusual. I will tell you, however. I left the house a little after eight o'clock this morning, in the character of a groom out of work. There is a wonderful sympathy and freemasonry among horsey men. Be one of them, and you will know all that there is to know. I soon found Briony Lodge. It is a bijou villa, with a garden at the back, but built out in front right up to the road, two stories. Chubb lock to the door. Large sitting-room on the right side, well furnished, with long windows almost to the floor, and those preposterous English window fasteners which a child could open. Behind there was nothing remarkable, save that the passage window could be reached from the top of the coach-house. I walked round it and examined it closely from every point of view, but without noting anything else of interest.

"I then lounged down the street, and found, as I expected, that there was a mews in a lane which runs down by one wall of the garden. I lent the ostlers a hand in rubbing down their horses, and I received in exchange twopence, a glass of half-and-half, two fills of shag tobacco and as much information as I could desire about Miss Adler, to say nothing of half a dozen other people in the neighbourhood in whom I was not in the least interested, but whose biographies I was compelled to listen to."

"And what of Irene Adler?" I asked.

"Oh, she has turned all the men's heads down in that part. She is the daintiest thing under a bonnet on this planet. So say the Serpentine Mews, to a man. She lives quietly, sings at concerts, drives out at five every day, and returns at seven sharp for dinner. Seldom goes out at other times, except when she sings. Has only one male visitor, but a good deal of him. He is dark, handsome, and dashing; never calls less than once a day, and often twice. He is a Mr. Godfrey Norton, of the Inner Temple. See the advantages of a cabman as a confidant. They had driven him home a dozen times from Serpentine Mews, and knew all about him. When I had listened to all that they had to tell, I began to walk up and down near Briony Lodge once more, and to think over my plan of campaign.

"This Godfrey Norton was evidently an important factor in the matter. He was a lawyer. That sounded ominous. What was the relation between them, and what the object of his repeated visits? Was she his client, his friend, or his mistress? If the former, she had probably transferred the photograph to his keeping. If the latter, it was less likely. On the issue of this question depended whether I should continue my work at Briony Lodge, or turn my attention to the gentleman's chambers in the Temple. It was a delicate point, and it widened the field of my inquiry. I fear that I bore you with these details, but I have to let you see my little difficulties, if you are to understand the situation."

"I am following you closely," I answered.

"I was still balancing the matter in my mind when a hansom cab drove up to Briony Lodge, and a gentleman sprang out. He was a remarkably handsome man, dark, aquiline, and moustached—evidently the man of whom I had heard. He appeared to be in a great hurry, shouted to the cabman to wait, and brushed past the maid who opened the door with the air of a man who was thoroughly at home.

"He was in the house about half an hour, and I could catch glimpses of him, in the windows of the sitting-room, pacing up and down, talking excitedly and waving his arms. Of her I could see nothing. Presently he emerged, looking even more flurried than before. As he stepped up to the cab, he pulled a gold watch from his pocket and looked at it earnestly. 'Drive like the devil,' he shouted, 'first to Gross and Hankey's in Regent Street, and then to the church of St. Monica in the Edgware Road. Half a guinea if you do it in twenty minutes!'

"Away they went, and I was just wondering whether I should not do well to follow them, when up the lane came a neat little landau, the coachman with his coat only half buttoned, and his tie under his ear, while all the tags of his harness were sticking out of the buckles. It hadn't pulled up before she shot out of the hall door and into it. I only caught a glimpse of her at the moment, but she was a lovely woman, with a face that a man might die for.

"'The Church of St. Monica, John,' she cried, 'and half a sovereign if you reach it in twenty minutes.'"

"This was quite too good to lose, Watson. I was just balancing whether I should run for it, or whether I should perch behind her landau, when a cab came through the street. The driver looked twice at such a shabby fare; but I jumped in before he could object. 'The Church of St. Monica,' said I, 'and half a sovereign if you reach it in twenty minutes.' It was twenty-five minutes to twelve, and of course it was clear enough what was in the wind.

"My cabby drove fast. I don't think I ever drove faster, but the others were there before us. The cab and the landau with their steaming horses were in front of the door when I arrived. I paid the man and hurried into the church. There was not a soul there save the two whom I had followed, and a surpliced clergyman, who seemed to be expostulating with them.

They were all three standing in a knot in front of the altar. I lounged up the side aisle like any other idler who has dropped into a church. Suddenly, to my surprise, the three at the altar faced round to me, and Godfrey Norton came running as hard as he could towards me.

" 'Thank God!' he cried. 'You'll do. Come! Come!' "

" 'What then?' " I asked.

" 'Come, man, come, only three minutes, or it won't be legal.' "

"I was half dragged up to the altar, and before I knew where I was, I found myself mumbling responses which were whispered in my ear, and vouching for things of which I knew nothing, and generally assisting in the secure tying up of Irene Adler, spinster, to Godfrey Norton, bachelor. It was all done in an instant, and there was the gentleman thanking me on the one side and the lady on the other, while the clergyman beamed on me in front. It was the most preposterous position in which I ever found myself in my life, and it was the thought of it that started me laughing just now. It seems that there had been some informality about their licence, that the clergyman absolutely refused to marry them without a witness of some sort, and that my lucky appearance saved the bridegroom from having to sally out into the streets in search of a best man. The bride gave me a sovereign, and I mean to wear it on my watch-chain in memory of the occasion."

"This is a very unexpected turn of affairs," said I; "and what then?"

"Well, I found my plans very seriously menaced. It looked as if the pair might take an immediate departure, and so necessitate very prompt and energetic measures on my part. At the church door, however, they separated, he driving back to the Temple, and she to her own house. 'I shall drive out in the Park at five as usual,' she said as she left him. I heard no more. They drove away in different directions, and I went off to make my own arrangements."

"Which are?"

"Some cold beef and a glass of beer," he answered, ringing the bell. "I have been too busy to think of food, and I am likely to be busier still this evening. By the way, Doctor, I shall want your co-operation."

"I shall be delighted."

"You don't mind breaking the law?"

"Not in the least."

"Nor running a chance of arrest?"

"Not in a good cause."

"Oh, the cause is excellent!"

"Then I am your man."

"I was sure that I might rely on you."

"But what is it you wish?"

"When Mrs. Turner has brought in the tray I will make it clear to you. Now," he said, as he turned hungrily on the simple fare that our landlady had provided, "I must discuss it while I eat, for I have not much time. It is nearly five now. In two hours we must be on the scene of action. Miss Irene, or Madame, rather, returns from her drive at seven. We must be at Briony Lodge to meet her."

"And what then?"

"You must leave that to me. I have already arranged what is to occur. There is only one point on which I must insist. You must not interfere, come what may. You understand?"

"I am to be neutral?"

"To do nothing whatever. There will probably be some small unpleasantness. Do not join in it. It will end in my being conveyed into the house. Four or five minutes afterwards the sitting-room window will open. You are to station yourself close to that open window."

"Yes."

"You are to watch for me, for I will be visible to you."

"Yes."

"And when I raise my hand—so—you will throw into the room what I give you to throw, and will, at the same time, raise the cry of fire. You quite follow me?"

"Entirely."

"It is nothing very formidable," he said, taking a long cigar-shaped roll from his pocket. "It is an ordinary plumber's smoke rocket, fitted with a cap at either end to make it self-lighting. Your task is confined to that. When you raise your cry of fire, it will be taken up by quite a number of people. You may then walk to the end of the street, and I will rejoin you in ten minutes. I hope that I have made myself clear?"

"I am to remain neutral, to get near the window, to watch you, and, at the signal, to throw in this object, then to raise the cry of fire, and to await you at the corner of the street."

"Precisely."

"Then you may entirely rely on me."

"That is excellent. I think perhaps it is almost time that I prepared for the new role I have to play."

He disappeared into his bedroom, and returned in a few minutes in the character of an amiable and simple-minded Nonconformist clergyman. His broad black hat, his baggy trousers, his white tie, his sympathetic smile, and general look of peering and benevolent curiosity, were such as

Mr. John Hare* alone could have equalled. It was not merely that Holmes changed his costume. His expression, his manner, his very soul seemed to vary with every fresh part that he assumed. The stage lost a fine actor, even as science lost an acute reasoner, when he became a specialist in crime.

It was a quarter past six when we left Baker Street, and it still wanted ten minutes to the hour when we found ourselves in Serpentine Avenue. It was already dusk, and the lamps were just being lighted as we paced up and down in front of Briony Lodge, waiting for the coming of its occupant. The house was just such as I had pictured it from Sherlock Holmes's succinct description, but the locality appeared to be less private than I expected. On the contrary, for a small street in a quiet neighbourhood, it was remarkably animated. There was a group of shabbily-dressed men smoking and laughing in a corner, a scissor-grinder with his wheel, two guardsmen who were flirting with a nurse-girl, and several well-dressed young men who were lounging up and down with cigars in their mouths.

"You see," remarked Holmes, as we paced to and fro in front of the house, "this marriage rather simplifies matters. The photograph becomes a double-edged weapon now. The chances are that she would be as averse to its being seen by Mr. Godfrey Norton, as our client is to its coming to the eyes of his Princess. Now the question is—Where are we to find the photograph?"

"Where, indeed?"

"It is most unlikely that she carries it about with her. It is cabinet size. To large for easy concealment about a woman's dress. She knows that the King is capable of having her waylaid and searched. Two attempts of the sort have already been made. We may take it then that she does not carry it about with her."

"Where, then?"

"Her banker or her lawyer. There is that double possibility. But I am inclined to think neither. Women are naturally secretive, and they like to do their own secreting. Why should she hand it over to anyone else? She could trust her own guardianship, but she could not tell what indirect or political influence might be brought to bear upon a business man. Besides, remember that she had resolved to use it within a few days. It must be where she can lay her hands upon it. It must be in her own house."

"But it has twice been burgled."

"Pshaw! They did not know how to look."

"But how will you look?"

---

*John Hare (1844–1921), later knighted, was a Victorian actor noted for his make-up in a variety of character roles, according to Laurence Senelick.

"I will not look."

"What then?"

"I will get her to show me."

"But she will refuse."

"She will not be able to. But I hear the rumble of wheels. It is her carriage. Now carry out my orders to the letter."

As he spoke, the gleam of the sidelights of a carriage came round the curve of the avenue. It was a smart little landau which rattled up to the door of Briony Lodge. As it pulled up, one of the loafing men at the corner dashed forward to open the door in the hope of earning a copper, but was elbowed away by another loafer who had rushed up with the same intention. A fierce quarrel broke out, which was increased by the two guardsmen, who took sides with one of the loungers, and by the scissors-grinder, who was equally hot upon the other side. A blow was struck, and in an instant the lady, who had stepped from her carriage, was the centre of a little knot of flushed and struggling men who struck savagely at each other with their fists and sticks. Holmes dashed into the crowd to protect the lady; but just as he reached her, he gave a cry and dropped to the ground, with the blood running freely down his face. At his fall the guardsmen took to their heels in one direction and the loungers in the other, while a number of better dressed people who had watched the scuffle without taking part in it, crowded in to help the lady and to attend to the injured man. Irene Adler, as I will still call her, had hurried up the steps; but she stood at the top with her superb figure outlined against the lights of the hall, looking back into the street.

"Is the poor gentleman much hurt?" she asked.

"He is dead," cried several voices.

"No, no, there's life in him," shouted another. "But he'll be gone before you can get him to hospital."

"He's a brave fellow," said a woman. "They would have had the lady's purse and watch if it hadn't been for him. They were a gang, and a rough one, too. Ah, he's breathing now."

"He can't lie in the street. May we bring him in, marm?"

"Surely. Bring him into the sitting-room. There is a comfortable sofa. This way, please!"

Slowly and solemnly he was borne into Briony Lodge, and laid out in the principal room, while I still observed the proceedings from my post by the window. The lamps had been lit, but the blinds had not been drawn, so that I could see Holmes as he lay upon the couch. I do not know whether he was seized with compunction at that moment for the part he was playing, but I know that I never felt more heartily ashamed of myself in my life than when I saw the beautiful creature against whom I was conspiring, or the grace and kindliness with which she waited upon the injured man. And yet it would be the blackest treachery to Holmes to draw back now from the part which he had entrusted to me. I hardened my heart and took the smoke rocket from under my ulster. After all, I thought, we are not injuring her. We are but preventing her from injuring another.

Holmes had sat up upon the couch, and I saw him motion like a man who is in want of air. A maid rushed across and threw open the window. At the same instant I saw him raise his hand, and at the signal I tossed my rocket into the room with a cry of "Fire." The word was no sooner out of my mouth than the whole crowd of spectators, well dressed and ill—gentlemen, ostlers, and servant maids—joined in a general shriek of "Fire." Thick clouds of smoke curled through the room, and out at the open window. I caught a glimpse of rushing figures, and a moment later the voice of Holmes from within, assuring them that it was a false alarm. Slipping through the shouting crowd I made my way to the corner of the street, and in ten minutes was rejoiced to find my friend's arm in mine, and to get away from the scene of the uproar. He walked swiftly and in silence for some few minutes, until we had turned down one of the quiet streets which lead towards the Edgware Road.

"You did it very nicely, Doctor," he remarked. "Nothing could have been better. It is all right."

"You have the photograph!"

"I know where it is."

"And how did you find out?"

"She showed me, as I told you that she would."

"I am still in the dark."

"I do not wish to make a mystery," said he, laughing. "The matter was perfectly simple. You, of course, saw that every one in the street was an accomplice. They were all engaged for the evening."

"I guessed as much."

"Then, when the row broke out, I had a little moist red paint in the palm of my hand. I rushed forward, fell down, clapped my hand to my face, and became a piteous spectacle. It is an old trick."

"That also I could fathom."

"Then they carried me in. She was bound to have me in. What else could she do? And into her sitting-room which was the very room which I suspected. It lay between that and her bedroom, and I was determined to see which. They laid me on a couch, I motioned for air, they were compelled to open the window and you had your chance."

"How did that help you?"

"It was all-important. When a woman thinks that her house is on fire, her instinct is at once to rush to the thing which she values most. It is a perfectly overpowering impulse, and I have more than once taken advantage of it. In the case of the Darlington Substitution Scandal it was of use to me, and also in the Arnsworth Castle business. A married woman grabs at her baby—an unmarried one reaches for her jewel box. Now it was clear to me that our lady of to-day had nothing in the house more precious to her than what we are in quest of. She would rush to secure it. The alarm of fire was admirably done. The smoke and shouting was enough to shake nerves of steel. She responded beautifully. The photograph is in a recess behind a sliding panel just above the right bell-pull. She was there in an instant, and I caught a glimpse of it as she half drew it out. When I cried out that it was a false alarm, she replaced it, glanced at the rocket, rushed from the room, and I have not seen her since. I rose, and, making my excuses, escaped from the house. I hesitated whether to attempt to secure the photograph at once; but the coachman had come in, and as he was watching me narrowly, it seemed safer to wait. A little over-precipitance may ruin all."

" 'And now?' " I asked.

"Our quest is practically finished. I shall call with the King to-morrow, and with you, if you care to come with us. We will be shown into the sitting-room to wait for the lady, but it is probable that when she comes she may find neither us nor the photograph. It might be a satisfaction to His Majesty to regain it with his own hands."

"And when will you call?"

"At eight in the morning. She will not be up, so that we shall have a clear field. Besides, we must be prompt, for this marriage may mean a complete change in her life and habits. I must wire to the King without delay."

We had reached Baker Street, and had stopped at the door. He was searching his pockets for the key, when some one passing said:

"Good night, Mister Sherlock Holmes."

There were several people on the pavement at the time, but the greeting appeared to come from a slim youth in an ulster who had hurried by.

"I've heard that voice before," said Holmes, staring down the dimly lit street. "Now, I wonder who the deuce that could have been."

III

I slept at Baker Street that night, and we were engaged upon our toast and coffee when the King of Bohemia rushed into the room.

"You have really got it!" he cried, grasping Sherlock Holmes by either shoulder, and looking eagerly into his face.

"Not yet."

"But you have hopes?"

"I have hopes."

"Then, come. I am all impatience to be gone."

"We must have a cab."

"No, my brougham is waiting."

"Then that will simplify matters."

We descended, and started off once more for Briony Lodge.

"Irene Adler is married," remarked Holmes.

"Married! When?"

"Yesterday."

"But to whom?"

"To an English lawyer named Norton."

"But she could not love him?"

"I am in hopes that she does."

"And why in hopes?"

"Because it would spare Your Majesty all fear of future annoyance. If the lady loves her husband, she does not love Your Majesty. If she does not love Your Majesty there is no reason why she should interfere with Your Majesty's plan."

"It is true. And yet—! Well! I wish she had been of my own station. What a queen she would have made!" He relapsed into a moody silence which was not broken until we drew up in Serpentine Avenue.

The door of Briony Lodge was open, and an elderly woman stood upon the steps. She watched us with a sardonic eye as we stepped from the brougham.

"Mr. Sherlock Holmes, I believe?" said she.

"I am Mr. Holmes," answered my companion, looking at her with a questioning and rather startled gaze.

"Indeed! My mistress told me that you were likely to call. She left this morning with her husband, by the 5.15 train from Charing Cross, for the Continent."

"What!" Sherlock Holmes staggered back, white with chagrin and surprise. "Do you mean that she has left England?"

"Never to return."

"And the papers?" asked the King hoarsely. "All is lost."

"We shall see." He pushed past the servant, and rushed into the drawing-room, followed by the King and myself. The furniture was scattered about in every direction, with dismantled shelves, and open drawers, as if the lady had hurriedly ransacked them before her flight. Holmes rushed at the bell-pull, tore back a small sliding shutter, and, plunging in his hand, pulled out a photograph and a letter. The photograph was of Irene Adler herself in evening dress, the letter was superscribed to 'Sherlock Holmes, Esq. To be left till called for.' My friend tore it open and we all three read it together. It was dated at midnight of the preceding night, and ran in this way:—

"My Dear Mr. Sherlock Holmes—You really did it very well. You took me in completely. Until after the alarm of fire, I had not a suspicion. But then, when I found how I had betrayed myself, I began to think. I had been warned against you months ago. I had been told that if the King employed an agent, it would certainly be you. And your address had been given me. Yet, with all this, you made me reveal what you wanted to know. Even after I became suspicious, I found it hard to think evil of such a dear, kind old clergyman. But, you know, I have been trained as an actress myself. Male costume is nothing new to me. I often take advantage of the freedom which it gives. I sent John, the coachman, to watch you, ran upstairs, got into my walking clothes, as I call them, and came down just as you departed.

"Well, I followed you to your door, and so made sure that I was really an object of interest to the celebrated Mr. Sherlock Holmes. Then I, rather imprudently, wished you good night, and started for the Temple to see my husband.

"We both thought the best resource was flight when pursued by so formidable an antagonist; so you will find the nest empty when you call to-morrow. As to the photograph, your client may rest in peace. I love and am loved by a better man than he. The King may do what he will without hindrance from one whom he has cruelly wronged. I keep it only to safeguard myself, and to preserve a weapon which will always secure me from any steps which he might take in the future. I leave a photograph which he might care to possess; and I remain, dear Mr. Sherlock Holmes, very truly yours,

IRENE NORTON, *née* ADLER."

"What a woman—oh, what a woman!" cried the King of Bohemia, when we had all three read this epistle. "Did I not tell you how quick and resolute she was? Would she not have made an admirable queen? Is it not a pity she was not on my level?"

"From what I have seen of the lady, she seems, indeed, to be on a very different level to Your Majesty," said Holmes, coldly. "I am sorry that I have not been able to bring Your Majesty's business to a more successful conclusion."

"On the contrary, my dear sir," cried the King. "Nothing could be more successful. I know that her word is inviolate. The photograph is now as safe as if it were in the fire."

"I am glad to hear Your Majesty say so."

"I am immensely indebted to you. Pray tell me in what way I can reward you. This ring—" He slipped an emerald snake ring from his finger and held it out upon the palm of his hand.

"Your Majesty has something which I should value even more highly," said Holmes.

"You have but to name it."

"This photograph!"

The King stared at him in amazement.

"Irene's photograph!" he cried. "Certainly, if you wish it."

"I thank Your Majesty. Then there is no more to be done in the matter. I have the honour to wish you a very good morning." He bowed, and, turning away without observing the hand which the King had stretched out to him, he set off in my company for his chambers.

And that was how a great scandal threatened to affect the kingdom of Bohemia, and how the best plans of Mr. Sherlock Holmes were beaten by a woman's wit. He used to make merry over the cleverness of women, but I have not heard him do it of late. And when he speaks of Irene Adler, or when he refers to her photograph, it is always under the honourable title of *the* woman.

THOMAS HARDY

AN IMAGINATIVE WOMAN

1 8 9 4

—————

The writings of Hardy (1840–1928) reveal a persistent interest in the imaginative uses of what he once called "the heliographic science."[1] *Though the author disparaged "photographic curiousness" and unselective realism, his own style can be considered markedly "photographic" with its use of framed settings, voyeuristic characters, decisive pictorial moments, and highly visual diction to portray the struggles of his typical characters against indifferent fate. Invented photographs often recur in Hardy's pessimistic poetry and fiction, variously serving as realistic or topical detail, plot device, means of characterization, thematic reinforcement, or iconic metaphor.*[2] *The photograph featured in this short masterpiece—apparently inspired by Hardy's frustrated passion for the married writer Florence Henniker—powerfully combines all these elements. The picture also enables the plot, which characteristically dramatizes the futility of matching private dreams with social realities, to frustrate the reader's conventional expectations.*[3] *Aside from his writing, however, Hardy didn't concern himself with photography either as an art form or even a document. But, though irritated when "Kodaked" by curious tourists, he proved a gracious sitter for serious photographers.*[4]

1. See Hardy, *A Laodicean* [1881] (London: Macmillan, 1975), Bk. 5, ch. 4, p. 311. See also Arlene M. Jackson, "Photography as Style and Metaphor in the Art of Thomas Hardy," *Thomas Hardy Annual* 2 (Atlantic Highlands, N.J.: Humanities Press, 1984), pp. 91–109, who discusses Hardy's use of photography throughout his works except for his poem "The Son's Portrait" (1924/1928), cited below in note 2. See also West, *Soft Murder by the Camera Eye*, pp. 20–21, 70–79, 136–52.

2. See Hardy's fiction, for examples: *Desperate Remedies* [1871] (London: Macmillan, 1975), ch. 17, pp. 319–21; ch. 18, pp. 324, 326, discussed in Jennifer M. Green, "Outside the Frame: The Photographer in Victorian Fiction," *Victorian Institute Jour-*

nal 19 (1991): 123-28; *A Laodicean* [1881] (London, 1975): Bk. 2: ch. 2-3, pp. 201-6; Bk. 5: ch. 4, pp. 310-11; ch. 6, p. 322; ch. 11, p. 353; ch. 13, pp. 366-67; and *Jude the Obscure* [1895], edited by Norman Page (New York: Norton, 1978): Pt. 1, ch. 11, pp. 60-61; Pt. 2, ch. 1, p. 72; ch. 2, p. 69; Pt. 3, ch. 1, p. 108; ch. 2, pp. 111-12; ch. 3, p. 113; ch. 6, p. 129; Pt. 4, ch. 1, p. 164, especially the telling scene (Pt. 1, ch. 11, p. 85) in which the title character discovers that his wife has sold — for the frame's value — the photograph of himself he gave her on their wedding day. This incident becomes the subject of a much later poem, "The Son's Portrait," mentioned by Hardy in 1924 but published posthumously in *Winter Words in Various Moods and Meters* (London: Macmillan, 1928), pp. 60-61. See also "The Photograph," mentioned in his letter to Ruth Head, August 7, 1921, in *The Collected Letters of Thomas Hardy*, edited by Richard Little Purdy and Michael Millgate (Oxford: Clarendon Press, 1987), vol. 6, p. 96; Jackson, "Photography as Style," p. 101, suggests this poem was originally composed between 1884 and 1890.

3. See Martin Seymour-Smith, *Hardy* (London: Bloomsbury, 1994), pp. 466, 496, 499-506, about Robert Trewe as a partial self-portrait of Hardy and about Florence Henniker, who "excited his lust, love and, later, involuntary resentment." These qualities are all expressed in "An Imaginative Woman," which Seymour-Smith terms "one of the few unequivocal masterpieces of comi-tragedy among [Hardy's] short stories"; he incorrectly asserts (p. 467), however, that the story, written in 1893 and published in 1894, did not appear until 1897. For other discussions of this story, see Martin Ray's comprehensive " 'An Imaginative Woman': From Manuscript to Wessex Edition," *Thomas Hardy Journal* 9 (October 1993): 76-83; and Ruth Essex's feminist piece, "Mrs. Marchmill, Mother and Poetess," *Thomas Hardy Journal* 10, no. 3 (October 1994): 64-66.

4. Quoted in Jackson, "Photography as Style," p. 91. See also Coburn's portrait of Hardy, October 13, 1913, originally published in *More Men of Mark*, Plate 13, and reproduced in Alvin Langdon Coburn, *Autobiography*, edited by Helmut and Alison Gernsheim, p. 98; and E. O. Hoppé's photograph of Hardy and his second wife (1914), reproduced in Michael Millgate, ed., *The Life and Work of Thomas Hardy* (Athens: University of Georgia Press, 1984), Fig. 13, following p. 305.

AN IMAGINATIVE WOMAN

W hen William Marchmill had finished his inquiries for lodgings at the well-known watering-place of Solentsea in Upper Wessex, he returned to the hotel to find his wife. She, with the children, had rambled along the shore, and Marchmill followed in the direction indicated by the military-looking hall-porter.

"By Jove, how far you've gone! I am quite out of breath," Marchmill said, rather impatiently, when he came up with his wife, who was reading as she walked, the three children being considerably further ahead with the nurse.

Mrs Marchmill started out of the reverie into which the book had thrown her. "Yes," she said, "you've been such a long time. I was tired of staying in that dreary hotel. But I am sorry if you have wanted me, Will."

"Well, I have had trouble to suit myself. When you see the airy and comfortable rooms heard of, you find they are stuffy and uncomfortable. Will you come and see if what I've fixed on will do? There is not much room, I am afraid; but I can light on nothing better. The town is rather full."

The pair left the children and nurse to continue their ramble, and went back together.

In age well-balanced, in personal appearance fairly matched, and in domestic requirements comfortable, in temper this couple differed, though even here they did not often clash, he being equable, if not lymphatic, and she decidedly nervous and sanguine. It was to their tastes and fancies, those smallest, greatest particulars, that no common denominator could be applied. Marchmill considered his wife's likes and inclinations somewhat silly; she considered his sordid and material. The husband's business was that of a gunmaker in a thriving city northwards, and his soul was in that business always; the lady was best characterized by that superannuated phrase of elegance "a votary of the muse". An impressionable, palpitating creature was Ella, shrinking humanely from detailed knowledge of her husband's trade whenever she reflected that everything he manufactured had for its purpose the destruction of life. She could only recover her equanimity by assuring herself that some, at least, of his weapons were sooner or later used for the extermination of horrid vermin and animals almost as cruel to their inferiors in species as human beings were to theirs.

She had never antecedently regarded this occupation of his as any objection to having him for a husband. Indeed, the necessity of getting life-leased at all cost, a cardinal virtue which all good mothers teach, kept her from thinking of it at all till she had closed with William, had passed the honeymoon, and reached the reflecting stage. Then, like a person who has stumbled upon some object in the dark, she wondered what she had got; mentally walked round it, estimated it; whether it were rare or common; contained gold, silver, or lead; were a clog or a pedestal, everything to her or nothing.

She came to some vague conclusions, and since then had kept her heart alive by pitying her proprietor's obtuseness and want of refinement, pitying herself, and letting off her delicate and ethereal emotions in imaginative occupations, day-dreams, and night-sighs, which perhaps would not much have disturbed William if he had known of them.

Her figure was small, elegant, and slight in build, tripping, or rather bounding, in movement. She was dark-eyed, and had that marvellously bright and liquid sparkle in each pupil which characterizes persons of Ella's cast of soul, and is too often a cause of heartache to the possessor's male friends, ultimately sometimes to herself. Her husband was a tall, long-featured man, with a brown beard; he had a pondering regard; and was, it must be added, usually kind and tolerant to her. He spoke in squarely shaped sentences, and was supremely satisfied with a condition of sublunary things which made weapons a necessity.

Husband and wife walked till they had reached the house they were in search of, which stood in a terrace facing the sea, and was fronted by a small garden of wind-proof and salt-proof evergreens, stone steps leading up to the porch. It had its number in the row, but, being rather larger than the rest, was in addition sedulously distinguished as Coburg House by its landlady, though everybody else called it "Thirteen, New Parade". The spot was bright and lively now; but in winter it became necessary to place sandbags against the door, and to stuff up the keyhole against the wind and rain, which had worn the paint so thin that the priming and knotting showed through.

The householder, who had been watching for the gentleman's return, met them in the passage, and showed the rooms. She informed them that she was a professional man's widow, left in needy circumstances by the rather sudden death of her husband, and she spoke anxiously of the conveniences of the establishment.

Mrs Marchmill said that she liked the situation and the house; but, it being small, there would not be accommodation enough, unless she could have all the rooms.

The landlady mused with an air of disappointment. She wanted the visitors to be her tenants very badly, she said, with obvious honesty. But unfortunately two of the rooms were occupied permanently by a bachelor gentleman. He did not pay season prices, it was true; but as he kept on his apartments all the year round, and was an extremely nice and interesting young man, who gave no trouble, she did not like to turn him out for a month's "let", even at a high figure. "Perhaps, however," she added, "he might offer to go for a time."

They would not hear of this, and went back to the hotel, intending to proceed to the agent's to inquire further. Hardly had they sat down to tea when the landlady called. Her gentleman, she said, had been so obliging as to offer to give up his rooms for three or four weeks rather than drive the new-comers away.

"It is very kind, but we won't inconvenience him in that way," said the Marchmills.

"O, it won't inconvenience him, I assure you!" said the landlady eloquently. "You see, he's a different sort of young man from most—dreamy, solitary, rather melancholy—and he cares more to be here when the southwesterly gales are beating against the door, and the sea washes over the Parade, and there's not a soul in the place, than he does now in the season. He'd just as soon be where, in fact, he's going temporarily, to a little cottage on the Island opposite, for a change." She hoped therefore that they would come.

The Marchmill family accordingly took possession of the house next day, and it seemed to suit them very well. After luncheon Mr Marchmill strolled out towards the pier, and Mrs Marchmill, having despatched the children to their outdoor amusements on the sands, settled herself in more completely, examining this and that article, and testing the reflecting powers of the mirror in the wardrobe door.

In the small back sitting-room, which had been the young bachelor's, she found furniture of a more personal nature than in the rest. Shabby books, of correct rather than rare editions, were piled up in a queerly reserved manner in corners, as if the previous occupant had not conceived the possibility that any incoming person of the season's bringing could care to look inside them. The landlady hovered on the threshold to rectify anything that Mrs Marchmill might not find to her satisfaction.

"I'll make this my own little room," said the latter, "because the books are here. By the way, the person who has left seems to have a good many. He won't mind my reading some of them, Mrs Hooper, I hope?"

"O dear no, ma'am. Yes, he has a good many. You see, he is in the literary line himself somewhat. He is a poet—yes, really a poet—and he has a little income of his own, which is enough to write verses on, but not enough for cutting a figure, even if he cared to."

"A poet! Oh, I did not know that."

Mrs Marchmill opened one of the books, and saw the owner's name written on the title-page. "Dear me!" she continued; "I know his name very well—Robert Trewe—of course I do; and his writings! And it is *his* rooms we have taken, and *him* we have turned out of his home?"

Ella Marchmill, sitting down alone a few minutes later, thought with interested surprise of Robert Trewe. Her own latter history will best explain that interest. Herself the only daughter of a struggling man of letters,

she had during the last year or two taken to writing poems, in an endeav-
our to find a congenial channel in which to let flow her painfully embayed
emotions, whose former limpidity and sparkle seemed departing in the
stagnation caused by the routine of a practical household and the gloom of
bearing children to a commonplace father. These poems, subscribed with
a masculine pseudonym, had appeared in various obscure magazines, and
in two cases in rather prominent ones. In the second of the latter the page
which bore her effusion at the bottom, in smallish print, bore at the top,
in large print, a few verses on the same subject by this very man, Robert
Trewe. Both of them had, in fact, been struck by a tragic incident reported
in the daily papers, and had used it simultaneously as an inspiration, the
editor remarking in a note upon the coincidence, and that the excellence
of both poems prompted him to give them together.

After that event Ella, otherwise "John Ivy", had watched with much attention the appearance anywhere in print of verse bearing the signature of
Robert Trewe, who, with a man's unsusceptibility on the question of sex,
had never once thought of passing himself off as a woman. To be sure, Mrs
Marchmill had satisfied herself with a sort of reason for doing the contrary
in her case; since nobody might believe in her inspiration if they found that
the sentiments came from a pushing tradesman's wife, from the mother of
three children by a matter-of-fact small-arms manufacturer.

Trewe's verse contrasted with that of the rank and file of recent minor
poets in being impassioned rather than ingenious, luxuriant rather than
finished. Neither *symboliste* nor *décadent*, he was a pessimist in so far as that
character applies to a man who looks at the worst contingencies as well as
the best in the human condition. Being little attracted by excellences of
form and rhythm apart from content, he sometimes, when feeling outran
his artistic speed, perpetrated sonnets in the loosely rhymed Elizabethan
fashion, which every right-minded reviewer said he ought not to have done.

With sad and hopeless envy Ella Marchmill had often and often scanned
the rival poet's work, so much stronger as it always was than her own feeble
lines. She had imitated him, and her inability to touch his level would send
her into fits of despondency. Months passed away thus, till she observed
from the publisher's list that Trewe had collected his fugitive pieces into
a volume, which was duly issued, and was much or little praised according
to chance, and had a sale quite sufficient to pay for the printing.

This step onward had suggested to "John Ivy" the idea of collecting her
pieces also, or at any rate of making up a book of her rhymes by adding
many in manuscript to the few that had seen the light, for she had been
able to get no great number into print. A ruinous charge was made for

costs of publication; a few reviews noticed her poor little volume; but nobody talked of it, nobody bought it, and it fell dead in a fortnight—if it had ever been alive.

The author's thoughts were diverted to another groove just then by the discovery that she was going to have a third child, and the collapse of her poetical venture had perhaps less effect upon her mind than it might have done if she had been domestically unoccupied. Her husband had paid the publisher's bill with the doctor's, and there it all had ended for the time. But, though less than a poet of her century, Ella was more than a mere multiplier of her kind, and latterly she had begun to feel the old afflatus once more. And now by an odd conjunction she found herself in the rooms of Robert Trewe.

She thoughtfully rose from her chair and searched the apartment with the interest of a fellow-tradesman. Yes, the volume of his own verse was among the rest. Though quite familiar with its contents, she read it here as if it spoke aloud to her, then called up Mrs Hooper, the landlady, for some trivial service, and inquired again about the young man.

"Well, I'm sure you'd be interested in him, ma'am, if you could see him, only he's so shy that I don't suppose you will." Mrs Hooper seemed nothing loth to minister to her tenant's curiosity about her predecessor. "Lived here long? Yes, nearly two years. He keeps on his rooms even when he's not here: the soft air of this place suits his chest, and he likes to be able to come back at any time. He is mostly writing or reading, and doesn't see many people, though, for the matter of that, he is such a good, kind young fellow that folks would only be too glad to be friendly with him if they knew him. You don't meet kind-hearted people every day."

"Ah, he's kind-hearted . . . and good."

"Yes; he'll oblige me in anything if I ask him. 'Mr Trewe,' I say to him sometimes, 'you are rather out of spirits.' 'Well, I am, Mrs Hooper,' he'll say, 'though I don't know how you should find it out.' 'Why not take a little change?' I ask. Then in a day or two he'll say that he will take a trip to Paris, or Norway, or somewhere; and I assure you he comes back all the better for it."

"Ah, indeed! His is a sensitive nature, no doubt."

"Yes. Still he's odd in some things. Once when he had finished a poem of his composition late at night he walked up and down the room rehearsing it; and the floors being so thin—jerry-built houses, you know, though I say it myself—he kept me awake up above him till I wished him further. . . . But we get on very well."

This was but the beginning of a series of conversations about the rising poet as the days went on. On one of these occasions Mrs Hooper drew Ella's attention to what she had not noticed before: minute scribblings in pencil on the wall-paper behind the curtains at the head of the bed.

"O! let me look," said Mrs Marchmill, unable to conceal a rush of tender curiosity as she bent her pretty face close to the wall.

"These," said Mrs Hooper, with the manner of a woman who knew things, "are the very beginnings and first thoughts of his verses. He has tried to rub most of them out, but you can read them still. My belief is that he wakes up in the night, you know, with some rhyme in his head, and jots it down there on the wall lest he should forget it by the morning. Some of these very lines you see here I have seen afterwards in print in the magazines. Some are newer; indeed, I have not seen that one before. It must have been done only a few days ago."

"O yes! . . ."

Ella Marchmill flushed without knowing why, and suddenly wished her companion would go away, now that the information was imparted. An indescribable consciousness of personal interest rather than literary made her anxious to read the inscription alone; and she accordingly waited till she could do so, with a sense that a great store of emotion would be enjoyed in the act.

Perhaps because the sea was choppy outside the Island, Ella's husband found it much pleasanter to go sailing and steaming about without his wife, who was a bad sailor, than with her. He did not disdain to go thus alone on board the steamboats of the cheap-trippers, where there was dancing by moonlight, and where the couples would come suddenly down with a lurch into each other's arms; for, as he blandly told her, the company was too mixed for him to take her amid such scenes. Thus, while this thriving manufacturer got a great deal of change and sea-air out of his sojourn here, the life, external at least, of Ella was monotonous enough, and mainly consisted in passing a certain number of hours each day in bathing and walking up and down a stretch of shore. But the poetic impulse having again waxed strong, she was possessed by an inner flame which left her hardly conscious of what was proceeding around her.

She had read till she knew by heart Trewe's last little volume of verses, and spent a great deal of time in vainly attempting to rival some of them, till, in her failure, she burst into tears. The personal element in the magnetic attraction exercised by this circumambient, unapproachable master of hers was so much stronger than the intellectual and abstract that she could not understand it. To be sure, she was surrounded noon and night by his customary environment, which literally whispered of him to her at every moment; but he was a man she had never seen, and that all that moved her was the instinct to specialize a waiting emotion on the first fit thing that came to hand did not, of course, suggest itself to Ella.

In the natural way of passion under the too practical conditions which civilization has devised for its fruition, her husband's love for her had not survived, except in the form of fitful friendship, any more than, or even so much as, her own for him; and, being a woman of very living ardours, that required sustenance of some sort, they were beginning to feed on this chancing material, which was, indeed, of a quality far better than chance usually offers.

One day the children had been playing hide-and-seek in a closet, whence, in their excitement, they pulled out some clothing. Mrs Hooper explained that it belonged to Mr Trewe, and hung it up in the closet again. Possessed of her fantasy, Ella went later in the afternoon, when nobody was in that part of the house, opened the closet, unhitched one of the articles, a mackintosh, and put it on, with the waterproof cap belonging to it.

"The mantle of Elijah!" she said. "Would it might inspire me to rival him, glorious genius that he is!"

Her eyes always grew wet when she thought like that, and she turned to look at herself in the glass. *His* heart had beat inside that coat, and *his* brain had worked under that hat at levels of thought she would never reach. The consciousness of her weakness beside him made her feel quite sick. Before she had got the things off her the door opened, and her husband entered the room.

"What the devil—"

She blushed, and removed them.

"I found them in the closet here," she said, "and put them on in a freak. What have I else to do? You are always away!"

"Always away? Well. . . ."

That evening she had a further talk with the landlady, who might herself have nourished a half-tender regard for the poet, so ready was she to discourse ardently about him.

"You are interested in Mr Trewe, I know, ma'am," she said; "and he has just sent to say that he is going to call to-morrow afternoon to look up some books of his that he wants, if I'll be in, and he may select them from your room?"

"O yes!"

"You could very well meet Mr Trewe then, if you'd like to be in the way!"

She promised with secret delight, and went to bed musing of him.

Next morning her husband observed: "I've been thinking of what you said, Ell: that I have gone about a good deal and left you without much to amuse you. Perhaps it's true. To-day, as there's not much sea, I'll take you with me on board the yacht."

For the first time in her experience of such an offer Ella was not glad. But she accepted it for the moment. The time for setting out drew near, and she went to get ready. She stood reflecting. The longing to see the poet she was now distinctly in love with overpowered all other considerations.

"I don't want to go," she said to herself. "I can't bear to be away! And I won't go."

She told her husband that she had changed her mind about wishing to sail. He was indifferent, and went his way.

For the rest of the day the house was quiet, the children having gone out upon the sands. The blinds waved in the sunshine to the soft, steady stroke of the sea beyond the wall; and the notes of the Green Silesian band, a troop of foreign gentlemen hired for the season, had drawn almost all the residents and promenaders away from the vicinity of Coburg House. A knock was audible at the door.

Mrs Marchmill did not hear any servant go to answer it, and she became impatient. The books were in the room where she sat; but nobody came up. She rang the bell.

"There is some person waiting at the door," she said.

"O no, ma'am! He's gone long ago. I answered it," the servant replied, and Mrs Hooper came in herself.

"So disappointing!" she said, "Mr Trewe not coming after all!"

"But I heard him knock, I fancy!"

"No; that was somebody inquiring for lodgings who came to the wrong house. I forgot to tell you that Mr Trewe sent a note just before lunch to say I needn't get any tea for him, as he should not require the books, and wouldn't come to select them."

Ella was miserable, and for a long time could not even re-read his mournful ballad on "Severed Lives", so aching was her erratic little heart, and so tearful her eyes. When the children came in with wet stockings, and ran up to her to tell her of their adventures, she could not feel that she cared about them half as much as usual.

"Mrs Hooper, have you a photograph of—the gentleman who lived here?" She was getting to be curiously shy in mentioning his name.

"Why, yes. It's in the ornamental frame on the mantelpiece in your own bedroom, ma'am."

"No; the Royal Duke and Duchess are in that."

"Yes, so they are; but he's behind them. He belongs rightly to that frame, which I bought on purpose; but as he went away he said: 'Cover me up from those strangers that are coming, for God's sake. I don't want them staring at me, and I am sure they won't want me staring at them.' So I slipped in the Duke and Duchess temporarily in front of him, as they had no frame, and Royalties are more suitable for letting furnished than a private young man. If you take 'em out you'll see him under. Lord, ma'am, he wouldn't mind if he knew it! He didn't think the next tenant would be such an attractive lady as you, or he wouldn't have thought of hiding himself, perhaps."

"Is he handsome?" she asked timidly.

"*I* call him so. Some, perhaps, wouldn't."

"Should I?" she asked, with eagerness.

"I think you would, though some would say he's more striking than handsome; a large-eyed, thoughtful fellow, you know, with a very electric flash in his eye when he looks round quickly, such as you'd expect a poet to be who doesn't get his living by it."

"How old is he?"

"Several years older than yourself, ma'am; about thirty-one or two, I think."

Ella was, as a matter of fact, a few months over thirty herself; but she did not look nearly so much. Though so immature in nature, she was entering on that tract of life in which emotional women begin to suspect that last love may be stronger than first love; and she would soon, alas! enter on the still more melancholy tract when at least the vainer ones of her sex shrink from receiving a male visitor otherwise than with their backs to the window or the blinds half down. She reflected on Mrs Hooper's remark, and said no more about age.

Just then a telegram was brought up. It came from her husband, who had gone down the Channel as far as Budmouth with his friends in the yacht, and would not be able to get back till next day.

After her light dinner Ella idled about the shore with the children till dusk, thinking of the yet uncovered photograph in her room, with a serene sense of something ecstatic to come. For, with the subtle luxuriousness of fancy in which this young woman was an adept, on learning that her husband was to be absent that night she had refrained from incontinently rushing upstairs and opening the picture-frame, preferring to reserve the inspection till she could be alone, and a more romantic tinge be imparted to the occasion by silence, candles, solemn sea and stars outside, than was afforded by the garish afternoon sunlight.

The children had been sent to bed, and Ella soon followed, though it was not yet ten o'clock. To gratify her passionate curiosity she now made her preparations, first getting rid of superfluous garments and putting on her dressing-gown, then arranging a chair in front of the table and reading several pages of Trewe's tenderest utterances. Next she fetched the portrait-frame to the light, opened the back, took out the likeness, and set it up before her.

It was a striking countenance to look upon. The poet wore a luxuriant black moustache and imperial, and a slouched hat which shaded the forehead. The large dark eyes described by the landlady showed an unlimited capacity for misery; they looked out from beneath well-shaped brows as if they were reading the universe in the microcosm of the confronter's face, and were not altogether overjoyed at what the spectacle portended.

Ella murmured in her lowest, richest, tenderest tone: "And it's *you* who've so cruelly eclipsed me these many times!"

As she gazed long at the portrait she fell into thought, till her eyes filled with tears, and she touched the cardboard with her lips. Then she laughed with a nervous lightness, and wiped her eyes.

She thought how wicked she was, a woman having a husband and three children, to let her mind stray to a stranger in this unconscionable manner. No, he was not a stranger! She knew his thoughts and feelings as well as she knew her own; they were, in fact, the self-same thoughts and feelings as hers, which her husband distinctly lacked; perhaps luckily for himself, considering that he had to provide for family expenses.

"He's nearer my real self, he's more intimate with the real me than Will is, after all, even though I've never seen him," she said.

She laid his book and picture on the table at the bedside, and when she was reclining on the pillow she re-read those of Robert Trewe's verses which she had marked from time to time as most touching and true. Putting these aside she set up the photograph on its edge upon the coverlet, and contemplated it as she lay. Then she scanned again by the light of the candle the half-obliterated pencillings on the wall-paper beside her head. There they were—phrases, couplets, *bouts-rimés*, beginnings and middles of lines, ideas in the rough, like Shelley's scraps, and the least of them so intense, so sweet, so palpitating, that it seemed as if his very breath, warm and loving, fanned her cheeks from those walls, walls that had surrounded his head times and times as they surrounded her own now. He must often have put up his hand so—with the pencil in it. Yes, the writing was sideways, as it would be if executed by one who extended his arm thus.

These inscribed shapes of the poet's world,

> "Forms more real than living man,
> Nurslings of immortality,"

were, no doubt, the thoughts and spirit-strivings which had come to him in the dead of night, when he could let himself go and have no fear of the frost of criticism. No doubt they had often been written up hastily by the light of the moon, the rays of the lamp, in the blue-grey dawn, in full daylight perhaps never. And now her hair was dragging where his arm had lain when he secured the fugitive fancies; she was sleeping on a poet's lips, immersed in the very essence of him, permeated by his spirit as by an ether.

While she was dreaming the minutes away thus, a footstep came upon the stairs, and in a moment she heard her husband's heavy step on the landing immediately without.

"Ell, where are you?"

What possessed her she could not have described, but, with an instinctive objection to let her husband know what she had been doing, she slipped the photograph under the pillow just as he flung open the door with the air of a man who had dined not badly.

"O, I beg pardon," said William Marchmill. "Have you a headache? I am afraid I have disturbed you."

"No, I've not got a headache," said she. "How is it you've come?"

"Well, we found we could get back in very good time after all, and I didn't want to make another day of it, because of going somewhere else to-morrow."

"Shall I come down again?"

"O no. I'm as tired as a dog. I've had a good feed, and I shall turn in straight off. I want to get out at six o'clock to-morrow if I can. . . . I shan't disturb you by my getting up; it will be long before you are awake." And he came forward into the room.

While her eyes followed his movements, Ella softly pushed the photograph further out of sight.

"Sure you're not ill?" he asked, bending over her.

"No, only wicked!"

"Never mind that." And he stooped and kissed her. "I wanted to be with you to-night."

Next morning Marchmill was called at six o'clock; and in waking and yawning she heard him muttering to himself: "What the deuce is this that's been crackling under me so?" Imagining her asleep he searched round him and withdrew something. Through her half-opened eyes she perceived it to be Mr Trewe.

"Well, I'm damned!" her husband exclaimed.

"What, dear?" said she.

"O, you are awake? Ha! ha!"

"What *do* you mean?"

"Some bloke's photograph—a friend of our landlady's, I suppose. I wonder how it came here; whisked off the mantelpiece by accident perhaps when they were making the bed."

"I was looking at it yesterday, and it must have dropped in then."

"O, he's a friend of yours? Bless his picturesque heart!"

Ella's loyalty to the object of her admiration could not endure to hear him ridiculed. "He's a clever man!" she said, with a tremor in her gentle voice which she herself felt to be absurdly uncalled for. "He is a rising poet—the gentleman who occupied two of these rooms before we came, though I've never seen him."

"How do you know, if you've never seen him?"

"Mrs Hooper told me when she showed me the photograph."

"O, well, I must up and be off. I shall be home rather early. Sorry I can't take you to-day, dear. Mind the children don't go getting drowned."

That day Mrs Marchmill inquired if Mr Trewe were likely to call at any other time.

"Yes," said Mrs Hooper. "He's coming this day week to stay with a friend near here till you leave. He'll be sure to call."

Marchmill did return quite early in the afternoon; and, opening some letters which had arrived in his absence, declared suddenly that he and his family would have to leave a week earlier than they had expected to do—in short, in three days.

"Surely, we can stay a week longer?" she pleaded. "I like it here."

"I don't. It is getting rather slow."

"Then you might leave me and the children!"

"How perverse you are, Ell! What's the use? And have to come to fetch you! No: we'll all return together; and we'll make out our time in North Wales or Brighton a little later on. Besides, you've three days longer yet."

It seemed to be her doom not to meet the man for whose rival talent she had a despairing admiration, and to whose person she was now absolutely attached. Yet she determined to make a last effort; and having gathered from her landlady that Trewe was living in a lonely spot not far from the fashionable town on the Island opposite, she crossed over in the packet from the neighbouring pier the following afternoon.

What a useless journey it was! Ella knew but vaguely where the house stood, and when she fancied she had found it, and ventured to inquire of a pedestrian if he lived there, the answer returned by the man was that he did not know. And if he did live there, how could she call upon him? Some women might have the assurance to do it, but she had not. How crazy he would think her. She might have asked him to call upon her, perhaps; but she had not the courage for that, either. She lingered mournfully about the picturesque seaside eminence till it was time to return to the town and enter the steamer for recrossing, reaching home for dinner without having been greatly missed.

At the last moment, unexpectedly enough, her husband said that he should have no objection to letting her and the children stay on till the end of the week, since she wished to do so, if she felt herself able to get home without him. She concealed the pleasure this extension of time gave her; and Marchmill went off the next morning alone.

But the week passed, and Trewe did not call.

On Saturday morning the remaining members of the Marchmill family departed from the place which had been productive of so much fervour in her. The dreary, dreary train; the sun shining in moted beams upon the hot cusions; the dusty permanent way; the mean rows of wire—these things were her accompaniment: while out of the window the deep blue sea-levels disappeared from her gaze, and with them her poet's home. Heavy-hearted, she tried to read, and wept instead.

Mr Marchmill was in a thriving way of business, and he and his family lived in a large new house, which stood in rather extensive grounds a few miles outside the midland city wherein he carried on his trade. Ella's life was lonely here, as the suburban life is apt to be, particularly at certain seasons; and she had ample time to indulge her taste for lyric and elegiac composition. She had hardly got back when she encountered a piece by Robert Trewe in the new number of her favourite magazine, which must have been written almost immediately before her visit to Solentsea, for it contained the very couplet she had seen pencilled on the wall-paper by the bed, and Mrs Hooper had declared to be recent. Ella could resist no longer, but seizing a pen impulsively, wrote to him as a brother-poet, using the name of John Ivy, congratulating him in her letter on his triumphant executions in metre and rhythm of thoughts that moved his soul, as compared with her own browbeaten efforts in the same pathetic trade.

To this address there came a response in a few days, little as she had dared to hope for it—a civil and brief note, in which the young poet stated that, though he was not well acquainted with Mr Ivy's verse, he recalled the name as being one he had seen attached to some very promising pieces; that he was glad to gain Mr Ivy's acquaintance by letter, and should certainly look with much interest for his productions in the future.

There must have been something juvenile or timid in her own epistle, as one ostensibly coming from a man, she declared to herself; for Trewe quite adopted the tone of an elder and superior in this reply. But what did it matter? He had replied; he had written to her with his own hand from that very room she knew so well, for he was now back again in his quarters.

The correspondence thus begun was continued for two months or more, Ella Marchmill sending him from time to time some that she considered to be the best of her pieces, which he very kindly accepted, though he did not say he sedulously read them, nor did he send her any of his own in return. Ella would have been more hurt at this than she was if she had not known that Trewe laboured under the impression that she was one of his own sex.

Yet the situation was unsatisfactory. A flattering little voice told her that, were he only to see her, matters would be otherwise. No doubt she would have helped on this by making a frank confession of womanhood, to begin with, if something had not happened, to her delight, to render it unnecessary. A friend of her husband's, the editor of the most important newspaper in their city and county, who was dining with them one day, observed during their conversation about the poet that his (the editor's) brother the landscape-painter was a friend of Mr Trewe's, and that the two men were at that very moment in Wales together.

Ella was slightly acquainted with the editor's brother. The next morning down she sat and wrote, inviting him to stay at her house for a short time on his way back, and requesting him to bring with him, if practicable, his companion Mr Trewe, whose acquaintance she was anxious to make. The answer arrived after some few days. Her correspondent and his friend Trewe would have much satisfaction in accepting her invitation on their way southward, which would be on such and such a day in the following week.

Ella was blithe and buoyant. Her scheme had succeeded; her beloved though as yet unseen was coming. "Behold, he standeth behind our wall; he looked forth at the windows, showing himself through the lattice," she thought ecstatically. "And, lo, the winter is past, the rain is over and gone, the flowers appear on the earth, the time of the singing of birds is come, and the voice of the turtle is heard in our land."

But it was necessary to consider the details of lodging and feeding him. This she did most solicitously, and awaited the pregnant day and hour.

It was about five in the afternoon when she heard a ring at the door and the editor's brother's voice in the hall. Poetess as she was, or as she thought herself, she had not been too sublime that day to dress with infinite trouble in a fashionable robe of rich material, having a faint resemblance to the *chiton* of the Greeks, a style just then in vogue among ladies of an artistic and romantic turn, which had been obtained by Ella of her Bond Street dressmaker when she was last in London. Her visitor entered the drawing-room. She looked towards his rear; nobody else came through the door. Where, in the name of the God of Love, was Robert Trewe?

"O, I'm sorry," said the painter, after their introductory words had been spoken. "Trewe is a curious fellow, you know, Mrs Marchmill. He said he'd come; then he said he couldn't. He's rather dusty. We've been doing a few miles with knapsacks, you know; and he wanted to get on home."

"He—he's not coming?"

"He's not; and he asked me to make his apologies."

"When did you p-p-part from him?" she asked, her nether lip starting off quivering so much that it was like a *tremolo*-stop opened in her speech. She longed to run away from this dreadful bore and cry her eyes out.

"Just now, in the turnpike road yonder there."

"What! he has actually gone past my gates?"

"Yes. When we got to them—handsome gates they are, too, the finest bit of modern wrought-iron work I have seen—when we came to them we stopped, talking there a little while, and then he wished me good-bye and went on. The truth is, he's a little bit depressed just now, and doesn't want to see anybody. He's a very good fellow, and a warm friend, but a little uncertain and gloomy sometimes; he things too much of things. His poetry is rather too erotic and passionate, you know, for some tastes; and he has just come in for a terrible slating from the —— *Review* that was published yesterday; he saw a copy of it at the station by accident. Perhaps you've read it?"

"No."

"So much the better. O, it is not worth thinking of; just one of those articles written to order, to please the narrow-minded set of subscribers upon whom the circulation depends. But he's upset by it. He says it is the misrepresentation that hurts him so; that, though he can stand a fair attack, he can't stand lies that he's powerless to refute and stop from spreading. That's just Trewe's weak point. He lives so much by himself that these things affect him much more than they would if he were in the bustle of fashionable or commercial life. So he wouldn't come here, making the excuse that it all looked so new and monied—if you'll pardon—"

"But—he must have known—there was sympathy here! Has he never said anything about getting letters from this address?"

"Yes, yes, he has, from John Ivy—perhaps a relative of yours, he thought, visiting her at the time?"

"Did he—like Ivy, did he say?"

"Well, I don't know that he took any great interest in Ivy."

"Or in his poems?"

"Or in his poems—so far as I know, that is."

Robert Trewe took no interest in her house, in her poems, or in their writer. As soon as she could get away she went into the nursery and tried to let off her emotion by unnecessarily kissing the children, till she had a sudden sense of disgust at being reminded how plain-looking they were, like their father.

The obtuse and single-minded landscape-painter never once perceived from her conversation that it was only Trewe she wanted, and not himself. He made the best of his visit, seeming to enjoy the society of Ella's husband, who also took a great fancy to him, and showed him everywhere about the neighbourhood, neither of them noticing Ella's mood.

The painter had been gone only a day or two when, while sitting upstairs alone one morning, she glanced over the London paper just arrived, and read the following paragraph:—

"SUICIDE OF A POET

"Mr Robert Trewe, who has been favourably known for some years as one of our rising lyrists, committed suicide at his lodgings at Solentsea on Saturday evening last by shooting himself in the right temple with a revolver. Readers hardly need to be reminded that Mr Trewe has recently attracted the attention of a much wider public than had hitherto known him, by his new volume of verse, mostly of an impassioned kind, entitled 'Lyrics to a Woman Unknown', which has been already favourably noticed in these pages for the extraordinary gamut of feeling it traverses, and which has been made the subject of a severe, if not ferocious, criticism in the —— *Review*. It is supposed, though not certainly known, that the article may have partially conduced to the sad act, as a copy of the review in question was found on his writing-table; and he has been observed to be in a somewhat depressed state of mind since the critique appeared."

Then came the report of the inquest, at which the following letter was read, it having been addressed to a friend at a distance:—

"DEAR ——,—Before these lines reach your hands I shall be delivered from the inconveniences of seeing, hearing, and knowing more of the things around me. I will not trouble you by giving my reasons for the step I have taken, though I can assure you they were sound and logical. Perhaps had I been blessed with a mother, or a sister, or a female friend of another sort tenderly devoted to me, I might have thought it worth while to continue my present existence. I have long dreamt of such an unattainable creature, as you know; and she, this undiscoverable, elusive one, inspired my last volume; the imaginary woman alone, for, in spite of what has been said in some quarters, there is no real woman behind the title. She has continued to the last unrevealed, unmet, unwon. I think it desirable to mention this in order that no blame may attack to any real woman as having been the cause of my decease by cruel or cavalier treatment of me. Tell my landlady that I am sorry to have caused her this unpleasantness; but my occupancy of the rooms will soon be forgotten. There are ample funds in my name at the bank to pay all expenses.

R. TREWE"

Ella sat for a while as if stunned, then rushed into the adjoining chamber and flung herself upon her face on the bed.

Her grief and distraction shook her to pieces; and she lay in this frenzy of sorrow for more than an hour. Broken words came every now and then from her quivering lips: "O, if he had only known of me—known of me—me! . . . O, if I had only once met him—only once; and put my hand upon his hot forehead—kissed him—let him know how I loved him—that I would have suffered shame and scorn, would have lived and died, for him! Perhaps it would have saved his dear life! . . . But no—it was not allowed! God is a jealous God; and that happiness was not for him and me!"

All possibilities were over; the meeting was stultified. Yet it was almost visible to her in her fantasy even now, though it could never be substantiated—

> "The hour which might have been, yet might not be,
> Which man's and woman's heart conceived and bore,
> Yet whereof life was barren."

She wrote to the landlady at Solentsea in the third person, in as subdued a style as she could command, enclosing a postal order for a sovereign, and informing Mrs Hooper that Mrs Marchmill had seen in the papers the sad account of the poet's death, and having been, as Mrs Hooper was aware, much interested in Mr Trewe during her stay at Coburg House, she would obliged if Mrs Hooper could obtain a small portion of his hair before his coffin was closed down, and send it her as a memorial of him, as also the photograph that was in the frame.

By the return-post a letter arrived containing what had been requested. Ella wept over the portrait and secured it in her private drawer; the lock of hair she tied with white ribbon and put in her bosom, whence she drew it nd kissed it every now and then in some unobserved nook.

"What's the matter?" said her husband, looking up from his newspaper on one of these occasions. "Crying over something? A lock of hair? Whose is it?"

"He's dead!" she murmured.

"Who?"

"I don't want to tell you, Will, just now, unless you insist!" she said, a sob hanging heavy in her voice.

"O, all right."

"Do you mind my refusing? I will tell you some day."

"It doesn't matter in the least, of course."

He walked away whistling a few bars of no tune in particular; and when he had got down to his factory in the city the subject came into Marchmill's head again.

He, too, was aware that a suicide had taken place recently at the house they had occupied at Solentsea. Having seen the volume of poems in his wife's hand of late, and heard fragments of the landlady's conversation about Trewe when they were her tenants, he all at once said to himself, "Why of course it's he! . . . How the devil did she get to know him? What sly animals women are!"

Then he placidly dismissed the matter, and went on with his daily affairs. By this time Ella at home had come to a determination. Mrs Hooper, in sending the hair and photograph, had informed her of the day of the funeral; and as the morning and noon wore on an overpowering wish to know where they were laying him took possession of the sympathetic woman. Caring very little now what her husband or anyone else might think of her eccentricities, she wrote Marchmill a brief note, stating that she was called away for the afternoon and evening, but would return on the following morning. This she left on his desk, and having given the same information to the servants, went out of the house on foot.

When Mr Marchmill reached home early in the afternoon the servants looked anxious. The nurse took him privately aside, and hinted that her mistress's sadness during the past few days had been such that she feared she had gone out to drown herself. Marchmill reflected. Upon the whole he thought that she had not done that. Without saying whither he was bound he also started off, telling them not to sit up for him. He drove to the railway-station, and took a ticket for Solentsea.

It was dark when he reached the place, though he had come by a fast train, and he knew that if his wife had preceded him thither it could only have been by a slower train, arriving not a great while before his own. The season at Solentsea was now past: the parade was gloomy, and the flys were few and cheap. He asked the way to the Cemetery, and soon reached it. The gate was locked, but the keeper let him in, declaring, however, that there was nobody within the precincts. Although it was not late, the autumnal darkness had now become intense; and he found some difficulty in keeping to the serpentine path which led to the quarter where, as the man had told him, the one or two interments for the day had taken place. He stepped upon the grass, and, stumbling over some pegs, stooped now and then to discern if possible a figure against the sky. He could see none; but lighting on a spot where the soil was trodden, beheld a crouching object beside a newly-made grave. She heard him, and sprang up.

"Ell, how silly this is!" he said indignantly. "Running away from home— I never heard such a thing! Of course I am not jealous of this unfortunate man; but it is too ridiculous that you, a married woman with three children and a fourth coming, should go losing your head like this over a dead lover! . . . Do you know you were locked in? You might not have been able to get out all night."

She did not answer.

"I hope it didn't go far between you and him, for your own sake."

"Don't insult me, Will."

"Mind, I won't have any more of this sort of thing; do you hear?"

"Very well," she said.

He drew her arm within his own, and conducted her out of the Cemetery. It was impossible to get back that night; and not wishing to be recognized in their present sorry condition he took her to a miserable little coffee-house close to the station, whence they departed early in the morning, travelling almost without speaking, under the sense that it was one of those dreary situations occurring in married life which words could not mend, and reaching their own door at noon.

The months passed, and neither of the twain ever ventured to start a conversation upon this episode. Ella seemed to be only too frequently in a sad and listless mood, which might almost have been called pining. The time was approaching when she would have to undergo the stress of childbirth for a fourth time, and that apparently did not tend to raise her spirits.

"I don't think I shall get over it this time!" she said one day.

"Pooh! what childish foreboding! Why shouldn't it be as well now as ever?"

She shook her head. "I feel almost sure I am going to die; and I should be glad, if it were not for Nelly, and Frank, and Tiny."

"And me!"

"You'll soon find somebody to fill my place," she murmured, with a sad smile, "And you'll have a perfect right to; I assure you of that."

"Ell, you are not thinking still about that—poetical friend of yours?"

She neither admitted nor denied the charge. "I am not going to get over my illness this time," she reiterated. "Something tells me I shan't."

This view of things was rather a bad beginning, as it usually is; and, in fact, six weeks later, in the month of May, she was lying in her room, pulse-less and bloodless, with hardly strength enough left to follow up one feeble breath with another, the infant for whose unnecessary life she was slowly parting with her own being fat and well. Just before her death she spoke to Marchmill softly:—

"Will, I want to confess to you the entire circumstances of that—about you know what—that time we visited Solentsea. I can't tell what possessed me—how I could forget you so, my husband! But I had got into a morbid state: I thought you had been unkind; that you have neglected me; that you weren't up to my intellectual level, while was, and far above it. I wanted a fuller appreciator, perhaps, rather than another lover—"

She could get no further then for very exhaustion; and she went off in a sudden collapse a few hours later, without having said anything more to her husband on the subject of her love for the poet. William Marchmill, in truth, like most husbands of several years' standing, was little disturbed by retrospective jealousies, and had not shown the least anxiety to press her for confessions concerning a man dead and gone beyond any power of inconveniencing him more.

But when she had been buried a couple of years it chanced one day that, in turning over some forgotten papers that he wished to destroy before his second wife entered the house, he lighted on a lock of hair in an envelope, with the photograph of the deceased poet, a date being written on the back in his late wife's hand. It was that of the time they spent at Solentsea.

Marchmill looked long and musingly at the hair and portrait, for something struck him. Fetching the little boy who had been the death of his mother, now a noisy toddler, he took him on his knee, held the lock of hair against the child's head, and set up the photograph on the table behind, so that he could closely compare the features each countenance presented. By a known but inexplicable trick of Nature there were undoubtedly strong traces of resemblance to the man Ella had never seen; the dreamy and peculiar expression of the poet's face sat, as the transmitted idea, upon the child's, and the hair was of the same hue.

"I'm damned if I didn't think so!" murmured Marchmill. "Then she *did* play me false with that fellow at the lodgings! Let me see: the dates—the second week in August . . . the third week in May . . . Yes . . . yes . . . Get away, you poor little brat! You are nothing to me!"

THOMAS MANN

GLADIUS DEI

1902

Mann (1875–1955) did not think highly of conventional photography to judge by
his use of the photographic reproduction of a painting in this early short story;
the photograph seems to embody the degeneration of art as well as the society that
produced it. The eminent German writer also represents the making and displaying of "exterior" photographs as merely the pastimes of the bored well-to-do in
his mature masterpiece The Magic Mountain (1924).[1] But his later fascination
with the spiritual and scientific revelations of the camera is evident both in his remarks on "phantom" photography in his study of the occult (1924) and in his use
of "interior" photographs (partly based on personal research in a hospital) made
by the X-ray machine in The Magic Mountain.[2] And around 1928, after further exposure to the portraits of E. O. Hoppé (1878–1972), the studies of August
Sander (1876–1964), and the still lifes of Albert Renger-Patzsch (1897–1966),
Mann enthusiastically raised his opinion of photography's aesthetic potential.[3] This
change of mind may partly explain why he subsequently became a willing subject
for the camera himself.[4]

1. See Mann, The Magic Mountain, translated by John E. Woods (New York:
Knopf, 1995), pp. 16, 20, 82, 252. See Erwin Koppen, Literatur und Photographie: Über
Geschichte und Thematik Einer Medienentdeckung (Stuttgart: J. B. Metzler, 1987), pp.
24–28, who notes that Mann's idol Goethe (1749–1832), by contrast, was long intrigued by the aesthetic and documentary revelations of the camera obscura.

2. See Mann, "Okkulte Erlebnisse" [Occult Experiences], Gesammelte Werke
(Frankfurt/M: S. Fischer, 1960), vol. 10, pp. 135–71; Mann, entry for February 24,
1920, in Diaries 1918–1939, edited by Hermann Kesten, translated by Richard and
Clara Winston (New York: Abrams, 1982), p. 86; and Mann, The Magic Mountain, pp.
193, 201–16, 334, 382, 429, 550, 656. Mann might have relished two of Alvarez Bravo's

photographs that incorporated X-rays—'Lucia, 1940s' and 'Flower and Rings, 1940'
—reproduced in *Revelaciones: The Art of Manuel Alvarez Bravo* (San Diego: Museum of
Photographic Art, 1990), pp. 87 and 119 respectively. See also Greenway, "Penetrat-
ing Surfaces: X-Rays, Strindberg and *The Ghost Sonata*," *Nineteenth-Century Studies* 5
(1991): 29–46, and William Dean Howells's relevant letter to Mark Twain, May 24,
1906, *Mark Twain-Howells Letters*, edited by Henry Nash Smith and William M.
Gibson (Cambridge: Belknap Press/Harvard University Press, 1960), vol. 2, p. 808,
in which he recommends a new book, comparing it to "a series of photographs taken
with Roentgen rays."

3. See Mann, "Die Welt ist schön" [The World Is Beautiful] (1928), *Gesammelte
Werke* (Frankfurt am Main: S. Fischer, 1960), vol. 10, pp. 901–4, and an excerpt from
his letter of January 6, 1930—praising August Sander's *Face of Our Time* (1929) to its
publisher, Kurt Wolff—quoted in *August Sander: Photographs of an Epoch* (Millerton,
N.Y.: Aperture/Philadelphia Museum of Art, 1980), p. 11.

4. Among the many portraits of Mann, who rather enjoyed the sittings (according
to the late Henry Hatfield in conversation with the editor on November 29, 1991)
see the 1936–38 series of him—some with his wife and brother—by Lotte Jacobi,
reproduced in *Lotte Jacobi*, edited by Kelly Wise, pp. 106–10; the 1946–47 series by
George Platt Lynes, reproduced in Diana Hulick, "George Platt Lynes: The Portrait
Series of Thomas Mann," *History of Photography* 15, no. 3 (Autumn 1991): 211–21; the
photograph mentioned in Carl Van Vechten's letter to Gertrude Stein, June 22, 1937,
in *The Letters of Carl Van Vechten*, edited by Bruce Kellner (New Haven, Conn.: Yale
University Press, 1987), pp. 152–53, reproduced in *Portraits: The Photography of Carl
Van Vechten*, compiled by Saul Mauriber (Indianapolis: Bobbs-Merrill, 1978), npn,
and Alfred A. Knopf, *Sixty Photographs* (New York: Knopf, 1975), which includes
some 1930's portraits of the author, whom the publisher had signed c. 1918 according
to Knopf's biographer, Peter Prescott, in conversation with the editor, December 2,
1991. Other Knopf portraits of Mann are at the Harry Ransom Humanities Research
Center, University of Texas at Austin, including one with a cigar—doubtless given to
him by the publisher, according to the late William Koshland in conversation with
the editor, October 23, 1992—which is reproduced in Rabb, *Literature and Photography*, p. 239.

GLADIUS DEI*

Munich was radiant. Above the gay squares and white columned
temples, the classicistic monuments and the baroque churches,
the leaping fountains, the palaces and parks of the Residence
there stretched a sky of luminous blue silk. Well-arranged leafy vistas

---

* *Gladius Dei* means the sword of God.

laced with sun and shade lay basking in the sunshine of a beautiful day in early June.

There was a twittering of birds and a blithe holiday spirit in all the little streets. And in the squares and past the rows of villas there swelled, rolled, and hummed the leisurely, entertaining traffic of that easy-going, charming town. Travellers of all nationalities drove about in the slow little droshkies, looking right and left in aimless curiosity in the house-fronts; they mounted and descended museum stairs. Many windows stood open and music was heard from within: practising on piano, cello, or violin—earnest and well-meant amateur efforts; while from the Odeon came the sound of serious work on several grand pianos.

Young people, the kind that can whistle the Nothung motif, who fill the pit of the Schauspielhaus every evening, wandered in and out of the University and Library with literary magazines in their coat pockets. A court carriage stood before the Academy, the home of the plastic arts, which spreads its white wings between the Türkenstrasse and the Siegestor. And colourful groups of models, picturesque old men, women and children in Albanian costume, stood or lounged at the top of the balustrade.

Indolent, unhurried sauntering was the mode in all the long streets of the northern quarter. There life is lived for pleasanter ends than the driving greed of gain. Young artists with little round hats on the backs of their heads, flowing cravats and no canes—carefree bachelors who paid for their lodgings with colour-sketches—were strolling up and down to let the clear blue morning play upon their mood, also to look at the little girls, the pretty, rather plump type, with the brunette bandeaux, the too large feet, and the unobjectionable morals. Every fifth house had studio windows blinking in the sun. Sometimes a fine piece of architecture stood out from a middle-class row, the work of some imaginative young architect; a wide front with shallow bays and decorations in a bizarre style very expressive and full of invention. Or the door to some monotonous façade would be framed in a bold improvisation of flowing lines and sunny colours, with bacchantes, naiads, and rosy-skinned nudes.

It was always a joy to linger before the windows of the cabinet-makers and the shops for modern articles *de luxe*. What a sense for luxurious nothings and amusing, significant line was displayed in the shape of everything! Little shops that sold picture-frames, sculptures, and antiques there were in endless number; in their windows you might see those busts of Florentine women of the Renaissance, so full of noble poise and poignant charm. And the owners of the smallest and meanest of these shops spoke of Mino da Fiesole* and Donatello† as though he had received the rights of reproduction from them personally.

But on the Odeonsplatz, in view of the mighty loggia with the spacious mosaic pavement before it, diagonally opposite to the Regent's palace, people were crowding round the large windows and glass show-cases of the big art-shop owned by M. Blüthenzweig. What a glorious display! There were reproductions of the masterpieces of all the galleries in the world, in costly decorated and tinted frames, the good taste of which was precious in its very simplicity. There were copies of modern paintings, works of a joyously sensuous fantasy, in which the antiques seemed born again in humorous and realistic guise; bronze nudes and fragile ornamental glassware; tall, thin earthenware vases with an iridescent glaze produced by a bath in metal steam; *éditions de luxe* which were triumphs of modern binding and presswork, containing the works of the most modish poets, set out with every possible advantage of sumptuous elegance. Cheek by jowl with these, the portraits of artists, musicians, philosophers, actors, writers, displayed to gratify the public taste for personalities.—In the first window, next the book-shop, a large picture stood on an easel, with a crowd of people in front of it, a fine sepia photograph in a wide old-gold frame, a very striking reproduction of the sensation at this year's great international exhibition, to which public attention is always invited by means of effective and artistic posters struck up everywhere on hoardings among concert programmes and clever advertisements of toilet preparations.

If you looked into the windows of the book-shop your eye met such titles as *Interior Decoration Since the Renaissance, The Renaissance in Modern Decorative Art, The Book as Work of Art, The Decorative Arts, Hunger for Art,* and many more. And you would remember that these thought-provoking pamphlets were sold and read by the thousand and that discussions on these subjects were the preoccupation of all the salons.

You might be lucky enough to meet in person one of the famous fair ones whom less fortunate folk know only through the medium of art; one of those rich and beautiful women whose Titian-blond colouring Nature's most sweet and cunning hand did *not* lay on, but whose diamond parures and beguiling charms had received immortality from the hand of some

---

*Mino da Fiesole (?1431–?1482) was an Italian sculptor of the early Renaissance who carved many monuments, reliefs, portrait busts, and the like.

†Donatello (?1386–1466) is considered the leading sculptor of the Italian Renaissance broke with classicism in favor of realistic actions and characterizations.

portrait-painter of genius and whose love-affairs were the talk of the town. These were the queens of the artist balls at carnival-time. They were a little painted, a little made up, full of haughty caprices, worthy of adoration, avid of praise. You might see a carriage rolling up the Ludwigstrasse, with such a great painter and his mistress inside. People would be pointing out the sight, standing still to gaze after the pair. Some of them would curtsy. A little more and the very policemen would stand at attention.

Art flourished, art swayed the destinies of the town, art stretched above it her rose-bound sceptre and smiled. On every hand obsequious interest was displayed in her prosperity, on every hand she was served with industry and devotion. There was a downright cult of line, decoration, form, significance, beauty. Munich was radiant.

A youth was coming down the Schellingstrasse. With the bells of cyclists ringing about him he strode across the wooden pavement towards the broad façade of the Ludwigskirche. Looking at him it was as though a shadow passed across the sky, or cast over the spirit some memory of melancholy hours. Did he not love the sun which bathed the lovely city in its festal light? Why did he walk wrapped in his own thoughts, his eyes directed on the ground?

No one in that tolerant and variety-loving town would have taken offence at his wearing no hat; but why need the hood of his ample black cloak have been drawn over his head, shadowing his low, prominent, and peaked forehead, covering his ears and framing his haggard cheeks? What pangs of conscience, what scruples and self-tortures had so availed to hollow out these cheeks? It is frightful, on such a sunny day, to see care sitting in the hollows of the human face. His dark brows thickened at the narrow base of his hooked and prominent nose. His lips were unpleasantly full, his eyes brown and close-lying. When he lifted them, diagonal folds appeared on the peaked brow. His gaze expressed knowledge, limitation, and suffering. Seen in profile his face was strikingly like an old painting preserved at Florence in a narrow cloister cell whence once a frightful and shattering protest issued against life and her triumphs.*

---

*This description of Hieronymus is doubtless intended to recall Savonarola (1453–98), a charismatic but fanatical Dominican friar who preached in Florence against the worldly corruptions of secular life, the ruling class, and the clergy. Seeking the establishment of a pure Christian state, he became a virtual dictator over the city in 1494. The aristocratic party eventually regained political power and the pope excommunicated him in 1497. After imprisonment and a trial for treason and heresy, Savonarola was tortured, hanged, and burned.

Hieronymus walked along the Schellingstrasse with a slow, firm stride, holding his wide cloak together with both hands from inside. Two little girls, two of those pretty, plump little creatures with the bandeaux, the big feet, and the unobjectionable morals, strolled towards him arm in arm, on pleasure bent. They poked each other and laughed, they bent double with laughter, they even broke into a run and ran away still laughing, at his hood and his face. But he paid them no heed. With bent head, looking neither to the right nor to the left, he crossed the Ludwigstrasse and mounted the church steps.

The great wings of the middle portal stood wide open. From somewhere within the consecrated twilight, cool, dank, incense-laden, there came a pale red glow. An old woman with inflamed eyes rose from a prayer-stool and slipped on crutches through the columns. Otherwise the church was empty.

Hieronymus sprinkled brow and breast at the stoup, bent the knee before the high altar, and then paused in the centre nave. Here in the church his stature seemed to have grown. He stood upright and immovable; his head was flung up and his great hooked nose jutted domineeringly above the thick lips. His eyes no longer sought the ground, but looked straight and boldly into the distance, at the crucifix on the high altar. Thus he stood awhile, then retreating he bent the knee again and left the church.

He strode up the Ludwigstrasse, slowly, firmly, with bent head, in the centre of the wide unpaved road, towards the mighty loggia with its statues. But arrived at the Odeonsplatz, he looked up, so that the folds came out on his peaked forehead, and checked his step, his attention being called to the crowd at the windows of the big art-shop of M. Blüthenzweig.

People moved from window to window, pointing out to each other the treasures displayed and exchanging views as they looked over one another's shoulders. Hieronymus mingled among them and did as they did, taking in all these things with his eyes, one by one.

He saw the reproductions of masterpieces from all the galleries in the world, the priceless frames so precious in their simplicity, the Renaissance sculpture, the bronze nudes, the exquisitely bound volumes, the iridescent vases, the portraits of artists, musicians, philosophers, actors, writers; he looked at everything and turned a moment of his scrutiny upon each object. Holding his mantle closely together with both hands from inside, he moved his hood-covered head in short turns from one thing to the next, gazing at each awhile with a dull, inimical, and remotely surprised air, lifting the dark brows which grew so thick at the base of the nose. At length he stood in front of the last window, which contained the startling picture.

For a while he looked over the shoulders of people before him and then in his turn reached a position directly in front of the window.

The large red-brown photograph in the choice old-gold frame stood on an easel in the centre. It was a Madonna, but an utterly unconventional one, a work of entirely modern feeling. The figure of the Holy Mother was revealed as enchantingly feminine and beautiful. Her great smouldering eyes were rimmed with darkness, and her delicate and strangely smiling lips were half-parted. Her slender fingers held in a somewhat nervous grasp the hips of the Child, a nude boy of pronounced, almost primitive leanness. He was playing with her breast and glancing aside at the beholder with a wise look in his eyes.

Two other youths stood near Hieronymus, talking about the picture. They were two young men with books under their arms, which they had fetched from the Library or were taking thither. Humanistically educated people, that is, equipped with science and with art.

"The little chap is in luck, devil take me!" said one.

"He seems to be trying to make one envious," replied the other. "A bewildering female!"

"A female to drive a man crazy! Gives you funny ideas about the Immaculate Conception."

"No, she doesn't look exactly immaculate. Have you seen the original?"

"Of course; I was quite bowled over. She makes an even more aphrodisiac impression in colour. Especially the eyes."

"The likeness is pretty plain."

"How so?"

"Don't you know the model? Of course he used his little dressmaker. It is almost a portrait, only with a lot more emphasis on the corruptible. The girl is more innocent."

"I hope so. Life would be altogether too much of a strain if there were many like this *mater amata.*"*

"The Pinakothek has bought it."

"Really? Well, well! They knew what they were about, anyhow. The treatment of the flesh and the flow of the linen garment are really first-class."

"Yes, an incredibly gifted chap."

"Do you know him?"

"A little. He will have a career, that is certain. He has been invited twice by the Prince Regent."

---

* *Mater amata* means beloved mother.

This last was said as they were taking leave of each other.

"Shall I see you this evening at the theatre?" asked the first. "The Dramatic Club is giving Machiavelli's *Mandragola*."

"Oh, bravo! That will be great, of course. I had meant to go to the Variété, but I shall probably choose our stout Niccolò after all. Good-bye."

They parted, going off to right and left. New people took their places and looked at the famous picture. But Hieronymus stood where he was, motionless, with his head thrust out; his hands clutched convulsively at the mantle as they held it together from inside. His brows were no longer lifted with that cool and unpleasantly surprised expression; they were drawn and darkened; his cheeks, half-shrouded in the black hood, seemed more sunken than ever and his thick lips had gone pale. Slowly his head dropped lower and lower, so that finally his eyes stared upwards at the work of art, while the nostrils of his great nose dilated.

Thus he remained for perhaps a quarter of an hour. The crowd about him melted away, but he did not stir from the spot. At last he turned slowly on the balls of his feet and went hence.

But the picture of the Madonna went with him. Always and ever, whether in his hard and narrow little room or kneeling in the cool church, it stood before his outraged soul, with its smouldering, dark-rimmed eyes, its riddlingly smiling lips—stark and beautiful. And no prayer availed to exorcize it.

But the third night it happened that a command and summons from on high came to Hieronymus, to intercede and lift his voice against the frivolity, blasphemy, and arrogance of beauty. In vain like Moses he protested that he had not the gift of tongues. God's will remained unshaken; in a loud voice He demanded that the faint-hearted Hieronymus go forth to sacrifice amid the jeers of the foe.

And since God would have it so, he set forth one morning and wended his way to the great art-shop of M. Blüthenzweig. He wore his hood over his head and held his mantle together in front from inside with both hands as he went.

The air had grown heavy, the sky was livid and thunder threatened. Once more crowds were besieging the show-cases at the art-shop and especially the window where the photograph of the Madonna stood. Hieronymus cast one brief glance thither; then he pushed up the latch of the glass door hung with placards and art magazines. "As God wills," said he, and entered the shop.

A young girl was somewhere at a desk writing in a big book. She was a pretty brunette thing with bandeaux of hair and big feet. She came up to him and asked pleasantly what he would like.

"Thank you," said Hieronymus in a low voice and looked her earnestly in the face, with diagonal wrinkles in his peaked brow. "I would speak not to you but to the owner of this shop, Herr Blüthenzweig."

She hesitated a little, turned away, and took up her work once more. He stood there in the middle of the shop.

Instead of the single specimens in the show-windows there was here a riot and a heaping-up of luxury, a fullness of colour, line, form, style, invention, good taste, and beauty. Hieronymus looked slowly round him, drawing his mantle close with both hands.

There were several people in the shop besides him. At one of the broad tables running across the room sat a man in a yellow suit, with a black goat's-beard, looking at a portfolio of French drawings, over which he now and then emitted a bleating laugh. He was being waited on by an undernourished and vegetarian young man, who kept on dragging up fresh portfolios. Diagonally opposite the bleating man sat an elegant old dame, examining art embroideries with a pattern of fabulous flowers in pale tones standing together on tall perpendicular stalks. An attendant hovered about her too. A leisurely Englishman in a travelling-cap, with his pipe in his mouth, sat at another table. Cold and smooth-shaven, of indefinite age, in his good English clothes, he sat examining bronzes brought to him by M. Blüthenzweig in person. He was holding up by the head the dainty figure of a nude young girl, immature and delicately articulated, her hands crossed in coquettish innocence upon her breast. He studied her thoroughly, turning her slowly about. M. Blüthenzweig, a man with a short, heavy brown beard and bright brown eyes of exactly the same colour, moved in a semicircle around him, rubbing his hands, praising the statuette with all the terms his vocabulary possessed.

"A hundred and fifty marks, sir," he said in English. "Munich art—very charming, in fact. Simply full of charm, you know. Grace itself. Really extremely pretty, good, admirable, in fact." Then he thought of some more and went on: "Highly attractive, fascinating." Then he began again from the beginning.

His nose lay a little flat on his upper lip, so that he breathed constantly with a slight sniff into his moustache. Sometimes he did this as he approached a customer, stooping over as though he were smelling at him. When Hieronymus entered, M. Blüthenzweig had examined him cursorily in this way, then devoted himself again to his Englishman.

The elegant old dame made her selection and left the shop. A man entered. M. Blüthenzweig sniffed briefly at him as though to scent out his capacity to buy and left him to the young book-keeper. The man purchased a faience bust of young Piero de' Medici, son of Lorenzo, and went out again. The Englishman began to depart. He had acquired the statuette of the young girl and left amid bowings from M. Blüthenzweig. Then the art-dealer turned to Hieronymus and came forward.

"You wanted something?" he said, without any particular courtesy.

Hieronymus held his cloak together with both hands and looked the other in the face almost without winking an eyelash. He parted his big lips slowly and said:

"I have come to you on account of the picture in the window there, the big photograph, the Madonna." His voice was thick and without modulation.

"Yes, quite right," said M. Blüthenzweig briskly and began rubbing his hands. "Seventy marks in the frame. It is unfadable—a first-class reproduction. Highly attractive and full of charm."

Hieronymus was silent. He nodded his head in the hood and shrank a little into himself as the dealer spoke. Then he drew himself up again and said:

"I would remark to you first of all that I am not in the position to purchase anything, nor have I the desire. I am sorry to have to disappoint your expectations. I regret if it upsets you. But in the first place I am poor and in the second I do not love the things you sell. No, I cannot buy anything."

"No? Well, then?" asked M. Blüthenzweig, sniffing a good deal. "Then may I ask—"

"I suppose," Hieronymus went on, "that being what you are you look down on me because I am not in a position to buy."

"Oh—er—not at all," said M. Blüthenzweig. "Not at all. Only—"

"And yet I beg you to hear me and give some consideration to my words."

"Consideration to your words. H'm—may I ask—"

"You may ask," said Hieronymus, "and I will answer you. I have come to beg you to remove that picture, the big photograph, the Madonna, out of your window and never display it again."

M. Blüthenzweig looked awhile dumbly into Hieronymus's face—as though he expected him to be abashed at the words he had just uttered. But as this did not happen he gave a violent sniff and spoke himself:

"Will you be so good as to tell me whether you are here in any official capacity which authorizes you to dictate to me, or what does bring you here?"

"Oh, no," replied Hieronymus, "I have neither office nor dignity from the state. I have no power on my side, sir. What brings me hither is my conscience alone."

M. Blüthenzweig, searching for words, snorted violently into his moustache. At length he said:

"Your conscience . . . well, you will kindly understand that I take not the faintest interest in your conscience." With which he turned round and moved quickly to his desk at the back of the shop, where he began to write. Both attendants laughed heartily. The pretty Fräulein giggled over her account-book. As for the yellow gentleman with the goat's beard, he was evidently a foreigner, for he gave no sign of comprehension but went on studying the French drawings and emitting from time to time his bleating laugh.

"Just get rid of the man for me," said M. Blüthenzweig shortly over his shoulder to his assistant. He went on writing. The poorly paid young vegetarian approached Hieronymus, smothering his laughter, and the other salesman came up too.

"May we be of service to you in any other way?" the first asked mildly. Hieronymus fixed him with his glazed and suffering eyes.

"No," he said, "you cannot. I beg you to take the Madonna picture out of the window, at once and forever."

"But—why?"

"It is the Holy Mother of God," said Hieronymus in a subdued voice.

"Quite. But you have heard that Herr Blüthenzweig is not inclined to accede to your request."

"We must bear in mind that it is the Holy Mother of God," said Hieronymus again and his head trembled on his neck.

"So we must. But should we not be allowed to exhibit any Madonnas— or paint any?"

"It is not that," said Hieronymus, almost whispering. He drew himself up and shook his head energetically several times. His peaked brow under the hood was entirely furrowed with long, deep cross-folds. "You know very well that it is vice itself that is painted there—naked sensuality. I was standing near two simple young people and overheard with my own ears that it led them astray upon the doctrine of the Immaculate Conception."

"Oh, permit me—that is not the point," said the young salesman, smiling. In his leisure hours he was writing a brochure on the modern movement in art and was well qualified to conduct a cultured conversation. "The picture is a work of art," he went on, "and one must measure it by the appropriate standards as such. It has been very highly praised on all hands. The state has purchased it."

"I know that the state has purchased it," said Hieronymus. "I also know that the artist has twice dined with the Prince Regent. It is common talk— and God knows how people interpret the fact that a man can become famous by such work as this. What does such a fact bear witness to? To the blindness of the world, a blindness inconceivable, if not indeed shamelessly hypocritical. This picture has its origin in sensual lust and is enjoyed in the same—is that true or not? Answer me! And you too answer me, Herr Blüthenzweig!"

A pause ensued. Hieronymus seemed in all seriousness to demand an answer to his question, looking by turns at the staring attendants and the round back M. Blüthenzweig turned upon him, with his own piercing and anguishing brown eyes. Silence reigned. Only the yellow man with the goat's beard, bending over the French drawings, broke it with his bleating laugh.

"It is true," Hieronymus went on in a hoarse voice that shook with his profound indignation. "You do not dare deny it. How then can honour be done to its creator, as though he had endowed mankind with a new ideal possession? How can one stand before it and surrender unthinkingly to the base enjoyment which it purveys, persuading oneself in all seriousness that one is yielding to a noble and elevated sentiment, highly creditable to the human race? Is this reckless ignorance of abandoned hypocrisy? My understanding falters, it is completely at a loss when confronted by the absurd fact that a man can achieve renown on this earth by the stupid and shameless exploitation of the animal instincts. Beauty? What is beauty? What forces are they which use beauty as their tool today—and upon what does it work? No one can fail to know this, Herr Blüthenzweig. But who, understanding it clearly, can fail to feel disgust and pain? It is criminal to play upon the ignorance of the immature, the led, the brazen, and the unscrupulous by elevating beauty into an idol to be worshipped, to give it even more power over those who know not affliction and have no knowledge of redemption. You are unknown to me, and you look at me with black looks—yet answer me! Knowledge, I tell you, is the profoundest torture in the world; but it is the purgatory without whose purifying pangs no soul can reach salvation. It is not infantile, blasphemous shallowness that can save us, Herr Blüthenzweig; only knowledge can avail, knowledge in which the passions of our loathsome flesh die away and are quenched."

Silence.—The yellow man with the goat's beard gave a sudden little bleat.

"I think you really must go now," said the underpaid assistant mildly.

But Hieronymus made no move to do so. Drawn up in his hooded cape, he stood with blazing eyes in the centre of the shop and his thick lips poured out condemnation in a voice that was harsh and rusty and clanking.

"Art, you cry; enjoyment, beauty! Enfold the world in beauty and endow all things with the noble grace of style!—Profligate, away! Do you think to wash over the lurid colours the misery of the world? Do you think with the sounds of feasting and music to drown out the voice of the tortured earth? Shameless one, you err! God lets not Himself be mocked, and your impudent deification of the glistering surface of things is an abomination in His eyes. You tell me that I blaspheme art. I say to you that you lie. I do not blaspheme art. Art is no conscienceless delusion, lending itself to re-inforce the allurements of the fleshly. Art is the holy torch which turns its light upon all the frightful depths, all the shameful and woeful abysses of life; art is the godly fire laid to the world that, being redeemed by pity, it may flame up and dissolve altogether with its shames and torments.—Take it out, Herr Blüthenzweig, take away the work of that famous painter out of your window—you would do well to burn it with a hot fire and strew its ashes to the four winds—yes, to all the four winds—"

His harsh voice broke off. He had taken a violent backwards step, snatched one arm from his black wrappings, and stretched it passionately forth, gesturing towards the window with a hand that shook as though pal-sied. And in this commanding attitude he paused. His great hooked nose seemed to jut more than ever, his dark brows were gathered so thick and high that folds crowded upon the peaked forehead shaded by the hood; a hectic flush mantled his hollow cheeks.

But at this point M. Blüthenzweig turned round. Perhaps he was out-raged by the idea of burning his seventy-mark reproduction; perhaps Hie-ronymus's speech had completely exhausted his patience. In any case he was a picture of stern and righteous anger. He pointed with his pen to the door of the shop, gave several short, excited snorts into his moustache, struggled for words, and uttered with the maximum of energy those which he found:

"My fine fellow, if you don't get out at once I will have my packer help you—do you understand?"

"Oh, you cannot intimidate me, you cannot drive me away, you can-not silence my voice!" cried Hieronymus as he clutched his cloak over his chest with his fists and shook his head doughtily. "I know that I am single-handed and powerless, but yet I will not cease until you hear me, Herr Blüthenzweig! Take the picture out of your window and burn it even today! Ah, burn not it alone! Burn all these statues and busts, the sight of which plunges the beholder into sin! Burn these vases and ornaments, these shameless revivals of paganism, these elegantly bound volumes of erotic verse! Burn everything in your shop, Herr Blüthenzweig, for it is a filthiness in God's sight. Burn it, burn it!" he shrieked, beside himself, describing a wild, all-embracing circle with his arm. "The harvest is ripe for the reaper, the measure of the age's shamelessness is full—but I say unto you—"

"Krauthuber!" Herr Blüthenzweig raised his voice and shouted towards a door at the back of the shop. "Come in here at once!"

And in answer to the summons there appeared upon the scene a massive overpowering presence, a vast and awe-inspiring, swollen human bulk, whose limbs merged into each other like links of sausage—a gigantic son of the people, malt-nourished and immoderate, who weighed in, with puffings, bursting with energy, from the packing-room. His appearance in the upper reaches of his form was notable for a fringe of walrus beard; a hide apron fouled with paste covered his body from the waist down, and his yellow shirt-sleeves were rolled back from his heroic arms.

"Will you open the door for this gentleman, Krauthuber?" said M. Blüthenzweig; "and if he should not find the way to it, just help him into the street."

"Huh," said the man, looking from his enraged employer to Hieronymus and back with his little elephant eyes. It was a heavy monosyllable, suggesting reserve force restrained with difficulty. The floor shook with his tread as he went to the door and opened it.

Hieronymus had grown very pale. "Burn—" he shouted once more. He was about to go on when he felt himself turned round by an irresistible power, by a physical preponderance to which no resistance was even thinkable. Slowly and inexorably he was propelled towards the door.

"I am weak," he managed to ejaculate. "My flesh cannot bear the force . . . it cannot hold its ground, no . . . but what does that prove? Burn—"

He stopped. He found himself outside the art-shop. M. Blüthenzweig's giant packer had let him go with one final shove, which set him down on the stone threshold of the shop, supporting himself with one hand. Behind him the door closed with a rattle of glass.

He picked himself up. He stood erect, breathing heavily, and pulled his cloak together with one fist over his breast, letting the other hang down inside. His hollow cheeks had a grey pallor; the nostrils of his great hooked nose opened and closed; his ugly lips were writhen in an expression of hatred and despair and his red-rimmed eyes wandered over the beautiful square like those of a man in a frenzy.

He did not see that people were looking at him with amusement and curiosity. For what he beheld upon the mosaic pavement before the great loggia were all the vanities of the world: the masked costumes of the artist balls, the decorations, vases and art objects, the nude statues, the female busts, the picturesque rebirths of the pagan age, the portraits of famous beauties by the hands of masters, the elegantly bound erotic verse, the art brochures—all these he saw heaped in a pyramid and going up in crackling flames amid loud exultations from the people enthralled by his own frightful words. A yellow background of cloud had drawn up over the Theatinerstrasse, and from it issued wild rumblings; but what he saw was a burning fiery sword, towering in sulphurous light above the joyous city.

"*Gladius Dei super terram* . . ." his thick lips whispered; and drawing himself still higher in his hooded cloak while the hand hanging down inside it twitched convulsively, he murmured, quaking: "*cito et velociter!*" *

---

* "*Gladius Dei super terram* . . . *Cito et velociter*" are phrases from a sentence in the Vulgate, the Latin translation of the Bible, meaning "May the sword of God come soon and swiftly over the earth." William Alfred kindly reviewed the editor's translation of this phrase and amplified its context.

WILLIAM FAULKNER

EVANGELINE

[1931], 1979

*Photographs intrigued the young Faulkner (1897–1962). The southern writer espe-
cially valued their ability to create legendary identities, judging by the portraits
he commissioned in 1928 of himself wearing various uniforms with unearned in-
signia from his brief service in the First World War.*[1] *Faulkner also became an
amateur photographer around this time, developing a particular fascination for
unusual cameras.*[2] *Throughout his early writing, his use of fictional pictures continued to reflect his interest in identity through portraits, such as the deceptive
photograph in the supernatural tale "The Leg" (1925) and the "Rogue's Gallery"
of family pictures in his first version of* Sanctuary *(1929).*[3] *A photograph protectively encased in metal provides the key to the complex plot in "Evangeline," a short
story written around 1931, but put away by the author after being rejected by two
magazines; it was only discovered by scholars four decades later. This photograph
was joined by others with various meanings when the short story evolved into the
more experimental novel-length work* Absalom, Absalom! *(1936); all possessed
the ability to ignite the passions of the central characters.*[4] *However, Faulkner subsequently gave up his own serious photography.*[5] *His use of fictional photographs
diminished in later work. His prose, increasingly proceeding by implication rather
than assertion, more often featured frozen "photographic" moments, variously
framed and interpreted by each character. But the writer remained sensitive to the
power of pictures. Even before winning the Nobel Prize in 1950, Faulkner continued trying to shape his public image, but not through portraits of himself; "no
photographs," he now insisted, wanting only to be remembered for his writing.*[6]

1. Joseph Blotner, *Faulkner, A Biography* (New York: Random House, 1974), vol. 1,
p. 232, describes the author's half-dozen poses, three of which are reproduced by

Judith Sensibar in "Popular Culture Invades Jefferson: Faulkner's Real and Imagined Photos of Desire," *Faulkner and Popular Culture*, edited by Doreen Fowles and Ann J. Abadie (Jackson: University of Mississippi Press, 1990), pp. 119, 124–25. Sensibar asserts that these "trick" photographs reinforced his wartime impostures—describing himself as English and fatherless to his fellow trainees, as an active pilot and an officer to his mother—in a later version of this article, "Faulkner's Fictional Photographs: Playing with Difference," in *Out of Bounds: Male Writers and Gender(ed) Criticism*, edited by Laura Claridge and Elizabeth Langland (Amherst: University of Massachusetts Press, 1990), pp. 300–302, 314, n. 38, and in "William Faulkner: Poet to Novelist: An Imposter Becomes an Artist," in *Psychoanalytic Studies of Biography*, no. 4, edited by George Moraitis and George H. Pollock (Madison, Conn.: International Universities Press, 1987), p. 309 and n. 3. Certainly such pictures reinforced the false impressions of military prowess Faulkner gave his mother; she painted portraits from photographs, using one from this series, according to James Dahl, "A Faulkner Reminiscence: Conversations with Mrs. M. F. Faulkner," *JML* 3, no. 4 (April 1974): 1027, 1030. But the local photographer J. R. "Colonel" Cofield—and perhaps also Faukner himself, who "clearly enjoyed the charade"—took this 1928 sitting less seriously, as described by Cofield, "Many Faces, Many Moods," in James W. Webb and A. Wigfall Green, eds., *William Faulkner of Oxford* (Baton Rouge: Louisiana State University Press, 1965), p. 109, and in Carvel Collins, introduction to Jack Cofield, *William Faulkner: The Cofield Collection* (Oxford, Miss.: Yoknapatawpha Press, 1978), p. 56.

2. Collins, in his introduction to *The Cofield Collection*, p. x, notes that in addition to making pictures of and for Faulkner, Cofield developed his film and advised him on camera techniques, impressed that the writer worked hard to perfect his hobby, though without much success. Cofield, in "Many Faces," pp. 109–10, recalls: "In the mid-thirties, Bill was a devout camera fiend. In his rambles in Europe, he had picked up a genuine old Zeiss Camera with one of the finest German mechanisms ever made, [but found it hard to operate and his results poor]. He finally gave it up in disgust, even though cameras always did fascinate him. . . . I never took a shot that he was not at my elbow taking in the complete procedure."

3. See Faulkner: "The Leg" in *Collected Stories of William Faulkner* (New York: Random House, 1950), pp. 841–42; and *Sanctuary, The Original Text*, edited by Noel Polk (New York: Random House, 1981), pp. 19 (2), 41 (2), 44 (2), 57–59, 63, 143 (2), 145, 146, 149, 167, 205 (2), 210 (1), 220 (2), 230; cf. the revised *Sanctuary* (1931) in Faulkner, *Novels 1930–1935*, edited by Joseph Blotner and Noel Polk (New York: Library of America, 1985), pp. 227, 294, 325, 333, 347, in which only the photograph of Horace's stepdaughter that repeatedly stimulates erotic fantasies is meaningfully retained. See also David Madden, "Photographs in the 1929 Version of *Sanctuary*," *Faulkner and Popular Culture*, edited by Fowles and Abadie, pp. 93–109, and Sensibar, *"Faulkner's Fictional Photographs,"* pp. 307–8.

4. See Elisabeth Muhlenfeld, *William Faulkner's Absalom, Absalom!: A Critical Casebook* (New York: Garland, 1984), pp. xiv–xxxv, for an account of the short story's subsequent evolution; Estella Schoenberg, *Old Tales and Talking: Quentin Compson in*

William Faulkner's Absalom, Absalom! and Related Works (Jackson: University Press of Mississippi, 1977), pp. 16–69, for a discussion of the relationship between the two works; and Brenda G. Cornell, "Faulkner's 'Evangeline': A Preliminary Stage," *Southern Quarterly* 22, no. 4 (Summer 1984): 22–41. See also Faulkner, *Absalom, Absalom!: The Corrected Text*, edited by Noel Polk (New York: Random House, 1986), pp. 146–47, for Rosa's moving recollection of a photograph of Charles; pp. 9, 236, 282, which mention the Sutpen family photograph—"strange, contradictory, bizarre, not quite comprehensible," according to Quentin Compson; and pp. 71, 73, 114, 121, 271, which mention the encased photograph which Rosa assumes must be a picture of her niece, Judith, Charles's fiancé, but which instead portrays Charles's octoroon woman (his wife in "Evangeline") and their son. For further discussion of Rosa's recollections, see Sensibar, *"Faulkner's Fictional Photographs,"* pp. 302–7. To locate Faulkner's use of photography in his other works, see Jack L. Capps et al., eds., *The Faulkner Concordances* (Ann Arbor, Mich.: UMI Research Press for the Faulkner Concordances Advisory Board, 1977–), 19 vols., in the indices under "Photography" and "Photographs."

5. The mature Faulkner, perhaps coping better or in different ways with his problems of identity and desire, focused his picture-taking on his young daughter. Jill Faulkner Summers recalled, in telephone conversations with the editor on January 8–9, 1993, that her father often took pictures of family members, friends, and favorite animals with a Leica; she has had some of the tiny prints enlarged for her family's enjoyment.

6. See Faulkner, letter to Malcolm Cowley, February 11, 1949, quoted in Cowley, ed., *The Faulkner-Cowley File: Letters and Memories, 1944–1962* (New York: Viking, 1957), p. 126. Cowley himself notes (pp. 66, 71, 75) that the author thought he wrote for enjoyment, couldn't bear to see his personal affairs discussed in print, and never corrected misstatements about himself, which may, as Sensibar suggests in "Faulkner's Fictional Photographs," p. 314, n. 38, relate to his earlier verbal and visual deceptions. Despite his dislike of portraits of himself, there is an undated one of him by Henri Cartier-Bresson in *Photoportraits* (London: Thames & Hudson, 1985), p. 165, and another taken in 1954 by Carl Van Vechten in *Portraits*, compiled by Mauriber, npn.

His writing inspired several photographic works about the so-called Faulkner Country, such as Walker Evans, "Faulkner's Mississippi," *Vogue* 112 (October 1, 1948): 144–49, reproduced with other Oxford scenes in *Walker Evans at Work* (New York: Harper & Row, 1982), pp. 170–79; Martin J. Dain, *Faulkner's County: Yoknapatawpha* (New York: Random House, 1964); Alain Desvergnes, *Yoknapatawpha: The Land of William Faulkner*, text by Régis Durand, translated by William Wheeler (Paris: Marval, 1989); Willie Morris and William Eggleston, *Faulkner's Mississippi* (Birmingham, Ala.: Oxmoor House, 1990); and Wright Morris's picture entitled "Faulkner Country, Near Oxford, Mississippi," 1939, which first appeared in *The Inhabitants* (New York: Scribner's, 1946), npn, and has been reproduced often in his subsequent books.

EVANGELINE

I

I had not seen Don in seven years and had not heard from him in six and a half when I got the wire collect: HAVE GHOST FOR YOU CAN YOU COME AND GET IT NOW LEAVING MYSELF THIS WEEK. And I thought at once, "What in the world do I want with a ghost?" and I reread the wire and the name of the place where it was sent—a Mississippi village so small that the name of the town was address sufficient for a person transient enough to leave at the end of the week—and I thought, "What in the world is he doing there?"

I found that out the next day. Don is an architect by vocation and an amateur painter by avocation. He was spending his two weeks' vacation squatting behind an easel about the countryside, sketching colonial porticoes and houses and negro cabins and heads—hill niggers, different from those of the lowlands, the cities.

While we were at supper at the hotel that evening he told me about the ghost. The house was about six miles from the village, vacant these forty years. "It seems that this bird—his name was Sutpen—"

"—Colonel Sutpen," I said.

"That's not fair," Don said.

"I know it," I said. "Pray continue."

"—seems that he found the land or swapped the Indians a stereopticon for it or won it at blackjack or something. Anyway—this must have been about '40 or '50—he imported him a foreign architect and built him a house and laid out a park and gardens (you can still see the old paths and beds, bordered with brick) which would be a fitten setting for his lone jewel—"

"—a daughter named—"

"Wait," Don said. "Here, now; I—"

"—named Azalea," I said.

"Now we're even," Don said.

"I meant Syringa," I said.

"Now I'm one up," Don said. "Her name was Judith."

"That's what I meant, Judith."

"All right. You tell, then."

"Carry on," I said. "I'll behave."

II

It seems that he had a son and a daughter both, as well as a wife—a florid, portly man, a little swaggering, who liked to ride fast to church of a Sunday. He rode fast there the last time he went, lying in a homemade coffin in his Confederate uniform, with his sabre and his embroidered gauntlets. That was in '70. He had lived for five years since the war in the decaying house, alone with his daughter who was a widow without having been a wife, as they say. All the livestock was gone then except a team of spavined work-horses and a pair of two year old mules that had never been in double harness until they put them into the light wagon to carry the colonel to town to the Episcopal chapel that day. Anyway, the mules ran away and turned the wagon over and tumbled the colonel, sabre and plumes and all, into the ditch; from which Judith had him fetched back to the house, and read the service for the dead herself and buried him in the cedar grove where her mother and her husband already lay.

Judith's nature had solidified a right smart by that time, the niggers told Don. "You know how women, girls, must have lived in those days. Sheltered. Not idle, maybe, with all the niggers to look after and such. But not breeding any highpressure real estate agents or lady captains of commerce. But she and her mother took care of the place while the men were away at the war, and after her mother died in '63 Judith stayed on alone. Maybe waiting for her husband to come back kept her bucked up. She knew he was coming back, you see. The niggers told me that never worried her at all. That she kept his room ready for him, same as she kept her father's and brother's rooms ready, changing the sheets every week until all the sheets save one set for each bed were gone to make lint and she couldn't change them anymore.

"And then the war was over and she had a letter from him—his name was Charles Bon, from New Orleans—written after the surrender. She wasn't surprised, elated, anything. 'I knew it would be all right,' she told the old nigger, the old one, the greatgrandmother, the one whose name was Sutpen too. 'They will be home soon now.' 'They?' the nigger said. 'You mean, him and Marse Henry too? That they'll both come back to the same roof after what has happened?' And Judith said, 'Oh. That. They were just children then. And Charles Bon is my husband now. Have you forgotten that?' And the nigger said, 'I aint forgot it. And Henry Sutpen aint forgot it neither.' And (they were cleaning up the room then) Judith says, 'They have got over that now. Dont you think the war could do that much?' And the nigger said, 'It all depends on what it is the war got to get over with.'

"What what was for the war to get over with?"

"That's it," Don said. "They didn't seem to know. Or to care, maybe it was. Maybe it was just so long ago. Or maybe it's because niggers are wiser than white folks and dont bother about *why* you do, but only about *what* you do, and not so much about that. This was what they told me. Not her, the old one, the one whose name was Sutpen too; I never did talk to her. I would just see her, sitting in a chair beside the cabin door, looking like she might have been nine years old when God was born. She's pretty near whiter than she is black; a regular empress, maybe because she is white. The others, the rest of them, of her descendants, get darker each generation, like stair-steps kind of. They live in a cabin about a half mile from the house—two rooms and an open hall full of children and grandchildren and greatgrand-children, all women. Not a man over eleven years old in the house. She sits there all day long where she can see the big house, smoking a pipe, her bare feet wrapped around a chair rung like an ape does, while the others work. And just let one stop, let up for a minute. You can hear her a mile, and her looking no bigger than one of these half lifesize dolls-of-all-nations in the church bazaar. Not moving except to take the pipe out of her mouth: 'You, Sibey!' or 'You, Abum!' or 'You, Rose!' That's all she has to say.

"But the others talked; the grandmother, the old one's daughter, of what she had seen as a child or heard her mother tell. She told me how the old woman used to talk a lot, telling the stories over and over, until about forty years ago. Then she quit talking, telling the stories, and the daughter said that sometimes the old woman would get mad and say such and such a thing never happened at all and tell them to hush their mouths and get out of the house. But she said that before that she had heard the stories so much that now she never could remember whether she had seen something or just heard it told. I went there several times, and they told me about the old days before the war, about the fiddles and the lighted hall and the fine horses and carriages in the drive, the young men coming thirty and forty and fifty miles, courting Judith. And one coming further than that: Charles Bon. He and Judith's brother were the same age. They had met one another at school—"

"University of Virginia," I said. "Bayard attenuated 1000 miles. Out of the wilderness proud honor periodical regurgitant."

"Wrong," Don said. "It was the University of Mississippi. They were of the tenth graduating class since its founding—almost charter members, you might say."

"I didn't know there were ten in Mississippi that went to school then."

"—you might say. It was not far from Henry's home, and (he kept a pair of saddle horses and a groom and a dog, descendant of a pair of shepherds which Colonel Sutpen had brought back from Germany: the first police dogs Mississippi, America, maybe, had ever seen) once a month perhaps he would make the overnight ride and spend Sunday at home. One weekend he brought Charles Bon home with him. Charles had probably heard of Judith. Maybe Henry had a picture of her, or maybe Henry had bragged a little. And maybe Charles got himself invited to go home with Henry without Henry being aware that this had happened. As Charles' character divulged (or became less obscure as circumstances circumstanced, you might say) it began to appear as if Charles might be that sort of a guy. And Henry that sort of a guy too, you might say.

"Now, get it. The two young men riding up to the colonial portico, and Judith leaning against the column in a white dress—"

"—with a red rose in her dark hair—"

"All right. Have a rose. But she was blonde. And them looking at one another, her and Charles. She had been around some, of course. But to other houses like the one she lived in, lives no different from the one she knew: patriarchal and generous enough, but provincial after all. And here was Charles, young—" We said, "and handsome" in the same breath. ("Dead heat," Don said) "and from New Orleans, prototype of what today would be a Balkan archduke at the outside. Especially after that visit. The niggers told how after that, every Tuesday A.M. Charles' nigger would arrive after his allnight ride, with a bouquet of flowers and a letter, and sleep for a while in the barn and then ride back again."

"Did Judith use the same column all the time, or would she change, say, twice a week?"

"Column?"

"To lean against. Looking up the road."

"Oh," Don said. "Not while they were away at the war, her father and brother and Charles. I asked the nigger what they—those two women—did while they were living there alone. 'Never done nothin. Jes hid de silver in de back gyarden, and et whut dey could git.' Isn't that fine? So simple. War is so much simpler than people think. Just bury the silver, and eat what you can git."

"Oh, the war," I said. "I think this should count as just one? Did Charles save Henry's life or did Henry save Charles' life?"

"Now I am two up," Don said. "They never saw each other during the war, until at the end of it. Here's the dope. Here are Henry and Charles, close as a married couple almost, rooming together at the university, spending their holidays and vacations under Henry's roof, where Charles was treated like a son by the old folks, and was the acknowledged railhorse of Judith's swains; even acknowledged so by Judith after a while. Over-came her maiden modesty, maybe. Or put down her maiden dissimulation, more like—"

"Ay. More like."

"Ay. Anyway, the attendance of saddle horses and fast buggies fell off, and in the second summer (Charles was an orphan, with a guardian in New Orleans—I never did find out just how Charles came to be in school way up in North Mississippi) when Charles decided that perhaps he had better let his guardian see him in the flesh maybe, and went home, he took with him Judith's picture in a metal case that closed like a book and locked with a key, and left behind him a ring.

"And Henry went with him, to spend the summer as Charles' guest in turn. They were to be gone all summer, but Henry was back in three weeks. They—the niggers—didn't know what had happened. They just knew that Henry was back in three weeks instead of three months, and that he tried to make Judith send Charles back his ring."

"And so Judith pined and died, and there's your unrequited ghost."

"She did no such thing. She refused to send back the ring and she dared Henry to tell what was wrong with Charles, and Henry wouldn't tell. Then the old folks tried to get Henry to tell what it was, but he wouldn't do it. So it must have been pretty bad, to Henry at least. But the engagement wasn't announced yet; maybe the old folks decided to see Charles and see if some explanation was coming forth between him and Henry, since whatever it was, Henry wasn't going to tell. It appears that Henry was that sort of a guy, too.

"Then fall came, and Henry went back to the university. Charles was there, too. Judith wrote to him and had letters back, but maybe they were waiting for Henry to fetch him at another weekend, like they used to do. They waited a good while; Henry's boy told how they didn't room together now and didn't speak when they met on the campus. And at home Judith wouldn't speak to him, either. Henry must have been having a fine time. Getting the full worth out of whatever it was he wouldn't tell.

"Judith might have cried some then at times, being as that was before her nature changed, as the niggers put it. And so maybe the old folks worked on Henry some, and Henry still not telling. And so at Thanksgiving they told Henry that Charles was coming to spend Christmas. They had it, then, Henry and his father, behind closed doors. But they said you could hear them through the door: 'Then I wont be here myself,' Henry says. 'You will be here, sir,' the colonel says. 'And you will give both Charles and your sister a satisfactory explanation of your conduct': something like that, I imagine.

"Henry and Charles explained it this way. There is a ball on Christmas eve, and Colonel Sutpen announces the engagement, which everybody knew about, anyway. And the next morning about daylight a nigger wakes the colonel and he comes charging down with his nightshirt stuffed into his britches and his galluses dangling and jumps on the mule bareback (the mule being the first animal the nigger came to in the lot) and gets down to the back pasture just as Henry and Charles are aiming at one another with pistols. And the colonel hasn't any more got there when here comes Judith, in her nightdress too and a shawl, and bareback on a pony too. And what she didn't tell Henry. Not crying, even though it wasn't until after the war that she gave up crying for good, her nature changing and all. 'Say what he has done,' she tells Henry. 'Accuse him to his face.' But still Henry wont tell. Then Charles says that maybe he had better clear off, but the colonel wont have it. And so thirty minutes later Henry rides off, without any breakfast and without even telling his mother goodbye, and they never saw him again for three years. The police dog howled a right smart at first; it wouldn't let anybody touch it or feed it. It got into the house and got into Henry's room and for two days it wouldn't let anybody enter the room.

"He was gone for three years. In the second year after that Christmas Charles graduated and went home. After Henry cleared out Charles' visits were put in abeyance, you might say, by mutual consent. A kind of probation. He and Judith saw one another now and then, and she still wore the ring, and when he graduated and went home, the wedding was set for that day one year. But when that day one year came, they were getting ready to fight Bull Run. Henry came home that spring, in uniform. He and Judith greeted one another: 'Good morning, Henry.' 'Good morning, Judith.' But that was about all. Charles Bon's name was not mentioned between them; maybe the ring on Judith's hand was mention enough. And then about three days after his arrival, a nigger rode out from the village, with a letter from Charles Bon, who had stopped tactfully you might say, at the hotel here, this hotel here.

"I dont know what it was. Maybe Henry's old man convinced him, or maybe it was Judith. Or maybe it was just the two young knights going off to battle; I think I told you Henry was that sort of a guy. Anyway, Henry rides into the village. They didn't shake hands, but after a while Henry and Charles come back together. And that afternoon Judith and Charles were married. And that evening Charles and Henry rode away together, to Tennessee and the army facing Sherman. They were gone four years.

"They had expected to be in Washington by July fourth of that first year and home again in time to lay-by the corn and cotton. But they were not in Washington by July fourth, and so in the late summer the colonel threw down his newspaper and went out on his horse and herded up the first three hundred men he met, trash, gentles and all, and told them they were a regiment and wrote himself a colonel's commission and took them to Tennessee too. Then the two women were left in the house alone, to 'bury the silver and eat what they could git.' Not leaning on any columns, looking up the road and not crying, either. That was when Judith's nature began to change. But it didn't change good until one night three years later.

"But it seemed that the old lady couldn't git enough. Maybe she wasn't a good forager. Anyway, she died, and the colonel couldn't get home in time and so Judith buried her and then the colonel got home at last and tried to persuade Judith to go into the village to live but Judith said she would stay at home and the colonel went back to where the war was, not having to go far, either. And Judith stayed in the house, looking after the niggers and what crops they had, keeping the rooms fresh and ready for the three men, changing the bedlinen each week as long as there was linen to change with. Not standing on the porch, looking up the road. Gittin something to eat had got so simple by then that it took all your time. And besides, she wasn't worried. She had Charles' monthly letters to sleep on, and besides she knew he would come through all right, anyway. All she had to do was to be ready and wait. And she was used to waiting by then.

"She wasn't worried. You have to expect, to worry. She didn't even expect when, almost as soon as she heard of the surrender and got Charles' letter saying that the war was over and he was safe, one of the niggers came running into the house one morning saying, 'Missy. Missy.' And she standing in the hall when Henry came onto the porch and in the door. She stood there, in the white dress (and you can still have the rose, if you like); she stood there; maybe her hand was lifted a little, like when someone threatens you with a stick, even in fun. 'Yes?' she says. 'Yes?'

" 'I have brought Charles home,' Henry says. She looks at him; the light is on her face but not on his. Maybe it is her eyes talking, because Henry says, not even gesturing with his head: 'Out there. In the wagon.'

" 'Oh,' she says, quite quiet, looking at him, not moving too. 'Was—was the journey hard on him?'

" 'It was not hard on him.'

" 'Oh,' she says. 'Yes. Yes. Of course. There must have been a last . . . last shot, so it could end. Yes. I had forgot.' Then she moves, quiet, deliberate. 'I am grateful to you. I thank you.' She calls then, to the niggers murmuring about the front door, peering into the hall. She calls them by name, composed, quiet: 'Bring Mr Charles into the house.'

"They carried him up to the room which she had kept ready for four years, and laid him on the fresh bed, in his boots and all, who had been killed by the last shot of the war. Judith walked up the stairs after them, her face quiet, composed, cold. She went into the room and sent the niggers out and she locked the door. The next morning, when she came out again, her face looked exactly as it had when she went into the room. And the next morning Henry was gone. He had ridden away in the night, and no man that knew his face ever saw him again."

"And which one is the ghost?" I said.

Don looked at me. "You are not keeping count anymore. Are you?"

"No," I said. "I'm not keeping count anymore."

"I dont know which one is the ghost. The colonel came home and died in '70 and Judith buried him beside her mother and her husband, and the nigger woman, the grandmother (not the old one, the one named Sutpen) who was a biggish girl then, she told how, fifteen years after that day, something else happened in that big decaying house. She told of Judith living there alone, busy around the house in an old dress like trash would wear, raising chickens, working with them before day and after dark. She told it as she remembered it, of waking on her pallet in the cabin one dawn to find her mother, dressed, crouched over the fire, blowing it alive. The mother told her to get up and dress, and she told me how they went up to the house in the dawn. She said she already knew it, before they got to the house and found another negro woman and two negro men of another family living three miles away already in the hall, their eyeballs rolling in the dusk, and how all that day the house seemed to be whispering: 'Shhhhhh. Miss Judith. Miss Judith. Shhhhhh.'

"She told me how she crouched between errands in the hall, listening to the negroes moving about upstairs, and about the grave. It was already dug, the moist, fresh earth upturned in slowly drying shards as the sun mounted. And she told me about the slow, scuffing feet coming down the stairs (she was hidden then, in a closet beneath the staircase); hearing the slow feet move across overhead, and pass out the door and cease. But she didn't come out, even then. It was late afternoon when she came out and found herself locked in the empty house. And while she was trying to get out she heard the sound from upstairs and she began to scream and to run. She said she didn't know what she was trying to do. She said she just ran, back and forth in the dim hall, until she tripped over something near the staircase and fell, screaming, and while she lay on her back beneath the stairwell, screaming, she saw in the air above her a face, a head upside down. Then she said the next thing she remembered was when she waked in the cabin and it was night, and her mother standing over her. 'You dreamed it,' the mother said. 'What is in that house belongs to that house. You dreamed it, you hear, nigger?'

"So the niggers in the neighborhood have got them a live ghost," I said. "They claim that Judith is not dead, eh?"

"You forget about the grave," Don said. "It's there to be seen with the other three."

"That's right," I said. "Besides those niggers that saw Judith dead."

"Ah," Don said. "Nobody but the old woman saw Judith dead. She laid out the body herself. Wouldn't let anybody in until the body was in the coffin and it fastened shut. But there's more than that. More than niggers." He looked at me. "White folks too. That is a good house, even yet. Sound inside. It could have been had for the taxes anytime these forty years. But there is something else." He looked at me. "There's a dog there."

"What about that?"

"It's a police dog. The same kind of dog that Colonel Sutpen brought back from Europe and that Henry had at the university with him—"

"—and has been waiting at the house forty years for Henry to come home. That puts us even. So if you'll just buy me a ticket home, I'll let you off about the wire."

"I dont mean the same dog. Henry's dog howled around the house for a while after he rode off that night, and died, and its son was an old dog when they had Judith's funeral. It nearly broke up the funeral. They had to drive it away from the grave with sticks, where it wanted to dig. It was the last of the breed, and it stayed around the house, howling. It would let no one approach the house. Folks would see it hunting in the woods, gaunt as a wolf, and now and then at night it would take a howling spell. But it was old then; after a while it could not get very far from the house, and I expect there were lots of folks waiting for it to die so they could get up there and give that house a prowl. Then one day a white man found the dog dead in a ditch it had got into hunting food and was too weak to get out again, and he thought, 'Now is my chance.' He had almost got to the porch when a police dog came around the house. Perhaps he watched it for a moment in a kind of horrid and outraged astonishment before he decided it wasn't a ghost and climbed a tree. He stayed there three hours, yelling, until the old nigger woman came and drove it away and told the man to get off the place and stay off."

"That's fine," I said. "I like the touch about the dog's ghost. I'll bet that

Sutpen ghost has got a horse, too. And did they mention the ghost of a demijohn, maybe?"

"That dog wasn't a ghost. Ask that man if it was. Because it died too. And then there was another police dog there. They would watch each dog in turn get old and die, and then on the day they would find it dead, another police dog would come charging full-fleshed and in midstride around the corner of the house like somebody with a wand or something had struck the foundation stone. I saw the present one. It isn't a ghost."

"A dog," I said. "A haunted house that bears police dogs like plums on a bush." We looked at one another. "And the old nigger woman could drive it away. And her name is Sutpen too. Who do you suppose is living in that house?"

"Who do you suppose?"

"Not Judith. They buried her."

"They buried something."

"But why should she want to make folks think she is dead if she isn't dead?"

"That's what I sent for you for. That's for you to find out."

"How find out?"

"Just go and see. Just walk up to the house and go in and holler: 'Hello. Who's at home?' That's the way they do in the country."

"Oh, is it?"

"Sure. That's the way. It's easy."

"Oh, is it."

"Sure," Don said. "Dogs like you, and you dont believe in haunts. You said so yourself."

And so I did what Don said. I went there and I entered that house. And I was right and Don was right. That dog was a flesh-and-blood dog and that ghost was a flesh-and-blood ghost. It had lived in that house for forty years, with the old negro woman supplying it with food, and no man the wiser.

III

While I stood in the darkness in a thick jungle of overgrown crepe myrtle beneath a shuttered window of the house, I thought, "I have only to get into the house. Then she will hear me and will call out. She will say 'Is that you?' and call the old negress by her name. And so I will find out what the old negress' name is too." That's what I was thinking, standing there beside the dark house in the darkness, listening to the diminishing rush of the dog fading toward the branch in the pasture.

So I stood there in the junglish overgrowth of the old garden, beside the looming and scaling wall of the house, thinking of the trivial matter of the old woman's name. Beyond the garden, beyond the pasture, I could see a light in the cabin, where in the afternoon I had found the old woman smoking in a wirebound chair beside the door. "So your name is Sutpen too," I said.

She removed the pipe. "And what might your name be?"

"I told her. She watched me, smoking. She was incredibly old: a small woman with a myriadwrinkled face in color like pale coffee and as still and cold as granite. The features were not negroid, the face in its cast was too cold, too implacable, and I thought suddenly, 'It's Indian blood. Part Indian and part Sutpen, spirit and flesh. No wonder Judith found her sufficient since forty years.' Still as granite, and as cold. She wore a clean calico dress and an apron. Her hand was bound in a clean white cloth. Her feet were bare. I told her my business, profession, she nursing the pipe and watching me with eyes that had no whites at all; from a short distance away she appeared to have no eyes at all. Her whole face was perfectly blank, like a mask in which the eyesockets had been savagely thumbed and the eyes themselves forgotten. "A which?" she said.

"A writer. A man that writes pieces for the newspapers and such."

She grunted. "I know um." She grunted again around the pipe stem, not ceasing to puff at it, speaking in smoke, shaping her words in smoke for the eye to hear. "I know um. You aint the first newspaper writer we done had dealings with."

"I'm not? When—"

She puffed, not looking at me. "Not much dealings, though. Not after Marse Henry went to town and horsewhupped him outen he own office, out into the street, wropping the whup around him like a dog." She smoked, the pipe held in a hand not much larger than the hand of a doll. "And so because you writes for the newspapers, you think you got lief to come meddling round Cunnel Sutpen's house?"

"It's not Colonel Sutpen's house now. It belongs to the state. To anybody."

"How come it does?"

"Because the taxes haven't been paid on it in forty years. Do you know what taxes are?"

She smoked. She was not looking at me. But it was hard to tell what she was looking at. Then I found what she was looking at. She extended her arm, the pipe stem pointing toward the house, the pasture. "Look yonder," she said. "Going up across the pahster." It was the dog. It looked as big as a calf: big, savage, lonely without itself being aware that it was lonely, like the house itself. "That dont belong to no state. You try it and see."

"Oh, that dog. I can pass that dog."

"How pass it?"

"I can pass it."

She smoked again. "You go on about your business, young white gentleman. You let what dont concern you alone."

"I can pass that dog. But if you'd tell me, I wouldn't have to."

"You get by that dog. Then we'll see about telling."

"Is that a dare?"

"You pass that dog."

"All right," I said. "I'll do that." I turned and went back to the road. I could feel her watching me. I didn't look back. I went on up the road. Then she called me, strongvoiced; as Don said, her voice would carry a good mile, and not full raised either. I turned. She still sat in the chair, small as a big doll, jerking her arm, the smoking pipe, at me. "You git out of here and stay out!" she shouted. "You go on away."

That's what I was thinking of while I stood there beside the house, hearing the dog. Passing it was easy: just a matter of finding where the branch ran, and a hunk of raw beef folded about a half can full of pepper. So I stood there, about to commit breaking and entering, thinking of the trivial matter of an old negress' name. I was a little wrought up; I was not too old for that. Not so old but what the threshold of adventure could pretty well deprive me of natural judgment, since it had not once occurred to me that one who had lived hidden in a house for forty years, going out only at night for fresh air, her presence known only to one other human being and a dog, would not need to call out, on hearing a noise in the house: "Is that you?"

So when I was in the dark hall at last, standing at the foot of the stairs where forty years ago the negro girl, lying screaming on her back, had seen the face upside down in the air above her, still hearing no sound, no voice yet saying, 'Is that you?' I was about ready to be tied myself. I was that young. I stood there for some time, until I found that my eyeballs were aching, thinking, 'What shall I do now? The ghost must be asleep. So I wont disturb her.'

Then I heard the sound. It was at the back of the house somewhere, and on the ground floor. I had a seething feeling, of vindication. I thought of myself talking to Don, telling him "I told you so! I told you all the time." Perhaps I had mesmerised myself and still had a hangover, because I imagine that judgment had already recognised the sound for that of a stiff key in a stiff lock; that someone was entering the house from the rear, in a logical flesh-and-blood way with a logical key. And I suppose that judgment knew who it was, remembering how the uproar of the creekward dog must have reached the cabin too. Anyway, I stood there in the pitch dark and heard her enter the hall from the back, moving without haste yet surely, as a blind fish might move surely about and among the blind rocks in a blind pool in a cave. Then she spoke, quietly, not loud, yet without lowering her voice: "So you passed the dog."

"Yes," I whispered. She came on, invisible.

"I told you," she said. "I told you not to meddle with what aint none of your concern. What have they done to you and yo'n?"

"Shhhhh," I whispered. "If she hasn't heard me yet maybe I can get out. Maybe she wont know—"

"He aint going to hear you. Wouldn't mind, if he did."

"He?" I said.

"Git out?" she said. She came on. "You done got this far. I told you not to, but you was bound. Gittin out is too late now."

"He?" I said. "He?" She passed me, without touching me. I heard her begin to mount the stairs. I turned toward the sound, as though I could see her. "What do you want me to do?"

She didn't pause. "Do? You done done too much now. I told you. But young head mulehard. You come with me."

"No; I'll—"

"You come with me. You done had your chance and you wouldn't take it. You come on."

We mounted the stairs. She moved on ahead, surely, invisible. I held to the railing, feeling ahead, my eyeballs aching: suddenly I brushed into her where she stood motionless. "Here's the top," she said. "Aint nothing up here to run into." I followed her again, the soft sound of her bare feet. I touched a wall and heard a door click and felt the door yawn inward upon a rush of stale, fetid air warm as an oven: a smell of old flesh, a closed room. And I smelled something else. But I didn't know what it was at the time, not until she closed the door again and struck a match to a candle fixed upright in a china plate. And I watched the candle come to life and I wondered quietly in that suspension of judgment how it could burn, live, at all in this dead room, this tomblike air. Then I looked at the room, the bed, and I went and stood above the bed, surrounded by that odor of stale and unwashed flesh and of death which at first I had not recognised. The woman brought the candle to the bed and set it on the table. On the table lay another object—a flat metal case. 'Why, that's the picture,' I thought. 'The picture of Judith which Charles Bon carried to the war with him and brought back.'

Then I looked at the man in the bed—the gaunt, pallid, skull-like head sur-rounded by long, unkempt hair of the same ivory color, and a beard reach-ing almost to his waist, lying in a foul, yellowish nightshirt on foul, yellow-ish sheets. His mouth was open, and he breathed through it, peaceful, slow, faint, scarce stirring his beard. He lay with closed eyelids so thin that they looked like patches of dampened tissue paper pasted over the balls. I looked at the woman. She had approached. Behind us our shadows loomed crouch-ing high up the scaling, fishcolored wall. "My God," I said. "Who is it?"

She spoke without stirring, without any visible movement of her mouth, in that voice not loud and not lowered either. "It's Henry Sutpen," she said.

I V

We were downstairs again, in the dark kitchen. We stood, facing one another. "And he's going to die," I said. "How long has he been like this?"

"About a week. He used to walk at night with the dog. But about a week ago one night I waked up and heard the dog howling and I dressed and come up here and found him laying in the garden with the dog standing over him, howling. And I brought him in and put him in that bed and he aint moved since."

"You put him to bed? You mean, you brought him into the house and up the stairs by yourself?"

"I put Judith into her coffin by myself. And he dont weigh nothing now. I going to put him in his coffin by myself too."

"God knows that will be soon," I said. "Why dont you get a doctor?"

She grunted; her voice sounded no higher than my waist. "He's the fourth one to die in this house without no doctor. I done for the other three. I reckon I can do for him too."

Then she told me, there in the dark kitchen, with Henry Sutpen upstairs in that foul room, dying quietly unknown to any man, including himself. "I got to get it off my mind. I done toted it a long time now, and now I going to lay it down." She told again of Henry and Charles Bon like two brothers until that second summer when Henry went home with Charles in turn. And how Henry, who was to be gone three months, was back home in three weeks, because he had found It out.

"Found what out?" I said.

It was dark in the kitchen. The single window was a pale square of sum-mer darkness above the shagmassed garden. Something moved beneath the window outside the kitchen, something big-soft-footed; then the dog barked once. It barked again, fulltongued now; I thought quietly, 'Now I haven't got any more meat and pepper. Now I am in the house and I cant get out.' The old woman moved; her torso came into silhouette in the window. "Hush," she said. The dog hushed for a moment, then as the woman turned away from the window it bayed again, a wild, deep, savage, reverberant sound. I went to the window.

"Hush," I said, not loud. "Hush, boy. Still, now." It ceased; the faint, soft-big sound of its feet faded and died. I turned. Again the woman was invisible. "What happened in New Orleans?" I said.

She didn't answer at once. She was utterly still; I could not even hear her breathe. Then her voice came out of the unbreathing stillness. "Charles Bon already had a wife."

"Oh," I said. "Already had a wife. I see. And so—"

She talked, not more rapidly, exactly. I dont know how to express it. It was like a train running along a track, not fast, but you got off the track, telling me how Henry had given Charles Bon his chance. Chance for what, to do what, never did quite emerge. It couldn't have been to get a divorce; she told me and Henry's subsequent actions showed that he could not have known there was an actual marriage between them until much later, perhaps during or maybe at the very end, of the war. It seemed that there was something about the New Orleans business that, to Henry anyway, was more disgraceful than the question of divorce could have been. But what it was, she wouldn't tell me. "You dont need to know that," she said. "It dont make no difference now. Judith is dead and Charles Bon is dead and I reckon she's done dead down yonder in New Orleans too, for all them lace dresses and them curly fans and niggers to wait on her, but I reckon things is different down there. I reckon Henry done told Charles Bon that at the time. And now Henry wont be living fore long, and so it dont matter."

"Do you think Henry will die tonight?"

Her voice came out of the darkness, hardly waisthigh. "If the Lord wills it. So he gave Charles Bon his chance. And Charles Bon never took it."

"Why didn't Henry tell Judith and his father what it was?" I said. "If it was reason enough for Henry, it would be reason enough for them."

"Would Henry tell his blooden kin something, withouten there wouldn't anything else do but telling them, that I wont tell you, a stranger? Aint I just telling you how Henry tried other ways first? and how Charles Bon lied to him?"

"Lied to him?"

"Charles Bon lied to Henry Sutpen. Henry told Charles Bon that them wasn't Sutpen ways, and Charles Bon lied to Henry. You reckon if Charles

Bon hadn't lied to Henry, that Henry would have let Charles Bon marry his sister? Charles Bon lied to Henry before that Christmas morning. And then he lied to Henry again after that Christmas morning; else Henry wouldn't have never let Charles Bon marry Judith."

"How lied?"

"Aint I just told you how Henry found out in New Orleans? Likely Charles Bon took Henry to see her, showing Henry how they did in New Orleans, and Henry told Charles Bon, 'Them ways aint Sutpen ways.' "

But still I couldn't understand it. If Henry didn't know they were married, it seemed to make him out pretty much of a prude. But maybe nowadays we can no longer understand people of that time. Perhaps that's why to us their written and told doings have a quality fustian though courageous, gallant, yet a little absurd. But that wasn't it either. There was something more than just the relationship between Charles and the woman; something she hadn't told me and had told me she was not going to tell and which I knew she would not tell out of some sense of honor or of pride; and I thought quietly, "And now I'll never know that. And without it, the whole tale will be pointless, and so I am wasting my time."

But anyway, one thing was coming a little clearer, and so when she told how Henry and Charles had gone away to the war in seeming amity and Judith with her hour old wedding ring had taken care of the place and buried her mother and kept the house ready for her husband's return, and how they heard that the war was over and that Charles Bon was safe and how two days later Henry brought Charles' body home in the wagon, dead, killed by the last shot of the war, I said, "The last shot fired by who?"

She didn't answer at once. She was quite still. It seemed to me that I could see her, motionless, her face lowered a little—that immobile, myriad face, cold, implacable, contained. "I wonder how Henry found out that they were married," I said.

She didn't answer that either. Then she talked again, her voice level, cold, about when Henry brought Charles home and they carried him up to the room which Judith had kept ready for him, and how she sent them all away and locked the door upon herself and her dead husband and the picture. And how she—the negress; she spent the night on a chair in the front hall—heard once in the night a pounding noise from the room above and how when Judith came out the next morning her face looked just like it had when she locked the door upon herself. "Then she called me and I went in and we put him in the coffin and I took the picture from the table and I said, 'Do you want to put this in, Missy?' and she said, 'I wont put that in,' and I saw how she had took the poker and beat that lock shut to where it wouldn't never open again.

"We buried him that day. And the next day I took the letter to town to put it on the train—"

"Who was the letter to?"

"I didn't know. I cant read. All I knew, it was to New Orleans because I knowed what New Orleans looked like wrote out because I used to mail the letters she wrote to Charles Bon before the war, before they was married."

"To New Orleans," I said. "How did Judith find where the woman lived?" Then I said: "Was there—There was money in that letter."

"Not then. We never had no money then. We never had no money to send until later, after Cunnel had done come home and died and we buried him too, and Judith bought them chickens and we raised them and sold them and the eggs. Then she could put money in the letters."

"And the woman took the money? She took it?"

She grunted. "Took it." She talked again; her voice was cold and steady as oil flowing. "And then one day Judith said, 'We will fix up Mr Charles' room.' 'Fix it up with what?' I said. 'We'll do the best we can,' she said. So we fixed up the room, and that day week the wagon went to town to meet the train and it come back with her in it from New Orleans. It was full of trunks, and she had that fan and that mosquito-bar umbrella over her head and a nigger woman, and she never liked it about the wagon. 'I aint used to riding in wagons,' she said. And Judith waiting on the porch in a old dress, and her getting down with all them trunks and that nigger woman and that boy—"

"Boy?"

"Hers and Charles Bon's boy. He was about nine years old. And soon as I saw her I knew, and soon as Judith saw her she knew too."

"Knew what?" I said. "What was the matter with this woman, anyway?"

"You'll hear what I going to tell you. What I aint going to tell you aint going to hear." She talked, invisible, quiet, cold. "She didn't stay long. She never liked it here. Wasn't nothing to do and nobody to see. She wouldn't get up till dinner. Then she would come down and set on the porch in one of them dresses outen the trunks, and fan herself and yawn, and Judith out in the back since daylight, in a old dress no better than mine, working.

"She never stayed long. Just until she had wore all the dresses outen the trunks one time, I reckon. She would tell Judith how she ought to have the house fixed up and have more niggers so she wouldn't have to fool with the chickens herself, and then she would play on the piano. But it never suited her neither because it wasn't tuned right. The first day she went out to see where Charles Bon was buried, with that fan and that umbrella that wouldn't stop no rain, and she come back crying into a lace handkerchief and laid down with that nigger woman rubbing her head with medicine. But at suppertime she come down with another dress on and said she never seed how Judith stood it here and played the piano and cried again, telling Judith about Charles Bon like Judith hadn't never seed him."

"You mean, she didn't know that Judith and Charles had been married too?"

She didn't answer at all. I could feel her looking at me with a kind of cold contempt. She went on: "She cried about Charles Bon a right smart at first. She would dress up in the afternoon and go promenading across to the burying ground, with that umbrella and the fan, and the boy and that nigger woman following with smelling bottles and a pillow for her to set on by the grave, and now and then she would cry about Charles Bon in the house, kind of flinging herself on Judith and Judith setting there in her old dress, straightbacked as Cunnel, with her face looking like it did when she come outen Charles Bon's room that morning, until she would stop crying and put some powder on her face and play on the piano and tell Judith how they done in New Orleans to enjoy themselves and how Judith ought to sell this old place and go down there to live.

"Then she went away, setting in the wagon in one of them mosquito-bar dresses too, with that umbrella, crying into the hankcher a while and then waving it at Judith standing there on the porch in that old dress, until the wagon went out of sight. Then Judith looked at me and she said, 'Raby, I'm tired. I'm awful tired.'"

"And I'm tired too. I done toted it a long time now. But we had to look after them chickens so we could put the money in the letter every month—"

"And she still took the money? even after she came and saw, she still took it? And after Judith saw, she still sent it?"

She answered immediately, abrupt, levelvoiced: "Who are you, questioning what a Sutpen does?"

"I'm sorry. When did Henry come home?"

"Right after she left, I carried two letters to the train one day. One of them had Henry Sutpen on it. I knowed how that looked wrote out, too."

"Oh. Judith knew where Henry was. And she wrote him after she saw the woman. Why did she wait until then?"

"Aint I told you Judith knew soon as she saw that woman, same as I knew soon as I saw?"

"But you never did tell me what. What is there about this woman? Dont you see, if you dont tell me that, the story wont make sense."

"It done made enough sense to put three folks in their graves. How much more sense you want it to make?"

"Yes," I said. "And so Henry came home."

"Not right then. One day, about a year after she was here, Judith gave me another letter with Henry Sutpen on it. It was all fixed up, ready to go on the train. "You'll know when to send it," Judith said. And I told her I would know the time when it come. And then the time come and Judith said, 'I reckon you can send that letter now' and I said 'I done already sent it three days ago.'

"And four nights later Henry rode up and we went to Judith in the bed and she said, 'Henry. Henry, I'm tired. I'm so tired, Henry.' And we never needed no doctor then and no preacher, and I aint going to need no doctor now and no preacher neither."

"And Henry has been here forty years, hidden in the house. My God."

"That's forty years longer than any of the rest of them stayed. He was a young man then, and when them dogs would begin to get old he would leave at night and be gone two days and come back the next night with another dog just like um. But he aint young now and last time I went myself to get the new dog. But he aint going to need no more dog. And I aint young neither, and I going soon too. Because I tired as Judith, too."

It was quiet in the kitchen, still, blackdark. Outside the summer midnight was filled with insects; somewhere a mockingbird sang. "Why did you do all this for Henry Sutpen? Didn't you have your own life to live, your own family to raise?"

She spoke, her voice not waisthigh, level, quiet. "Henry Sutpen is my brother."

V

We stood in the dark kitchen. "And so he wont live until morning. And nobody here but you."

"I been enough for three of them before him."

"Maybe I'd better stay too. Just in case . . ."

Her voice came level, immediate: "In case what?" I didn't answer. I could not hear her breathe at all. "I been plenty enough for three of them. I dont need no help. You done found out now. You go on away from here and write your paper piece."

"I may not write it at all."

"I bound you wouldn't, if Henry Sutpen was in his right mind and strength. If I was to go up there now and say, 'Henry Sutpen, here a man going to write in the papers about you and your paw and your sister.' what you reckon he'd do?"

"I dont know. What would he do?"

"Nummine that. You done heard now. You go away from here. You let Henry Sutpen die quiet. That's all you can do for him."

"Maybe that's what I doing, anyway. You go away from here."

So that's what I did. She called the dog to the kitchen window and I could hear her talking to it quietly as I let myself out the front door and went on down the drive. I expected the dog to come charging around the house after me and tree me too, but it didn't. Perhaps that was what decided me. Or perhaps it was just that human way of justifying meddling with the humanities. Anyway, I stopped where the rusted and now hingeless iron gate gave upon the road and I stood there for a while, in the myriad, peaceful, summer country midnight. The lamp in the cabin was black now, and the house too was invisible beyond the cedartunnelled drive, the massed cedars which hid it shaggy on the sky. And there was no sound save the bugs, the insects silversounding in the grass, and the senseless mockingbird. And so I turned and went back up the drive to the house.

I still expected the dog to come charging around the corner, barking. "And then she will know I didn't play fair," I thought. "She will know I lied to her like Charles Bon lied to Henry Sutpen." But the dog didn't come. It didn't appear until I had been sitting on the top step for some time, my back against a column. Then it was there: it appeared without a sound, standing on the earth below the steps, looming, shadowy, watching me. I made no sound, no move. After a while it went away, as silent as it came. The shadow of it made one slow dissolving movement and disappeared.

It was quite still. There was a faint constant sighing high in the cedars, and I could hear the insects and the mockingbird. Soon there were two of them, answering one another, brief, quiring, risinginflectioned. Soon the sighing cedars, the insects and the birds became one peaceful sound bowled inside the skull in monotonous miniature, as if all the earth were contracted and reduced to the dimensions of a baseball, into and out of which shapes, fading, emerged fading and faded emerging:

"And you were killed by the last shot fired in the war?"

"I was so killed. Yes."

"Who fired the last shot fired in the war?"

"Was it the last shot you fired in the war, Henry?"

"I fired a last shot in the war; yes."

"You depended on the war, and the war betrayed you too; was that it?"

"Was that it, Henry?"

"What was wrong with that woman, Henry? There was something the matter that was worse to you than the marriage. Was it the child? But Raby said the child was nine after Colonel Sutpen died in '70. So it must have been born after Charles and Judith married. Was that how Charles Bon lied to you?"

"What was it that Judith knew and Raby knew as soon as they saw her?"

"Yes."

"Yes what?"

"Yes."

"Oh. And you have lived hidden here for forty years."

"I have lived here forty years."

"Were you at peace?"

"I was tired."

"That's the same thing, isn't it? For you and Raby too."

"Same thing. Same as me. I tired too."

"Why did you do all this for Henry Sutpen?"

"He was my brother."

V I

The whole thing went off like a box of matches. I came out of sleep with the deep and savage thunder of the dog roaring over my head and I stumbled past it and down the steps running before I was good awake, awake at all, perhaps. I remember the thin, mellow, farcarrying negro voices from the cabin beyond the pasture, and then I turned still half asleep and saw the façade of the house limned in fire, and the erstblind sockets of the windows, so that the entire front of the house seemed to loom stooping above me in a wild and furious exultation. The dog, howling, was hurling itself against the locked front door, then it sprang from the porch and ran around toward the back.

"I followed, running; I was shouting too. The kitchen was already gone, and the whole rear of the house was on fire, and the roof too; the light, longdried shingles taking wing and swirling upward like scraps of burning paper, burning out zenithward like inverted shooting stars. I ran back toward the front of the house, still yelling. The dog passed me, fulltongued, frantic; as I watched the running figures of negro women coming up across the redglared pasture I could hear the dog hurling itself again and again against the front door.

The negroes came up, the three generations of them, their eyeballs white, their open mouths pinkly cavernous. "They're in there, I tell you!" I was yelling. "She set fire to it and they are both in there. She told me Henry Sutpen would not be alive by morning, but I didn't—" In the roaring I could scarce hear myself, and I could not hear the negroes at all for a time. I could only see their open mouths, their fixed, whitecircled eyeballs. Then the roaring reached that point where the ear loses it and it rushes soundless up and away, and I could hear the negroes. They were making a long, concerted, wild, measured wailing, in harmonic pitch from the treble of the children to the soprano of the oldest woman, the daughter of the woman in the burning house; they might have rehearsed it for years, waiting for this irrevocable moment out of all time. Then we saw the woman in the house.

We were standing beneath the wall, watching the clapboards peel and melt away, obliterating window after window, and we saw the old negress come to the window upstairs. She came through fire and she leaned for a moment in the window, her hands on the burning ledge, looking no bigger than a doll, as impervious as an effigy of bronze, serene, dynamic, musing in the foreground of Holocaust. Then the whole house seemed to collapse, to fold in upon itself, melting; the dog passed us again, not howling now. It came opposite us and then turned and sprang into the roaring dissolution of the house without a sound, without a cry.

I think I said that the sound had now passed beyond the outraged and surfeited ear. We stood there and watched the house dissolve and liquefy and rush upward in silent and furious scarlet, licking and leaping among the wild and blazing branches of the cedars, so that, blazing, melting too, against the soft, mildstarred sky of summer they too wildly tossed and swirled.

V I I

Just before dawn it began to rain. It came up fast, without thunder or lightning, and it rained hard all forenoon, lancing into the ruin so that above the gaunt, unfallen chimneys and the charred wood a thick canopy of steam unwinded floated. But after a while the steam dispersed and we could walk among the beams and plank ends. We moved gingerly, however, the negroes in nondescript outer garments against the rain, quiet too, not chanting now, save the oldest woman, the grandmother, who was singing a hymn monotonously as she moved here and there, pausing now and then to pick up something. It was she who found the picture in the metal case, the picture of Judith which Charles Bon had owned. "I'll take that," I said.

She looked at me. She was a shade darker than the mother. But there was still the Indian, faintly; still the Sutpen, in her face. "I dont reckon mammy would like that. She particular about Sutpen property."

"I talked to her last night. She told me about it, about everything. It'll be all right." She watched me, my face. "I'll buy it from you, then."

"It aint none of mine to sell."

"Just let me look at it, then.I'll give it back. I talked to her last night. It'll be all right."

She gave it to me then. The case was melted a little; the lock which Judith had hammered shut for all time melted now into a thin streak along the seam, to be lifted away with a knifeblade, almost. But it took an axe to open it.

The picture was intact. I looked at the face and I thought quietly, stupidly (I was a little idiotic myself, with sleeplessness and wet and no breakfast)— I thought quietly, "Why, I thought she was blonde. They told me Judith was blonde. . . ." Then I came awake, alive. I looked quietly at the face: the smooth, oval, unblemished face, the mouth rich, full, a little loose, the hot, slumbrous, secretive eyes, the inklike hair with its faint but un- mistakable wiriness—all the ineradicable and tragic stamp of negro blood. The inscription was in French: *A mon mari. Toujours. 12 Aout, 1860*. And I looked again quietly at the doomed and passionate face with its thick, sur- feitive quality of magnolia petals—the face which had unawares destroyed three lives—and I knew now why Charles Bon's guardian had sent him all the way to North Mississippi to attend school, and what to a Henry Sut- pen born, created by long time, with what he was and what he believed and thought, would be worse than the marriage and which compounded the bigamy to where the pistol was not only justified, but inescapable.

"That's all there is in it," the negro woman said. Her hand came out from beneath the worn, mudstained khaki army overcoat which she wore across her shoulders. She took the picture. She glanced once at it before closing it: a glance blank or dull, I could not tell which. I could not tell if she had ever seen the photograph or the face before, or if she was not even aware that she had never seen either of them before. "I reckon you better let me have it."

THE PHOTOGRAPH

[c. 1933], 1992

*Bing Xin, born Xie Wanying (1900–), survived China's political vicissitudes—
sometimes as an activist, more often as an observer—to become the "grand old
lady" of its modern literature. She began writing in 1919 as a university student involved in the May 4th movement, which ignited a political and intellectual protest against corrupt traditional Chinese culture. Under the pen name of
Bing Xin, which means "pure heart," she wrote in the vernacular and often in
forms traditionally disdained rather than in the language and genres previously
used for the elite readers of Chinese literature.[1] Her short epigrammatic poems
established her reputation as a pioneer of modern Chinese poetry. Her "Letters
to Young Readers" are generally considered the earliest children's literature in
modern China. Meanwhile, her short stories documented the changing nature of
Chinese society—often through a single family or relationship as the one here—
sometimes advocating resignation rather than struggle. Bing Xin sought a new
role for the Chinese writer, based partly on Western models, which she further
studied in a master's program at Wellesley College (1923–26). This story apparently reflects aspects of her relationship with Grace Boynton, her former English
teacher and later colleague and translator in China, as well as Boynton's New
England family, which provided a home for the young writer in America.[2] Even
before her cherished "hundreds of photographs" were destroyed during the Second
World War, Bing Xin had registered her sensitivity to these images in some of her
short stories,[3] especially this one, where the photograph becomes the locus of a cluster of universal issues between generations and cultures.*

1. See Wendy Larson, "Female Subjectivity and Gender Relations: The Early
Stories of Lu Yin and Bing Xin," in *Politics, Ideology, and Literary Discourse in Modern*

China: Theoretical Interventions and Cultural Critique, edited by Kang Liu and Xiao-
bing Tang (Durham, N.C.: Duke University Press, 1993), pp. 124–43, for the position
of women writers encountered by Bing Xin. Patrick Hanan and Raymond Lum provided the editor with helpful translations of the story's Chinese terms, and Benjamin
Schwartz and Ross Terrill contributed information about its political, social, and
cultural context.

2. See Charlotte Boynton, "The Bridge of Love: Thirty Years of Friendship between Poet and Translator," from her introduction to Bing Xin, "Selections from
Spring Water," translated by Grace Boynton, in *Renditions* 32 (Autumn 1989): 92–97.

3. See Bing Xin, "Treasures Imperishable," p. 109, and see also her use of photo-
graphs in "Returning South," p. 73, "Our Madam's Parlour," pp. 261–62, and "My
Most Unforgettable Experience," pp. 347, 355–56, all in *The Photograph* (Beijing:
Panda, 1992).

THE PHOTOGRAPH

Madam Simpson had spent twenty-eight years of her life in China.
Those twenty-eight years had flown by like a leaf on a gust
of autumn wind, and the days were now but one long line of
memories that had all but blurred together. Yet, at times, it seemed as if the
years had passed as slowly as a cloud in a sultry summer sky, with each and
every occasion of those days a clear and vivid memory. Her home—New
England—had become to her nothing more than a distant place of towering buildings, a place where people rushed everywhere and women powdered their noses in buses on the way to work, of apartment buildings built
one on top of the other like pigeon coops. Even the memories had become
a source of irritation. When she went home every seventh year, the so-
called rest period was filled with nothing but pain and sorrow for her. Every
trip back there she realized that more of her old friendships had withered.
Friends and relatives had spouses she had never met, children she had never
seen. Nieces would bring their friends for her to meet, and she abhorred
their arrogance and frivolous pursuits. That was the worst part, by far—the
young people. Every time she returned, it seemed, they had become less
sympathetic to their elders, less respectful to them. Oh, they would put on
a thin front of courtesy, but thin it was indeed. They would quite quickly
show their lack of interest or respect, and on occasions would even laugh
and sneer at her. At times like that Madam Simpson would retreat in herself with thoughts, fond thoughts, of another place far to the east, where
she truly felt at home. The small but stately house was located in an ancient

city, at the end of a long and lonely lane, having two venerable willow trees like giant sentries at either side of the front gate. Inside the courtyard, rows of lilac bushes bordered the flagstone walkway that led under a rose-bush trellis band up to the front porch. A large door opened to a small but friendly hallway, and on both sides of the hallway there were small rooms, each one of them containing a fireplace, bookshelves, a few antiques, a painting or two. . . . Everything about the house was tasteful and pleasant, but more than anything else the place possessed a "homey" atmosphere. It was in that place that she had raised the quiet and virtuous Shuzhen.

Madam Simpson was only 25 years old when she first arrived in China; it was late summer, almost fall. Northern China is a place full of brilliant light at that time of year—whether it is the crisp and vivid light of day or the flashing, boisterous lightning of late summer storms—and truly a delightful and often exhilarating time and place. Miss Simpson would often walk just around with her pink dress and golden hair, an angelic smile across her lovely face, as she took in the wonder of it all. Miss Simpson was the music teacher at the missionary school, and she lived in a little house in the east corner of the campus. The small building was a dormitory for Western single women who taught at the school, and Miss Simpson was the youngest, the prettiest, the gentlest one of them all, and all the students simply adored her. The affections of a middle school student, though often hidden and usually awkward if ever expressed, always run deep. That is particularly true of girls' feelings toward their teachers; though their love for them may border on worship, they usually can never find the courage to say or even write what they feel. Madam Simpson lived on the first floor of the little dormitory, and nearly every night she would sit at her desk in front of the window to write letters or check homework. Often she would catch a glimpse of someone hiding in the shadows outside, some adolescent hoping to catch a glimpse of his teacher's golden hair and beautiful countenance as she looked down at the work on her desk. Sometimes the rustling of the ivy leaves on the wall would call her attention to white, skinny arms reaching over the top as a boy peered in innocent awe at the young and lovely teacher. Sometimes she could even hear them sigh. Miss Simpson would look up, and with a sad smile simply push back the hair out of her eyes with her pencil and continue her work.

She had plenty of admirers off campus as well. Many of the students firmly believed that Pastor Bintrim would be her future husband. He was a well-built and handsome young man, and forever wearing the blissful smile of one in love. Every Sunday after his sermon, the pastor would tuck his Bible under his arm and step down to the piano to escort Madam Simpson out of the church. And he was often seen sitting on the front steps of the teacher's dorm. Three years later, it was time for Reverend Bintrim to return to his homeland for a holiday. When he came back, he brought with him a pretty and vivacious young wife. The students were crushed. Never again would they enjoy the sight of lovely Miss Simpson and handsome Reverend Bintrim walking beneath the crimson leaves of the autumn trees. Time marched on like the steps of a camel; slow and heavy, yet strong and steady the days came and went. Other teachers came; Madam Simpson was no longer the youngest girl in the little dorm, and slowly the students' affections turned toward the newer ones. The golden hair slowly turned grey. Madam Simpson moved to a little house on a lane off campus where she kept a puppy, grew some flowers. In her free time she would take strolls around Longfu Temple or Changdian Fair. She would buy antiques at a very good price now and then and display them on her mantel or bookshelves. These she enjoyed very much, and students who visited her home would always compliment her fine taste in ancient artifacts. In the spring she would rest outside by the flowers and on winter evenings she would sit inside by the fireplace. Secretly she despaired. Her life was stagnating like a pond in summer with no source water and no outlet; was this how she would spend her remaining days on earth?

One summer day, like a dainty willow blossom borne on a summer breeze, Shuzhen fell gently into the courtyard of her heart. Shuzhen's father, one Mister Wang, had earned the honorable if not illustrious scholarly rank of *xiucai** during the Qing Dynasty, and had worked directly under a *yamen*† during that time. For the last thirty years, thanks to some friends who helped make the connections, he had made a living by teaching foreigners Mandarin. His second student had been Madam Simpson. Madam Simpson believed that Mister Wang was the most refined Chinese scholar she had ever met; he certainly was above any political ambitions or material pursuits. Outside of class, Mister Wang was taciturn, and quite uncomfortable when Madam Simpson would hand him his tutoring pay in a sealed envelope. He would stand there awkwardly, and with red face accept the envelope with a kind of embarrassed resignation: Sometimes for a holiday or special occasion Mister Wang would give Madam Simpson a handbag or other object handmade by Mrs Wang with Mrs Wang's own poems em-

---

* "Cultivated talent," e.g., the lowest level attained on the civil service exam, which was abolished in 1905.
† The local magistrate's office.

broidered on them. Through conversations Madam Simpson found out that Mrs Wang was from an eminent family, and the only child at that.

One winter day fifteen years before, Mister Wang had asked for ten days of leave from his work. When he returned, he was despondent, haggard, and grey. Madam Simpson found out that he had taken the time off to bury his wife who had died of pneumonia and to take his three-year-old daughter, Shuzhen, to live with her grandmother for the time being.

Mister Wang never recovered from the death of his wife. Each day he grew more withdrawn and melancholy and feeble. Even his voice, once so clear and strong, now sounded like a late autumn wind rustling a cluster of dead leaves. Madam Simpson worried about Mister Wang and felt sorry for him, and she took every opportunity to encourage him and lift his spirits. The man would force a weak smile for her, but it was quite evident that his body and spirit had given up on life. Five years later, Mister Wang suffered a case of heat stroke and did not recover.

Madam Simpson found out from Mister Wang's neighbours about his sudden death, and attended his funeral at his house. It was her first visit to the Wang's home. Inside the main gate stood a large crock with goldfish swimming around the dark green water plants. Growing around the huge crock were four pots of oleander. Several stands of bamboo huddled close to the wall and shaded the courtyard; beneath them grew wild jasmine. The bamboo curtain of the north door opened into a large study where there was shelf after shelf of books. On each wall hung one or two long painting scrolls. Madam Simpson quietly followed the other mourners through the study and entered another room. There, in the bedroom, the body of Mister Wang rested on the *kang*. A quilt covered him up to his chest, and his face was under a white piece of paper. An old, grey-haired woman, dressed in white and with eyes puffy and bloodshot from weeping, sat beside the *kang*. When Madam Simpson walked into the room, the elderly lady stood to her feet. Someone standing by introduced the foreigner to Mister Wang's mother-in-law, Mrs Huang. Mrs Huang took the hand of a young girl who was stooping over the *kang* crying and said to the foreign visitor, "This is Shuzhen." The girl was as frail as a willow blossom, thin, sickly, and pale. But there was something about this young thing that so contrasted with the dark and lifeless atmosphere around her that Madam Simpson could not forget the little girl named Shuzhen.

Except for paintings and some old books, Mister Wang owned absolutely nothing, so Madam Simpson paid all the funeral and burial expenses. After Mister Wang was buried, Madam Simpson offered Mrs Huang some money to help with Shuzhen's care and education. Mrs Huang would not hear of it, however, telling her would-be benefactor to wait until they were really in need. Madam Simpson waited several months and heard nothing. Worried for the family, she asked some of the neighbours about Mrs Huang and discovered that the old woman was actually taking care of quite a few children, so many in fact, that she could not possibly give Shuzhen the kind of care she needed. So, on the night before Christmas, Madam Simpson brought Shuzhen to her home to live.

Moonlight played off the thin layer of snow outside. It was past midnight, and the Christmas carolers had not yet passed by. Large red candles shed hot tears as they burned in solemn silence in each window. Shuzhen sat in front of the fireplace beside Madam Simpson. In the light of the blazing fire the older woman looked into the gaunt and timid face and those deep-set black eyes: there was something so mysterious, so desolate in this tiny thing. Madam Simpson slowly reached out and touched the hand of the girl. She did not move back, nor did she show any sign of feeling. She wanted to talk to the little girl, but did not know where to begin. And then, as she clung to the tiny hand in the warm glow of the parlor fireplace, she slowly began to sense that it was not just the hand of a little girl that she was holding: she was now grasping Mister Wang's poetry, Mrs Wang's exquisite embroidery; she was holding the very essence of Eastern womanhood, all the silent mystery of ancient China. . . .

And so for the next ten years Shuzhen grew up at the side of Madam Simpson. The girl was like a stream in a meadow, its slow water too deep to gurgle, too placid to be heard. Although well cared for, Shuzhen remained a short and skinny girl, and her face was always a sad, pale shade. She never showed sorrow, never showed joy. She answered when spoken to, but no more, and she went around the house as silently as if she were on tiptoes. She was a model student at school and all the teachers praised her, but she did not have one little friend, nor did she like the things that other children played with.

"She has Mister Wang's values and Mrs Wang's virtues, a perfect blend of the two!" Madam Simpson thought to herself. The girl had a certain quality and character that simply could not be found in Western girls. She possessed a quiet depth, but she was not aloof. She radiated a self-assured peace and strength, but was at the same time humble and compassionate. Whenever Madam Simpson was sick, the lass would quietly and meticulously take care of the older woman with gentleness an genuine feeling. Whenever Madam Simpson would look up from her bed, Shuzhen was always sitting at her side. The girl would look up from a book she was read-ing and smile warmly. "You're like an angel sent from Heaven!" Madam Simpson would always want to say, but as she looked into that ashen face and sorrowful eyes, she would hold back her words.

Old Mrs Huang died the second year. Shuzhen was with Madam Simpson, and Madam Simpson took her to the funeral. After that, Shuzhen never went anywhere except to school and to church every Sunday. On the Pure Brightness,* Madam Simpson took Shuzhen to her parents' graves to sweep the site and place flowers, as was the custom. Both of them cried. Madam Simpson held the little girl's hand tightly as they walked back from the cemetery. Both of them felt like outcasts in the world, lonely fragments that fit only into each other. The sense of loss and loneliness brought them closer together that day. As they walked home, Shuzhen could feel herself being bathed in the motherly love and compassion that Madam Simpson had for her. They never went out much; Madam Simpson slowly lost con-tact with most of her friends, and she even lost interest in collecting an-tiques. Her life was now centered on this fair and delicate willow blossom, Shuzhen; in the girl Madam Simpson found contentment and purpose. At times she wondered to herself, what would she do if Shuzhen later decided to marry? That was natural and expected for all young women. What a lovely thought, to see Shuzhen holding a fair-skinned, chubby little baby in her arms; what a sweet picture that produced in her mind. And yet there was something in that thought that froze her heart. "What if Shu-zhen decides to marry?" Loneliness, a chilling sadness overwhelmed her as she mumbled those words to herself. She trembled as she pushed the white hairs back from her temple, forced herself to smile and pushed that terri-fying thought out of her mind.

Everyone praised Madam Simpson for how she raised Shuzhen; for the ten years that she took care of her in China, Shuzhen remained entirely Chinese in looks, action, and spirit. She never wore Western clothes. Ex-cept when with folks who could not understand Chinese, Madam Simp-son never spoke to the girl in English. If any of the boys from the school came to their house for an occasional party, Shuzhen would timidly stay at the Madam's side and would never enter into the games or bantering. Even when she passed the candied fruit or other refreshments, she would always keep her eyes modestly downcast and speak in a whisper. The get-togethers that most young people enjoy so much were uncomfortable times

---

*A day to mourn the dead, usually falling on April 4 or 5.

for Shuzhen, and she never liked them. If an older Chinese woman ever mentioned to Madam Simpson that Shuzhen ought to marry someday, or if one of the girl's male classmates talked frankly to her about his love for Shuzhen, Madam Simpson would simply smile smugly, and with practiced tact change the subject.

Shuzhen graduated from middle school when she was eighteen, the same time that Madam Simpson was due to go back to the U.S. for a furlough. She had left Shuzhen with friends the last time she had gone home, but this time she wanted to take the girl with her. She wanted Shuzhen to see something of the world, and, anyway, she knew she would be lonely without the girl's companionship. Madam Simpson decided to ask Shuzhen if she would like to accompany her across the sea. Much to Madam Simpson surprise, the normally sober face lit up with joy and she said, "Mama, all I want to do is be with you. I'll go anywhere you go!" Madam Simpson hugged her adopted daughter and said, "Oh, thank you! I know you'll enjoy seeing where I grew up, and if you really like America, maybe we can arrange for you to go to college there. . . ."

Madam Simpson and Shuzhen made a new home in a small American town. Around the small and stout New England home were large lawns shaded by old and long-armed oaks. It was early fall when they arrived, and the leaves were turning their brilliant fall colours. There was a damp and earthy fragrance under the big, shady trees. The house had originally been owned by Madam Simpson's father, a pastor of the local church. The place still had the family's big oak beds, heavy rugs, high bookcases loaded with books, and the study still had the lingering odor of tobacco. The hallways were so high that footsteps echoed in them, and on the walls were hung various paintings. The windows were hung with dark, heavy curtains, so the rooms became dark even before the sun had set. When they arrived, Madam Simpson gave Shuzhen a tour of the house. There, in the study in front of the fireplace, was the large, stuffed chair where her father had sat every night to study the Bible; in the parlor stood a bookcase and a small walnut desk that her mother had used to keep the family books; upstairs, facing east, was her own bedroom when she was growing up; on the third floor was her older brother James' bedroom. . . . The house had belonged to her brother James and his family after their parents' deaths, but James had died that same spring and his wife and son had moved to a new house not far away. They were going to sell the old house, but Madam Simpson wrote James' wife a letter asking her not to put the house up for sale, that she and Shuzhen hoped to live in it for a year. She said she hoped to relive one more time some of the dreams of her home and youth.

Few people came to visit them in the old house, and except to venture out once a week to attend church, Madam Simpson and Shuzhen spent each and every day reading, playing the piano, or doing some knitting or other craft. Occasionally Madam Simpson was asked to speak at the church on the present situation in China. Shuzhen would quietly sit and listen, then everyone would shake hands with Madam Simpson and Shuzhen after the service. If anyone asked Shuzhen about China, she would timidly give a short answer and then fall silent again. Everyone thought she was adorable. Her quiet and respectful disposition was especially admired by the older women who showered the girl with little gifts.

Every Sunday evening, James' wife and her son, Peter, came over for dinner. James' wife was a thin and tall woman. Her face was wrinkled and she always wore a lot of make-up to try to cover up that fact. She was an incessant talker, and her endless speech wearied the normally patient Madam Simpson. Peter was a red-haired, rambunctious young man of twenty-two who, in Shuzhen's eyes, behaved like a child. There was never a moment of peace in the house once he stepped in the door. The first time they met, Peter called out her name and said, "So this is my aunt's Chinese daughter! I think we'll become the best of friends!" The fellow stood there with a simpleton's smile stretched across his face waiting for a response. Madam Simpson saw that Shuzhen did not know how to react and was feeling quite uncomfortable, so she walked up and said with a smile, "Peter, calm down a little! Don't frighten the girl!" Turning to Shuzhen she explained, "This is just how Americans act when they are trying to be cordial. If we want to show ourselves friendly to someone, we do not bother using 'Mister' or 'Miss'. You can just call him Peter." Shuzhen's face turned red as she smiled.

Shuzhen's quietness was totally unappreciated by Peter, and after dinner on Sunday nights he would leave early on some pretext. Madam Simpson and her sister-in-law would then struggle through a conversation about the old days which neither of them found very interesting. Shuzhen found the experience boring, and would often stare out the window at the people passing by on the sidewalk under the street lamp with their yellow hair and green eyes. The evening breeze carried their words, English words, their sound even more foreign than usual. She felt something unsettling inside her, and indescribable sadness. . . .

One Sunday evening, just as James' wife was ready to leave, she suddenly smiled at Shuzhen and said, "Next Sunday evening you'll have a chance to speak Chinese with someone. I found out about a certain Reverend Li who teaches at the seminary. His son, Tianxi, is a student there. I have already asked them to come here for dinner next Sunday night. I hope you will enjoy that." Shuzhen looked over to see Madam Simpson's response. "I've met them at the seminary library several times," Madam Simpson said. "Reverend Li is a kind and amiable old gentleman, and Tianxi is a very serious and quiet young man. I have been thinking myself that we really ought to ask them over. They must be lonely living abroad, and we should try to make their lives a little more pleasant." Shuzhen nodded her head in agreement.

The next Sunday, Madam Simpson and Shuzhen prepared a table of Chinese food and set out chopsticks and some tall red candles. Madam Simpson changed into a Chinese gown, put on a jade bracelet, and told Shuzhen to listen for the door bell. When Reverend Li came, she told her, she would answer the door and let Reverend Li hear genuine Chinese for the first time in quite a while. Shuzhen smiled broadly.

When the doorbell rang, Shuzhen jumped to her feet and ran to welcome their company. Peter came charging through the door first, then after him came his mother. Finally, behind them, entered a thin, pale middle-aged man with dark black hair. Peter grabbed Shuzhen's arm, pulled her in front of the man and said to her, "This is Reverend Li! It's great you can meet each other!" Then pulling the young man behind Reverend Li towards the girl, Peter said loudly, "This is Mister Li Tianxi! Mr Li, this is Miss Wang, our Shuzhen that you've heard about." Reverend Li smiled warmly and shook hands with Shuzhen as he said, "It is so wonderful to meet someone from home! What a privilege this is!" Tianxi bowed politely to everyone as Madam Simpson came, then they all went into the dining room.

There was plenty of talk and activity at the table. Reverend Li and Madam Simpson had a lively discussion about China and other affairs as well as about preaching. The sister-in-law joined in enthusiastically, Peter fought to keep a piece of pork on his chopsticks, but the meat rolled on the table. Shuzhen, a faint smile on her face, tried to give him some instructions. Tianxi quietly ate his meal, answering any questions politely but briefly. His voice had a clear and confident ring to it, however, that reflected warmth and maturity. Peter's mother looked at the two young men at the table then said to Reverend Li, "I really respect how you Chinese raise your children; just look at how quiet and mature Shuzhen and Tianxi are; they're nothing like our restless kids. Just look at Peter!" Peter had just managed to get a meatball in his chopsticks, and as he looked up at the mention of his name, the ball fell again. Peter roared with laughter and everyone laughed with him.

After dinner, everyone went into the parlor for coffee. Shuzhen and Tianxi sat silently listening to the other three talk. After a few minutes Peter yawned, then stood to his feet and said, "Mama, you can go on talking. I have to get going; I have class tomorrow morning!" His mother looked at him and smiled. "So what's your hurry? You never seem to mind staying up late going to the theatre or the cinema. I don't if you'll go directly to bed if you leave now!" But even as she spoke, she was standing up getting ready to leave. Tianxi rose slightly from his chair and looked at his father and said, "Papa, perhaps we should be going, too." Madam Simpson spoke up hurriedly, "Oh, no, it is much too early for you to leave. Besides, your father has not yet seen my father's collection of theology books!" Peter laughed, picked up his hat and said, "I hope I haven't wrecked the evening for you all. Please, everybody, sit back down and enjoy yourselves." He took his mother by the arm as he shook everyone's hand and said good-bye.

Madam Simpson saw the two of them to the door, then came back and said to Reverend Li with a smile, "Why don't you come with me to the study. Almost all of Father's books are there. Shuzhen, please entertain Tianxi. Both of you are in a foreign country now, so I hope you will forget the old Chinese customs for a few minutes and actually talk to each other for a while!" Both Shuzhen and Tianxi bowed to their elders as they left the room.

The two turned around and sat down. Somehow Tianxi's quietness and reserve had reduced Shuzhen's timidity, and she began asking the young man when he came to America, where he lived. By the warm light of the parlor lamp, Shuzhen looked attentively at this young man from her homeland: His thick, black hair was well-groomed and cut, but had no hair oil. He had a wide forehead, a small, fine nose, lively eyes, and a small mouth that curled up at the end almost like a little girl's. He wore a dark blue suit and black tie and shoes which set off radiance of his light yellow face. Looking at him, one felt the whole room suddenly take on an oriental atmosphere.

Tianxi smiled and asked, "Miss Wang has been here quite a while now; do you often go out for some fun?" Shuzhen sighed slightly and lowered her head.

"No, I never go out, except to go to church. I'm not sure why, but I've found the foreigners I've met here are quite different from the foreigners

I knew in China. Here, I never know what to say when I'm around them; I feel so awkward, so lost." Shuzhen was surprised at herself for saying that, especially to a young man she had hardly met.

Tianxi was quiet for a moment then said, "Perhaps it's because Chinese and foreigners are so different in character. Anyway, I often feel the very same way. Sometimes I don't even like going to church!" Shuzhen looked up and said, "But I thought it wasn't necessary to talk to anyone in church, that you shouldn't; why do you feel—" As she looked for words she was thinking, "This is a pastor's son speaking. . . ."

Tianxi jumped to his feet and paced in front of the fireplace. After a minute or two he stopped and stood in front of Shuzhen's chair, stood very close to her. Shuzhen felt herself shrinking back slightly. Tianxi put his hands in his pockets, and with his eyes now blazing he said, "Miss Wang, you'll have to excuse me for being so frank with someone I have just met, but five minutes after I met you I knew that you were the same as I. . . . Exactly the same as I, that here you feel lonely and out of place. I have never told anyone that, not even my own father." Shuzhen looked up in shocked attention.

"My grandfather was a *Jinshi**—one of the highest ranking scholars in the Qing Dynasty, as you probably know. In his later years he was a frustrated man with little to do and not much money, so he took up teaching; later he even taught foreigners and helped compile a Chinese dictionary. My father got to know many of these foreigners through Grandfather's connections, and he studied the Bible in their school and got baptized. I also am the product of a missionary school, but I have always enjoyed the classics that grandfather used to read, and I would really like to study art. Last year the church sent Father here to study more theology, and they also have supplied me with a very generous stipend so I can come and attend classes. The sad part is that I would prefer to study art, but because of the conditions set up by the church, I must attend classes on theology. They want to make me into a pastor, of course, but I have no desire to wear a black robe and stand behind a pulpit all my life! I want to express love and glorify God's creation through art, not with words in a sermon but people have something else in mind!

"To speak at the church and have people come up to me afterwards and ask questions about China scares me to death. From my scant twenty years of life, what do I know about four thousand years of Chinese history and what it means to us today? The very idea of doing that annoys me, fright-

---

*"Metropolitan graduate," e.g., attained the highest level on the civil service exam.

ens me. What rattles me even more is when people say that China had no culture before the coming of Christianity. At the seminary they dote over me to no good end and call me a 'model Chinese youth.' Some of the educators who have been in China and who go around raising money for the work there like to take me with them on their fund-raising campaigns. After they have given their rousing speeches they ask me up to the front and introduce me to the audience with something like, 'Just look at the kind of Chinese youth our education there has produced!' Isn't that just the way a circus man shows his trained monkey to the crowds? I tell you one thing, if there is anything praiseworthy about me, it is not thanks to these people!"

Shuzhen was now sitting forward in her chair. She felt as if there was standing before her a glowing image, an illuminating light so warm and powerful that it penetrated and enveloped her very soul. As she looked into Tianxi's face, his cheeks burning and eyes blazing with passion for the truth he spoke, tears began to well up in her eyes. Tears of sympathy? Love for her homeland? She herself did not know. To keep those tears from rolling down her cheek, she kept her head looking up at the young man.

Tianxi sighed and said, "Really, you should see it when the church has a meeting to ordain a missionary to go to China to preach. The missionary candidate stands up and says a final sad but stirring farewell, and everyone shows the person the utmost respect and pity as if the fellow was heading for some disease-infested jungle full of savages! Missionaries make sacrifices, I admit that, but foreigners in China have it better off than Chinese in foreign countries—at least materially, wouldn't you say?" Shuzhen smiled a little and nodded her head. She stood up straightening her dress a bit and said softly, "You are no doubt right on that, but the way I see it, these people are acting out of good motives. I admit there are some things here that make me discouraged and even afraid, and I sometimes have a bad feeling towards those who are really trying to help me. But if we can just control ourselves and not get flustered, we can learn from all these negative experiences. When we return to our homeland, we will be able to better help the future young people to better cope with the outside world. We will be able to make China a stronger, better place, and we ourselves will be better for it. . . . Don't you think so?"

Tianxi sat down and took a handkerchief from his pocket. As he wiped the sweat from his brow, the red in his face began to disappear and his eyes became peaceful and friendly again. He pulled the chair a little closer and said faintly, "I am terribly sorry, Miss Wang, I never imagined that I would become so excited and act so childishly the first time I met you! Generally speaking, I am a quiet fellow; I just miss the land of my fathers. Tonight when we met, I could immediately sense the "new China" in you—a dynamic and progressive China. You seemed like the embodiment of all that our land could be. I impulsively vented all my pent-up frustrations, and in the process managed to ruin this evening for you. I am sorry, sincerely sorry for my behaviour." The young man's face turned red, this time with embarrassment, and he was quiet.

Shuzhen's face flushed with embarrassment as well, and she looked down at the arm of the chair and fingered the doily as she said, "I have said too much tonight. I must admit myself, since my father died, I have always felt like no one could understand me in my silence. . . . Tonight . . . Maybe it's just hearing Chinese in a strange land. . . . I . . ." The more Shuzhen talked the less she was saying. Finally her voice faded to a whisper, then she was quiet. For a long time not a sound was heard in the room.

When Shuzhen finally looked up, Tianxi's face was as solemn as it had been during dinner; there was not a trace of the fervour and passion that had possessed him moments before. A smile came to the young man again as he said, "I believe we ought to use our time abroad to read, to travel. . . . I have always respected Westerners' courage and zest for life. I very rarely find an American young person perpetually somber and pensive like we are. I have some friends from the art school and the seminary, many of them young ladies, who get together every Saturday afternoon to discuss issues or just go on an outing. I often join them. It is quite interesting, honestly. Miss Wang, I really think you ought to join them sometime; it would really broaden your horizons. Father often goes along; I think Madam Simpson would certainly approve."

Shuzhen's eyes radiated thanks and joy as she said excitedly, "Thank you for the idea. I'll be going to college next year, and I have been thinking that before I attend college I should make some contact with young people my age. Otherwise, I may not be able to adjust myself to living with so many other people my age while studying."

"What college were you thinking about attending?" Tianxi asked. Shuzhen shrugged her shoulders. "I don't know. Madam Simpson may go back to China next year or she may not. She hasn't said much about it lately and I haven't asked. If she goes back, I suppose I ought to go back with her, but . . . now . . . I'm thinking about going to school here. . . ."

Just then the door opened, and in walked Madam Simpson with Reverend Li behind her with a load of books under his arm. Madam Simpson smiled and said to Tianxi, "We lost all track of time looking through the books. Did you have a good chat, the two of you?" Tianxi stood up and said with a smile, "We had such a good talk that we forgot about the time ourselves." Reverend Li picked up his hat and said, "Now we really must be going! Madam Simpson, thank you so much for a most enjoyable evening, and thank you for your good food and for these books. I hope we soon will have another chance to meet again." Madam Simpson smiled and shook hands with her two guests and told them, "You must come more often. Shuzhen is so lonely here; to talk with another Chinese does her so much good!" Shuzhen stood beside her, her face red as she smiled silently. Tianxi took some books from under his father's arm and bowed to his hostesses as he followed his father out the door. Madam Simpson and Shuzhen saw their guests to the front gate.

The two returned to the parlor and collected the tea set to wash. Madam Simpson stifled a yawn and said, "Aren't Reverend Li and his son lovable people? That Tianxi is a real gentleman; not a thing frivolous about that young man. Did you have a good chat with him?" Shuzhen handed her a tray of cups, looked into her eyes and paused for just a moment. The girl's face turned a little red as she spun around to pick up some saucers. Yes, she told Madam Simpson, she had had a very good chat with the reverend's son.

It was early spring now, and Madam Simpson and Shuzhen had been in America for half a year already. Not much had changed at the old house, except that Reverend Li and his son, Peter and his mother joined the family for their Sunday evening dinners. Sometimes all six of them would join the group of college students on their outings. Also, during the same time, Shuzhen was filling out physically; she was beginning to look like a young woman. Madam Simpson saw the change in her, the shapelier figure, the robust cheeks, but most of all the new gleam in her eye, the easy smile and laughter. Although the girl managed to keep her Chinese sense of reserve and propriety in front of Reverend Li and his son, she noticed a big difference in how the girl acted around Peter, now freely talking and joking with him. Madam Simpson felt a strange sort of comfort from all this. Shuzhen had always been too reserved, too reticent; a young person ought to be alive and expressive. . . . With a new and lively spirit inside that maturing body, Shuzhen would become a different person. . . . What if . . . Madam Simpson refused to think further. Rubbing her forehead lightly, she rose to her feet shaking her head as if remorseful for something and looked out the window. There remained in the yard a few patches of snow, the remnants of the winter that was now quickly retreating.

The weather of her home, New England, was unkind to Madam Simpson in her old age, and the months leading up to spring had been hard on her physically. The last big snow of winter was melting quickly in a balmy spring breeze, but the added humidity in the air seemed to make the heavy and dark curtains of the house even heavier and darker. Madam Simpson sluggishly sat up in her bed. Downstairs she could hear Shuzhen's footsteps echoing down the hall as she hurried about dusting and cleaning. She heard the doorbell and Shuzhen's voice as she greeted someone at the front door. A little while later Shuzhen appeared at her bedroom door with breakfast on a tray. She placed the tray on a table and placed a little stand on Madam Simpson's lap so she could have her breakfast in bed. Shuzhen fluffed up the pillow and got the Madam comfortably seated against them, then pulled out an envelope from her pocket and laid it in front of Madam Simpson. "Look, Mama," she laughed. "Take a look at these photos! They're of that last picnic we went on. . . . There's one there that young Mr. Li took before I realized what he was doing. I look so ridiculous!" She got the tray of food and placed it on the little table above Madam Simpson's lap, then turned around and left.

Madam Simpson slowly opened the envelope and took out the photographs, all eight of them, and held them up to look at. There was James' wife and Peter, one of Reverend Li and his son, another of Shuzhen and herself, and a couple more of the other young people that had gone on that excursion. When she came to the last photograph, however, Madam Simpson suddenly froze in shock!

In the background was the thick, gnarled bough of an old oak, its branches adorned with new leaves, at the bottom was lush green lawn, and in the middle was Shuzhen. Her hands were on a picnic basket that she was opening and she had just spun around when the picture was snapped. Her sleeves were rolled up and her hair was let down; her face reflected all the young woman's spirit, personality, and joy. Her perfect smile revealed her beautiful white teeth, and in her eyes there was a vitality that Madam Simpson had never seen in the girl for the ten years she had known her!

Madam Simpson trembled slightly. A deep and dark feeling suddenly seized her. It was not fear, not was it anger, it was not even remorse. . . . She clutched the photograph tightly as she stared at it. . . .

She had been sick when the group came by to pick Shuzhen up for the picnic. She was going to ask Shuzhen to stay home and take care of her, but afraid that the girl's presence would be missed too much by the others, and because she assumed Shuzhen would not go alone anyway, she said half-heartedly that the girl should go on ahead with them, that she could manage allright by herself. The girl hesitated for a while, then looked out the door; Li Tianxi was waiting on the front porch with his hat in his hands.

She smiled and told the group she would join them, and they all ran down the porch steps and disappeared in the car.

She stared for a long time at the photograph, but she was no longer seeing Shuzhen. Before her eyes swam the image of Pastor Bintrim's loving smile, Mister Wang's somber face, an ancient city, a city wall, a little courtyard, a rose trellis. . . . She relaxed her grip and the photograph dropped to the floor. Madam Simpson's eyes suddenly filled with tears.

The door quietly opened, and Shuzhen came tip-toeing in with a pot of coffee and set it down on the table beside the bed. The girl moved quickly around the room, cleaning and straightening things, smiling as she worked. Madam Simpson looked up from the bed and silently watched her. Shuzhen was wearing a white silk gown today. Her full, mature breasts rose and fell rhythmically as she caught her breath from running up the stairs. Her hair, slightly curled, framed her rosy cheeks, and when she turned around, Madam Simpson could see just what an attractive figure the young woman had recently developed. Through the white silk the old woman could see the pink and smooth skin of a young lady. . . . There was the sudden fragrance of spring in the room, the fragrance of youth. . . .

She looked across the room at the mirror on her vanity. Her hair was dishevelled, she was wearing a flannel nightgown, and her face was ashen white. She peered at her own bloodshot eyes, and at the wrinkled face. . . .

Shuzhen came skipping into the room and stood in front of the bed. She picked up the photographs off the table and looked at them. She laughed and said to Madam Simpson as she shuffled through them, "Madam, aren't these young people fun and lovable? You know, we are talking about going to college together, really. . . ."

Madam Simpson said nothing. Shuzhen looked up at the old woman, and her smile faded. Madam Simpson bit her lips and tried to blink back the tears that filled her eyes as she gazed mournfully out the window. Shuzhen leaned over the bed and asked softly, "Mother, what are you thinking?"

Madam Simpson kept staring out the window as she took Shuzhen's hand in hers. "I'm thinking, daughter," she said through her tears, "about returning to China."

THE LITTLE PHOTOGRAPHER

1952

Du Maurier (1907–89) was the granddaughter of the artist-writer George Du Maurier (photographed by his friend Julia Margaret Cameron)[1] *and the daughter of the actor Gerald Du Maurier, one of whose famous roles was that of Raffles, the character based on E. W. Hornung's stories. She made her own name a household word, creating compelling novels like* Rebecca *(1938), which made her the most highly paid woman writer in England. Her four collections of short stories (1952–81) are less well known but similarly express her dark creativity. This macabre narrative portrays the extravagant way of life the author probably witnessed on family trips abroad; it also reflects the low social status of most professional photographers and their dependence on the often insensitive rich. Later in life, Du Maurier collaborated with her son Christopher Brown, a photographer, on* Vanishing Cornwall, *a nonfiction work about the region where she had spent most of her adulthood. Brown approved the posthumous publication of her* Enchanted Cornwall, *a volume with photographs by Nick Wright, which illustrated his mother's life as a writer.*[2]

1. Cameron quotes George Du Maurier as saying her photography *"charms* me," in Helmut Gernsheim, *Julia Margaret Cameron* (Millerton, N.Y.: Aperture, 1975), p. 46; see also p. 47. Cameron's portrait of Du Maurier with his wife and daughter is reproduced in Judith Cook, *Daphne: A Portrait of Daphne Du Maurier* (London: Bantam Press, 1991), facing p. 146.

2. See Du Maurier: *Vanishing Cornwall* (London: Gollancz, 1981), and *Enchanted Cornwall*, edited by Piers Dudgeon (London: Joseph and Pilot, 1989).

THE LITTLE PHOTOGRAPHER

The Marquise lay on her chaise longue on the balcony of the hotel. She wore only a wrapper, and her sleek gold hair, newly set in pins, was bound close to her head in a turquoise bandeau that matched her eyes. Beside her chair stood a little table, and on it were three bottles of nail varnish all of a different shade.

She had dabbed a touch of colour on to three separate fingernails, and now she held her hand in front of her to see the effect. No, the varnish on the thumb was too red, too vivid, giving a heated look to her slim olive hand, almost as if a spot of blood had fallen there from a fresh-cut wound.

In contrast, her forefinger was a striking pink, and this too seemed to her false, not true to her present mood. It was the elegant rich pink of drawing-rooms, of ball gowns, of herself standing at some reception, slowly moving to and fro her ostrich feather fan, and in the distance the sound of violins.

The middle finger was touched with a sheen of silk neither crimson nor vermilion, but somehow softer, subtler; the sheen of a peony in bud, not yet opened to the heat of the day but with the dew of the morning upon it still. A peony, cool and close, looking down upon lush grass from some terraced border, and later, at high noon, the petals unfolding to the sun.

Yes, that was the colour. She reached for cotton wool and wiped away the offending varnish from her other fingernails, and then slowly, carefully, she dipped the little brush into the chosen varnish and, like an artist, worked with swift, deft strokes.

When she had finished she leant back in her chaise longue, exhausted, waving her hands before her in the air to let the varnish harden—a strange gesture, like that of a priestess. She looked down at her toes, appearing from her sandals, and decided that presently, in a few moments, she would paint them too; olive hands, olive feet, subdued and quiet, surprised into sudden life.

Not yet, though. She must rest, relax. It was too hot to move from the supporting back of the chaise longue and lean forward, crouching, Eastern fashion, for the adorning of her feet. There was plenty of time. Time, in fact, stretched before her in an unwinding pattern through the whole long, languorous day.

She closed her eyes.

The distant sound of hotel life came to her as in a dream, and the sounds were hazy, pleasant, because she was part of that life yet free as well, bound no longer to the tyranny of home. Someone on a balcony above scraped

back a chair. Below, on the terrace, the waiters set up the gay striped um-
brellas over the little luncheon tables; she could hear the maître d'hôtel
call directions from the dining-room. The *femme de chambre* was doing
the rooms in the adjoining suite. Furniture was moved, a bed creaked, the
valet de chambre came out on to the next balcony and swept the boards with
a straw brush. Their voices murmured, grumbled. Then they went away.
Silence again. Nothing but the lazy splash of the sea as effortlessly it licked
the burning sand; and somewhere, far away, too distant to make an irritation, the laughter of children playing, her own amongst them.

A guest ordered coffee on the terrace below. The smoke of his cigar
came floating upwards to the balcony. The Marquise sighed, and her lovely
hands drooped down like lilies on either side of the chaise longue. This
was peace, this was contentment. If she could hold the moment thus for
one more hour . . . But something warned her, when the hour was past, the
old demon of dissatisfaction, of tedium, would return, even here where she
was free at last, on holiday.

A bumblebee flew on to the balcony, hovered over the bottle of nail varnish, and entered the open flower, picked by one of the children, lying beside it. His humming ceased when he was inside the flower. The Marquise
opened her eyes and saw the bee crawl forth, intoxicated. Then dizzily
once more he took the air and hummed his way. The spell was broken. The
Marquise picked up the letter from Edouard, her husband, that had fallen
on to the floor of the balcony. ". . . And so, my dearest, I find it impossible
to get to you and the children after all. There is so much business to attend
to here at home, and you know I can rely on no one but myself. I shall, of
course, make every effort to come and fetch you at the end of the month.
Meanwhile, enjoy yourself, bathing and resting. I know the sea air will do
you good. I went to see Maman yesterday, and Madeleine, and it seems the
old curé . . ."

The Marquise let the letter fall back again on to the balcony floor. The
little droop at the corner of her mouth, the one telltale sign that spoilt the
smooth lovely face, intensified. It had happened again. Always his work.
The estate, the farms, the forests, the businessmen that he must see, the
sudden journeys that he must take, so that in spite of his devotion for her
he had no time to spare, Edouard, her husband.

They had told her, before her marriage, how it would be. *"C'est un
homme très sérieux, Monsieur le Marquis, vous comprenez."* How little she
had minded, how gladly she had agreed, for what could be better in life
than a marquis who was also *un homme sérieux?* What more lovely than
that château and those vast estates? What more imposing than the house

in Paris, the retinue of servants, humble, bowing, calling her Madame la Marquise? A fairy-tale world to someone like herself, brought up in Lyons, the daughter of a hard-working surgeon, an ailing mother. But for the sudden arrival of Monsieur le Marquis she might have found herself married to her father's young assistant, and that same day-by-day in Lyons continuing forever.

A romantic match, surely. Frowned on at first by his relatives, most certainly. But Monsieur le Marquis, *homme sérieux*, was past forty. He knew his own mind. And she was beautiful. There was no further argument. They married. They had two little girls. They were happy. Yet sometimes . . . The Marquise rose from the chaise longue and, going into the bedroom, sat down before the dressing table and removed the pins from her hair. Even this effort exhausted her. She threw off her wrapper and sat naked before her mirror. Sometimes she found herself regretting that day-by-day in Lyons. She remembered the laughter, the joking with other girls, the stifled giggles when a passing man looked at them in the street, the confidences, the exchange of letters, the whispering in bedrooms when her friends came to tea.

Now, as Madame la Marquise, she had no one with whom to share confidences, laughter. Everyone about her was middle-aged, dull, rooted to a life long-lived that never changed. Those interminable visits of Edouard's relatives to the château. His mother, his sisters, his brothers, his sisters-in-law. In the winter, in Paris, it was just the same. Never a new face, never the arrival of a stranger. The only excitement was the appearance, perhaps, at luncheon of one of Edouard's business friends, who, surprised at her beauty when she entered the salon, flickered a daring glance of admiration, then bowed and kissed her hand.

Watching such a one during luncheon, she would make a fantasy to herself of how they would meet in secret, how a taxi would take her to his apartment, and, entering a small, dark *ascenseur*, she would ring a bell and vanish into a strange unknown room. But, the long luncheon over, the business friend would bow and go his way. And afterwards she would think to herself he was not even passably good-looking; even his teeth were false. But the glance of admiration, swiftly suppressed — she wanted that.

Now she combed her hair before the mirror and, parting it on one side, tried a new effect; a ribbon, the colour of her fingernails, threaded through the gold. Yes, yes . . . And the white frock, later, and that chiffon scarf, thrown carelessly over the shoulders, so that when she went out on to the terrace, followed by the children and the English governess, and the maître d'hôtel, bowing, led the way to the little table at the corner under the striped umbrella, people would stare, would whisper, and the eyes would follow her as deliberately she would stoop to one of the children, pat its curls in a fond maternal gesture, a thing of grace, of beauty.

But now, before the mirror, only the naked body and the sad, sulky mouth. Other women would have lovers. Whispers of scandal came to her ears, even during those long heavy dinners, with Edouard at the far end of the table. Not only in the smart riffraff society to which she never penetrated, but even amongst the old noblesse to which she now belonged. "*On dit, vous savez . . .*" and the suggestion, the murmur, passed from one to the other, with a lifted eyebrow, a shrug of the shoulder.

Sometimes, after a tea party, a guest would leave early, before six o'clock, giving as an excuse that she was expected elsewhere, and the Marquise, echoing regrets, bidding the guest au revoir, would wonder, "Is she going to a rendezvous?" Could it be that in twenty minutes — less, perhaps — that dark, rather ordinary little comtesse would be shivering, smiling secretly, as she let her clothes slip to the floor?

Even Elise, her friend of lycée days in Lyons, married now six years, had a lover. She never wrote of him by name. She always called him "*mon ami.*" Yet they managed to meet twice a week, on Mondays and Thursdays. He had a car and drove her into the country, even in winter. And Elise would write to the Marquise and say, "But how plebeian my little affair must seem to you, in high society. How many admirers you must have, and what adventures! Tell me of Paris, and the parties, and who is the man of your choice this winter." The Marquise would reply, hinting, suggesting, laughing off the question, and launch into a description of her frock, worn at some reception. But she did not say that the reception ended at midnight, that it was formal, dull, and that all she, the Marquise, knew of Paris was the drives she took in the car with the children, and the drives to the couturier to be fitted for yet another frock, and the drives to the coiffeur to have her hair rearranged and set to perhaps a different style. As to life at the château, she would describe the rooms, yes, the many guests, the solemn long avenue of trees, the acres of woodland; but not the rain in spring, day after day, nor the parching heat of early summer, when silence fell upon the place like a great white pall.

"*Ah! Pardon, je croyais que Madame était sortie . . .*" He had come in without knocking, the *valet de chambre*, his straw brush in his hand, and now he backed out of the room again, discreetly, but not before he had seen her there, naked before the mirror. And surely he must have known she had not gone out, when only a few moments before she had been lying on the balcony? Was it compassion she saw in his eyes as well as admiration before he left the room? As though to say, "So beautiful, and all alone? We are not used to that in this hotel, where people come for pleasure. . . ."

Heavens, it was hot. No breeze even from the sea. Trickles of perspiration ran down from her arms to her body.

She dressed languidly, putting on the cool white dress, and then, strolling out on to the balcony once more, pulled up the sun blind, let the full heat of the day fall upon her. Dark glasses hid her eyes. The only touch of colour lay on her mouth, her feet, her hands, and in the scarf thrown about her shoulders. The dark lenses gave a deep tone to the day. The sea, by natural eye a periwinkle blue, had turned to purple, and the white sands to olive brown. The gaudy flowers in their tubs upon the terrace had a tropical texture. As the Marquise leant upon the balcony the heat of the wooden rail burnt her hands. Once again the smell of a cigar floated upwards from some source unknown. There was a tinkle of glasses as a waiter brought apéritifs to a table on the terrace. Somewhere a woman spoke, and a man's voice joined with the woman's, laughing.

An Alsatian dog, his tongue dripping moisture, padded along the terrace towards the wall, searching for a cold stone slab on which to lie. A group of young people, bare and bronzed, the salt from the warm sea scarce dried upon their bodies, came running up from the sands, calling for martinis. Americans, of course. They flung their towels upon the chairs. One of them whistled to the Alsatian, who did not move. The Marquise looked down upon them with disdain, yet merged with her disdain was a kind of envy. They were free to come and go, to climb into a car, to move onward to some other place. They lived in a state of blank, ferocious gaiety. Always in groups. Six or eight of them. They paired off, of course; they pawed each other, forming into couples. But—and here she gave full play to her contempt—their gaiety held no mystery. In their open lives there could be no moment of suspense. No one waited, in secret, behind a half-closed door.

The savour of a love affair should be quite otherwise, thought the Marquise, and breaking off a rose that climbed the trellis of the balcony, she placed it in the opening of her dress, below her neck. A love affair should be a thing of silence, soft, unspoken. No raucous voice, no burst of sudden laughter, but the kind of stealthy curiosity that comes with fear, and when the fear has gone, a brazen confidence. Never the give-and-take between good friends, but passion between strangers.

One by one they came back from the sands, the visitors to the hotel. The tables began to fill up. The terrace, hot and deserted all the morning, became alive once more. And guests, arriving by car for luncheon only, mingled with the more familiar figures belonging to the hotel. A party of six in the right-hand corner. A party of three below. And now more bustle, more chatter, more tinkling of glasses and clatter of plates, so that the splash of the sea, which had been the foremost sound since early morning, now seemed secondary, remote. The tide was going out, the water rippling away across the sands.

Here came the children with their governess, Miss Clay. They prinked their way like little dolls across the terrace, followed by Miss Clay in her striped cotton dress, her crimped hair straggling from her bathe, and suddenly they looked up to the balcony, they waved their hands. "Maman . . . Maman . . ." She leant down, smiling at them; and then, as usual, the little clamour brought distraction. Somebody glanced up with the children, smiling, some man at a left-hand table laughed and pointed to his companion, and it began, the first wave of admiration that would come again in full measure when she descended, the Marquise, the beautiful Marquise and her cherubic children, whispers wafting towards her in the air like the smoke from the cigarettes, like the conversation the guests at the other tables shared with one another. This, then, was all that déjeuner on the terrace would bring to her, day after day, the ripple of admiration, respect, and then oblivion. Each and all went his way, to swim, to golf, to tennis, to drive, and she was left, beautiful, unruffled, with the children and Miss Clay.

"Look, Maman, I found a little starfish on the beach. I am going to take him home with me when we go."

"No, no, that isn't fair, it's mine. I saw it first."

The little girls, with flushed faces, fell out with one another.

"Hush, Céleste and Hélène: you make my head ache."

"Madame is tired? You must rest after lunch. It will do you good, in such heat." Miss Clay, tactful, bent down to scold the children. "Everyone is tired. It will do us all good to rest," she said.

Rest . . . "But," thought the Marquise, "I never do anything else. My life is one long rest." *Il faut reposer. Repose-toi, ma chérie, tu as mauvaise mine.* Winter and summer, those were the words she heard. From her husband, from the governess, from sisters-in-law, from all those aged, tedious friends. Life was one long sequence of resting, of getting up, and of resting again. Because with her pallor, with her reserve, they thought her delicate. Heavens above, the hours of her married life she had spent resting, the bed turned down, the shutters closed. In the house in Paris, in the château in the country. Two to four, resting, always resting.

"I'm not in the least tired," she said to Miss Clay, and for once her voice, usually melodious and soft, was sharp, high-pitched. "I shall go walking after lunch. I shall go into the town."

The children stared at her, round-eyed, and Miss Clay, her goat-face startled to surprise, opened her mouth in protest.

"You'll kill yourself, in the heat. Besides, the few shops always close between one and three. Why not wait until after tea? Surely it would be wiser to wait until after tea? The children could go with you and I could do some ironing."

The Marquise did not answer. She rose from the table, and now, because the children had lingered over déjeuner—Céleste was always slow with her food—the terrace was almost deserted. No one of any importance would watch the progress back to the hotel.

The Marquise went upstairs and once again touched her face with powder, circled her mouth, dipped her forefinger in scent. Next door she could hear the droning of the children as Miss Clay settled them to rest and closed the shutters. The Marquise took her handbag, made of plaited straw, put in it her purse, a roll of film, a few odds and ends, and, tiptoeing past the children's room, went downstairs again and out of the hotel grounds to the dusty road.

The gravel forced its way at once into her open sandals, and the glare of the sun beat down upon her head, and at once what had seemed to her, on the spur of the moment, an unusual thing to do struck her now, in the doing of it, as foolish, pointless. The road was deserted, the sands were deserted, the visitors who had played and walked all morning, while she had lain idle on her balcony, were now taking their ease in their rooms, like Miss Clay and the children. Only the Marquise trod the sun-baked road into the little town.

And here it was even as Miss Clay had warned her. The shops were closed, the sun blinds were all down, the hour of siesta, inviolate, unbroken, held sway over the shops and their inhabitants.

The Marquise strolled along the street, her straw handbag swinging from her hand, the one walker in a sleeping, yawning world. Even the café at the corner was deserted, and a sand-coloured dog, his face between his paws, snapped with closed eyes at the flies that bothered him. Flies were everywhere. They buzzed at the window of the *pharmacie*, where dark bottles, filled with mysterious medicine, rubbed glass shoulders with skin tonic, sponges, and cosmetics. Flies danced behind the panes of the shop filled with sunshades, spades, pink dolls, and rope-soled shoes. They crawled upon the empty bloodstained slab of the butcher's shop, behind the iron shutter. From above the shop came the jarring sound of the radio, suddenly switched off, and the heavy sigh of someone who would sleep and would not be disturbed. Even the *bureau de poste* was shut. The Marquise, who had thought to buy stamps, rattled the door to no purpose.

Now she could feel the sweat trickling under her dress, and her feet, in the thin sandals, ached from the short distance she had walked. The sun was too strong, too fierce, and as she looked up and down the empty street, and at the houses, with the shops between, every one of them closed from her, withdrawn into the blessed peace of their siesta, she felt a sudden longing for any place that might be cool, that might be dark—a cellar, perhaps, where there was dripping water from a tap. The sound of water falling to a stone floor would soothe her nerves, now jagged from the sun.

Frustrated, almost crying, she turned into an alleyway between two shops. She came to steps leading down to a little court where there was no sun, and paused there a moment, her hand against the wall, so cold and firm. Beside her there was a window, shuttered, against which she leant her head, and suddenly, to her confusion, the shutter was withdrawn and a face looked out upon her from some dark room within.

"*Je regrette . . .*" she began, swept to absurdity that she should be discovered here, intruding, like one peering into the privacy and squalor of life below a shop. And then her voice dwindled and died away, foolishly, for the face that looked out upon her from the open window was so unusual, so gentle, that it might have come straight from a stained-glass saint in a cathedral. His face was framed in a cloud of dark curled hair, his nose was small and straight, his mouth a sculptured mouth, and his eyes, so solemn, brown, and tender, were like the eyes of a gazelle.

"*Vous désirez, Madame la Marquise?*" he said in answer to her unfinished words.

He knows me, she thought in wonder, he has seen me before, but even this was not so unexpected as the quality of his voice, not rough, not harsh, not the voice of someone in a cellar under a shop, but cultivated, liquid, a voice that matched the eyes of the gazelle.

"It was so hot up in the street," she said. "The shops were closed and I felt faint. I came down the steps. I am very sorry, it is private, of course."

The face disappeared from the window. He opened a door somewhere that she had not seen, and suddenly she found a chair beneath her and she was sitting down, inside the doorway, and it was dark and cool inside the room, even like the cellar she had imagined, and he was giving her water from an earthenware cup.

"Thank you," she said, "thank you very much." Looking up, she saw that he was watching her, with humility, with reverence, the pitcher of water in his hand; and he said to her in his soft, gentle voice, "Is there anything else I can get for you, Madame la Marquise?"

She shook her head, but within her stirred the feeling she knew so well, the sense of secret pleasure that came with admiration, and, conscious of herself for the first time since he had opened the window, she drew her scarf closer about her shoulders, the gesture deliberate, and she saw the gazelle eyes fall to the rose tucked in the bodice of her dress.

She said, "How do you know who I am?"

He answered, "You came into my shop three days ago. You had your children with you. You bought a film for your camera."

She stared at him, puzzled. She remembered buying the film from the little shop that advertised Kodaks in the window, and she remembered too the ugly, shuffling, crippled woman who had served her behind the counter. The woman had walked with a limp, and afraid that the children would notice and laugh, and that she herself, from nervousness, would be betrayed to equally heartless laughter, she had ordered some things to be sent to the hotel, and then departed.

"My sister served you," he said in explanation. "I saw you from the inner room. I do not often go behind the counter. I take photographs of people, of the countryside, and then they are sold to the visitors who come here in the summer."

"Yes," she said, "I see, I understand."

And she drank again from the earthenware cup, and drank, too, the adoration in his eyes.

"I have brought a film to be developed," she said. "I have it here in my bag. Would you do that for me?"

"Of course, Madame la Marquise," he said. "I will do anything for you, whatever you ask. Since that day you came into my shop I . . ." Then he stopped, a flush came over his face, and he looked away from her, deeply embarrassed.

The Marquise repressed a desire to laugh. It was quite absurd, his admiration. Yet, funny . . . it gave her a sense of power.

"Since I came into your shop, what?" she asked.

He looked at her again. "I have thought of nothing else, but nothing," he said to her, and with such intensity that it almost frightened her.

She smiled; she handed back the cup of water. "I am quite an ordinary woman," she said. "If you knew me better, I should disappoint you." How odd it is, she thought to herself, that I am so much mistress of this situation, I am not at all outraged or shocked. Here I am, in the cellar of a shop, talking to a photographer who has just expressed his admiration for me. It is really most amusing, and yet he, poor man, is in earnest, he really means what he says.

"Well," she said, "are you going to take my film?"

It was as though he could not drag his eyes away from her, and boldly she stared him out of face, so that his eyes fell and he flushed again.

"If you will go back the way you came," he said, "I will open up the shop for you." And now it was she who let her eyes linger upon him; the open vest, no shirt, the bare arms, the throat, the head of curling hair, and she said, "Why cannot I give you the film here?"

"It would not be correct Madame la Marquise," he said to her.

She turned, laughing, and went back up the steps to the hot street. She stood on the pavement, she heard the rattle of the key in the door behind, she heard the door open. And then presently, in her own time, having deliberately stood outside to keep him waiting, she went into the shop, which was stuffy now, and close, unlike the cool quiet cellar.

He was behind the counter and she saw, with disappointment, that he had put on his coat, a grey cheap coat worn by any man serving in a shop, and his shirt was much too stiff, and much too blue. He was ordinary, a shopkeeper, reaching across the counter for the film.

"When will you have them ready?" she said.

"Tomorrow," he answered, and once again he looked at her with his dumb brown eyes. And she forgot the common coat and the blue stiff shirt, and saw the vest under the coat, and the bare arms.

"If you are a photographer," she said, "why don't you come to the hotel and take some photographs of me and my children?"

"You would like me to do that?" he asked.

"Why not?" she answered.

A secret look came into his eyes and went again, and he bent below the counter, pretending to search for string. But she thought, smiling to herself, "This is exciting to him, his hands are trembling"; and for the same reason her heart beat faster than before.

"Very well, Madame la Marquise," he said, "I will come to the hotel at whatever time is convenient to you."

"The morning, perhaps, is best," she said, "at eleven o'clock."

Casually she strolled away. She did not even say good-bye.

She walked across the street and, looking for nothing in the window of a shop opposite, she saw, through the glass, that he had come to the door of his own shop and was watching her. He had taken off his jacket and his shirt. The shop would be closed again, the siesta was not yet over. Then she noticed, for the first time, that he too was crippled, like his sister. His right foot was encased in a high fitted boot. Yet, curiously, the sight of this did not repel her, nor bring her to nervous laughter, as it had done before when she had seen the sister. His high boot had a fascination, strange, unknown.

The Marquise walked back to the hotel along the dusty road.

At eleven o'clock the next morning the concierge of the hotel sent up word that Monsieur Paul, the photographer, was below in the hall, and awaited the instructions of Madame la Marquise. The instructions were sent back that Madame la Marquise would be pleased if Monsieur Paul would go upstairs to the suite. Presently she heard the knock on the door, hesitant, timid.

"*Entrez*," she called, and standing, as she did, on the balcony, her arms around the two children, she made a tableau, ready set, for him to gaze upon.

Today she was dressed in silk shantung the colour of chartreuse, and her hair was not the little-girl hair of yesterday, with the ribbon, but parted in the centre and drawn back to show her ears, with the gold clips upon them.

He stood in the entrance of the doorway, he did not move. The children, shy, gazed with wonder at the high boot, but they said nothing. Their mother had warned them not to mention it.

"These are my babies," said the Marquise. "And now you must tell us how to pose, and where you want us placed."

The children did not make their usual curtsey, as they did to guests. Their mother had told them it would not be necessary. Monsieur Paul was a photographer, from the shop in the little town.

"If it would be possible, Madame la Marquise," he said, "to have one pose just as you are standing now. It is quite beautiful. So very natural, so full of grace."

"Why, yes, if you like. Stand still, Hélène."

"Pardon. It will take a few moments to fix the camera."

His nervousness had gone. He was busy with the mechanical tricks of his trade. And as she watched him set up the tripod, fix the velvet cloth, make the adjustments to his camera, she noticed his hands, deft and efficient, and they were not the hands of an artisan, of a shopkeeper, but the hands of an artist.

Her eyes fell to the boot. His limp was not so pronounced as the sister's, he did not walk with that lurching, jerky step that produced stifled hysteria in the watcher. His step was slow, more dragging, and the Marquise felt a kind of compassion for his deformity, for surely the misshapen foot beneath the boot must pain him constantly, and the high boot, especially in hot weather, crush and sear his flesh.

"Now, Madame la Marquise," he said, and guiltily she raised her eyes from the boot and struck her pose, smiling gracefully, her arms embracing the children.

"Yes," he said, "just so. It is very lovely."

The dumb brown eyes held hers. His voice was low, gentle. The sense of pleasure came upon her just as it had done in the shop the day before. He pressed the bulb. There was a little clicking sound.

"Once more," he said.

She went on posing, the smile on her lips; and she knew that the reason he paused this time before pressing the bulb was not from professional necessity, because she or the children had moved, but because it delighted him to gaze upon her.

"There," she said, and breaking the pose, and the spell, she moved towards the balcony, humming a little song.

After half an hour the children became tired, restless.

The Marquise apologised. "It's so very hot," she said, "you must excuse them. Céleste, Hélène, get your toys and play on the other corner of the balcony."

They ran chattering to their own room. The Marquise turned her back upon the photographer. He was putting fresh plates into his camera.

"You know what it is with children," she said. "For a few minutes it is a novelty, then they are sick of it, they want something else. You have been very patient, Monsieur Paul."

She broke off a rose from the balcony and, cupping it in her hands, bent her lips to it.

"Please," he said with urgency, "if you would permit me, I scarcely like to ask you . . ."

"What?" she said.

"Would it be possible for me to take one or two photographs of you alone, without the children?"

She laughed. She tossed the rose over the balcony to the terrace below.

"But of course," she said, "I am at your disposal. I have nothing else to do."

She sat down on the edge of the chaise longue and, leaning back against the cushion, rested her head against her arm.

"Like this?" she said.

He disappeared behind the velvet cloth, and then, after an adjustment to the camera, came limping forward.

"If you will permit me," he said, "the hand should be raised a little, so . . . And the head, just slightly on one side."

He took her hand and placed it to his liking; and then gently, with hesitation, put his hand under her chin, lifting it. She closed her eyes. He did not take his hand away. Almost imperceptibly his thumb moved, lingering, over the long line of her neck, and his fingers followed the movement of the thumb. The sensation was featherweight, like the brushing of a bird's wing against her skin.

"Just so," he said, "that is perfection."

She opened her eyes. He limped back to his camera.

The Marquise did not tire as the children had done. She permitted Monsieur Paul to take one photograph, then another, then another. The children returned, as she had bidden them, and played together at the far end of the balcony, and their chatter made a background to the business of the photography, so that, both smiling at the prattle of the children, a kind of adult intimacy developed between the Marquise and the photographer, and the atmosphere was not so tense as it had been.

He became bolder, more confident of himself. He suggested poses and she acquiesced, and once or twice she placed herself badly and he told her of it.

"No, Madame la Marquise. Not like that. Like this."

Then he would come over to the chair, kneel beside her, move her foot perhaps, or turn her shoulder, and each time he did so his touch became more certain, became stronger. Yet when she forced him to meet her eyes he looked away, humble and diffident, as though he was ashamed of what he did, and his gentle eyes, mirroring his nature, would deny the impulse of his hands. She sensed a struggle within him, and it gave her pleasure.

At last, after he rearranged her dress the second time, she noticed that he had gone quite white and there was perspiration on his forehead.

"It is very hot," she said, "perhaps we have done enough for today."

"If you please, Madame la Marquise," he answered, "it is indeed very warm. I think it is best that we should stop now."

She rose from the chair, cool and at her ease. She was not tired, nor was she troubled. Rather was she invigorated, full of a new energy. When he had gone she would walk down to the sea and swim. It was very different for the photographer. She saw him wipe his face with his handkerchief, and as he packed up his camera and his tripod, and put them in the case, he looked exhausted and dragged his high boot more heavily than before.

She made a pretence of glancing through the snapshots he had developed for her from her own film.

"These are very poor," she said lightly. "I don't think I handle my camera correctly. I should take lessons from you."

"It is just a little practice that you need, Madame la Marquise," he said. "When I first started I had a camera much the same as yours. Even now, when I take exteriors, I wander out on the cliffs above the sea, with a small camera, and the effects are just as good as with the larger one."

She put the snapshots down on the table. He was ready to go. He carried the case in his hand.

"You must be very busy in the season," she said. "How do you get time to take exteriors?"

"I make time, Madame la Marquise," he said. "I prefer it, actually, to taking studio portraits. It is only occasionally that I find true satisfaction in photographing people. Like, for instance, today."

She looked at him and she saw again the devotion, the humility, in his eyes. She stared at him until he dropped his eyes, abashed.

"The scenery is very beautiful along the coast," he said. "You must have noticed it, when walking. Most afternoons I take my small camera and go out on to the cliffs, above the big rock that stands there so prominent, to the right of the bathing beach."

He pointed from the balcony, and she followed the direction of his hand. The green headland shimmered hazily in the intense heat.

"It was only by chance that you found me at home yesterday," he said. "I was in the cellar, developing prints that had been promised for visitors who were to leave today. But usually I go walking on the cliffs at that time."

"It must be very hot," she said.

"Perhaps," he answered. "But above the sea there is a little breeze. And best of all, between one and four there are so few people. They are all taking their siesta in the afternoon. I have all that beautiful scenery to myself."

"Yes," said the Marquise, "I understand."

For a moment they both stood silent. It was as though something unspoken passed between them. The Marquise played with her chiffon handkerchief, then tied it loosely round her wrist, a casual, lazy gesture.

"Sometime I must try it for myself," she said at last, "walking in the heat of the day."

Miss Clay came on to the balcony, calling the children to come and be washed before déjeuner. The photographer stepped to one side, deferential, apologising. And the Marquise, glancing at her watch, saw that it was already *midi*, and that the tables below on the terrace were filled with people and the usual bustle and chatter were going on, the tinkle of glasses, the rattle of plates, and she had noticed none of it.

She turned her shoulder to the photographer, dismissing him, deliberately cool and indifferent now that the session was over and Miss Clay had come to fetch the children.

"Thank you," she said. "I shall call in at the shop to see the proofs in a few days' time. Good morning."

He bowed, he went away, an employee who had fulfilled his orders.

"I hope he has taken some good photographs," said Miss Clay. "The Marquis will be very pleased to see the results."

The Marquise did not answer. She was taking off the gold clips from her ears that now, for some reason, no longer matched her mood. She would go down to déjeuner without jewellery, without rings; she felt, for today, her own beauty would suffice.

Three days passed, and the Marquise did not once descend into the little town. The first day she swam, she watched the tennis in the afternoon. The second day she spent with the children, giving Miss Clay leave of absence to take a tour by charabanc to visit the old walled cities, further inland, along the coast. The third day she sent Miss Clay and the children into the town to enquire for the proofs, and they returned with them wrapped in a neat package. The Marquise examined them. They were very good indeed, and the studies of herself the best she had ever had taken.

Miss Clay was in raptures. She begged for copies to send home to England. "Who would believe it," she exclaimed, "that a little photographer by the sea like this could take such splendid pictures? And then you go and pay heaven knows what to real professionals in Paris."

"They are not bad," said the Marquise, yawning. "He certainly took a lot of trouble. They are better of me than they are of the children." She folded the package and put it away in a drawer. "Did Monsieur Paul seem pleased with them himself?" she asked the governess.

"He did not say," replied Miss Clay. "He seemed disappointed that you had not gone down for them yourself; he said they had been ready since yesterday. He asked if you were well, and the children told him Maman had been swimming. They were quite friendly with him."

"It's much too hot and dusty down in the town," said the Marquise.

The next afternoon, when Miss Clay and the children were resting and the hotel itself seemed asleep under the glare of the sun, the Marquise changed into a short sleeveless frock, very simple and plain, and softly, so as not to disturb the children, went downstairs, her small box camera slung over her arm, and, walking through the hotel grounds on to the sands, she followed a narrow path that led upwards, to the greensward above. The sun was merciless. Yet she did not mind. Here on the springy grass there was no dust, and presently, by the cliff's edge, the bracken, growing thicker, brushed her bare legs.

The little path wound in and out amongst the bracken, at times coming so close to the cliff's edge that a false step, bringing a stumble, would spell danger. But the Marquise, walking slowly, with the lazy swing of the hips peculiar to her, felt neither frightened nor exhausted. She was merely intent on reaching a spot that overlooked the great rock standing out from the coast in the middle of the bay. She was quite alone on the headland. No one was in sight. Away behind her, far below, the white walls of the hotel and the rows of bathing cabins on the beach looked like bricks played with by children. The sea was very smooth and still. Even where it washed upon the rock in the bay it left no ripple.

Suddenly the Marquise saw something flash in the bracken ahead of her. It was the lens of a camera. She took no notice. Turning her back, she pretended to examine her own camera, and took up a position as though to photograph the view. She took one, took another, and then she heard the swish of someone walking towards her through the bracken.

She turned, surprised. "Why, good afternoon, Monsieur Paul," she said.

He had discarded the cheap stiff jacket and the bright blue shirt. He was not on business. It was the hour of the siesta, when he walked, as it were, incognito. He wore only the vest and a pair of dark blue trousers, and the grey squash hat, which she had noticed with dismay the morning he had come to the hotel, was also absent. His thick dark hair made a frame to his gentle face. His eyes had such a rapturous expression at the sight of her that she was forced to turn away to hide her smile.

"You see," she said lightly, "I have taken your advice, and strolled up here to look at the view. But I am sure I don't hold my camera correctly. Show me how."

He stood beside her and, taking her camera, steadied her hands, moving them to the correct position.

"Yes, of course," she said, and then moved away from him, laughing a little, for it had seemed to her that when he stood beside her and guided her hands she had heard his heart beating, and the sound brought excitement, which she wished to conceal from him.

"Have you your own camera?" she said.

"Yes, Madame la Marquise," he answered. "I left it over in the bracken there, with my coat. It is a favourite spot of mine, close to the edge of the cliff. In spring I come here to watch the birds and take photographs of them."

"Show me," she said.

He led the way, murmuring "Pardon," and the path he had made for himself took them to a little clearing, like a nest, hidden on all sides by bracken that was now waist-high. Only the front of the clearing was open, and this was wide to the cliff face and the sea.

"But how lovely," she said, and, passing through the bracken into the hiding place, she looked about her, smiling, and sitting down, gracefully, naturally, like a child at a picnic, she picked up the book that was lying on top of his coat beside his camera.

"You read much?" she said.

"Yes, Madame la Marquise," he answered. "I am very fond of reading." She glanced at the cover, and read the title. It was a cheap romance, the sort of book she and her friends had smuggled into their satchels at the lycée in old days. She had not read that sort of stuff for years. Once again she had to hide her smile. She put the book back on the coat.

"Is it a good story?" she asked him.

He looked down at her solemnly, with his great eyes like a gazelle's.

"It is very tender, Madame la Marquise," he said.

Tender . . . What an odd expression. She began to talk about the proofs of the photographs, and how she preferred one to another, and all the while she was conscious of an inner triumph that she was in such command of the situation. She knew exactly what to do, what to say, when to smile, when to look serious. It reminded her strangely of childhood days, when she and her young friends would dress up in their mothers' hats and say, "Let's pretend to be ladies." She was pretending now; not to be a lady, as then, but to be—what? She was not sure. But something other than the self who now, for so long, was in truth a real lady, sipping tea in the salon at the château, surrounded by so many ancient things and people that each one of them had the mustiness of death.

The photographer did not talk much. He listened to the Marquise. He agreed, nodded his head, or simply remained silent, and she heard her own voice trilling on in a sort of wonder. He was merely a witness she could ignore, a nonentity, while she listened to the brilliant, charming woman that had suddenly become herself.

At last there came a pause in the one-sided conversation, and he said to her shyly, "May I dare to ask you something?"

"Of course," she said.

"Could I photograph you here, alone, with this background?"

Was that all? How timid he was, and how reluctant. She laughed.

"Take as many as you want," she said. "It is very pleasant sitting here. I may even go to sleep."

"*La belle au bois dormant*," he said quickly, and then, as if ashamed of his familiarity, he murmured "Pardon" once more and reached for the camera behind her.

This time he did not ask her to pose, to change position. He photographed her as she sat, lazily nibbling at a stem of grass, and it was he who moved, now here, now there, so that he had shots of her from every angle, full-face, profile, three-quarter.

She began to feel sleepy. The sun beat down upon her uncovered head, and the dragonflies, gaudy and green and gold, swung and hovered before her eyes. She yawned and leant back against the bracken.

"Would you care for my coat as a pillow for your head, Madame la Marquise?" he asked her.

Before she could reply he had taken his coat, folded it neatly, and placed it in a little roll against the bracken. She leant back against it, and the despised grey coat made a softness to her head, easy and comfortable.

He knelt beside her, intent upon his camera, doing something to the film, and she watched him, yawning, between half-closed eyes, and noticed that as he knelt he kept his weight upon one knee only, thrusting the deformed foot in the high boot to one side. Idly, she wondered if it hurt to lean upon it. The boot was highly polished, much brighter than the leather shoe upon the left foot, and she had a sudden vision of him taking great pains with the boot every morning when he dressed, polishing it, rubbing it, perhaps, with a wash-leather cloth.

A dragonfly settled on her hand. It crouched, waiting, a sheen upon its wing. What was it waiting for? She blew upon it and it flew away. Then it came back again, hovering, insistent.

Monsieur Paul had put aside his camera, but he was still kneeling in the bracken beside her. She was aware of him, watching her, and she thought to herself, "If I move he will get up, and it will be all over."

She went on staring at the glittering, shivering dragonfly, but she knew that in a moment or two she must look somewhere else, or the dragonfly would go, or the present silence would become so tense and so strained that she would break it with a laugh and so spoil everything. Reluctantly, against her will, she turned to the photographer, and his large eyes, humble and devoted, were fixed upon her with all the deep abasement of a slave.

"Why don't you kiss me?" she said, and her own words startled her, shocked her into sudden apprehension.

He said nothing. He did not move. He went on gazing at her. She closed her eyes, and the dragonfly went from her hand.

Presently, when the photographer bent to touch her, it was not what she expected. There was no sudden crude embrace. It was just as though the dragonfly had returned, and now with silken wings brushed and stroked the smooth surface of her skin.

When he went away it was with tact and delicacy. He left her to herself so that there should be no aftermath of awkwardness, of embarrassment, no sudden strain of conversation.

The Marquise lay back in the bracken, her hands over her eyes, thinking about what had happened to her, and she had no sense of shame. She was clear-headed and quite calm. She began to plan how she would walk back to the hotel in a little while, giving him good time to gain the sands before her, so that if by chance people from the hotel should see him they would not connect him with her, who would follow after, say in half an hour.

She got up, rearranged her dress, took out her powder compact from her pocket, with her lipstick, and, having no mirror, judged carefully how much powder to put upon her face. The sun had lost its power, and a cool breeze blew inland from the sea.

"If the weather holds," thought the Marquise as she combed her hair, "I can come out here every day, at the same time. No one will ever know. Miss Clay and the children always rest in the afternoon. If we walk separately and go back separately, as we have done today, and come to this same place, hidden by the bracken, we cannot possibly be discovered. There are over three weeks still to the holiday. The great thing is to pray for this hot weather to continue. If it should rain . . ."

As she walked back to the hotel she wondered how they would manage, should the weather break. She could not very well set out to walk the cliffs in a mackintosh, and then lie down while the rain and the wind beat the bracken. There was of course the cellar, beneath the shop. But she might be seen in the village. That would be dangerous. No, unless it rained in torrents, the cliff was safest.

That evening she sat down and wrote a letter to her friend Elise. ". . . This is a wonderful place," she wrote, "and I am amusing myself as usual, and without my husband, *bien entendu!*" But she gave no details of her conquest, though she mentioned the bracken and the hot afternoon. She felt that if she left it vague Elise would picture to herself some rich American, traveling for pleasure, alone, without his wife.

The next morning, dressing herself with great care—she stood for a long while before her wardrobe, finally choosing a frock rather more elaborate than was usual for the seaside, but this was deliberate on her part—she went down into the little town, accompanied by Miss Clay and the children. It was market day, and the cobbled streets and the square were full of people. Many came from the countryside around, but there were quantities of visitors, English and American, who strolled to see the sights, to buy souvenirs and picture-postcards, or to sit down at the café at the corner and look about them.

The Marquise made a striking figure, walking in her indolent way in her lovely dress, hatless, carrying a sunshade, with the two little girls prancing beside her. Many people turned to look at her, or even stepped aside to let her pass, in unconscious homage to her beauty. She dawdled in the market place and made a few purchases, which Miss Clay put into the shopping bag she carried, and then, still casual, still answering with gay, lazy humour the questions of the children, she turned into the shop which displayed Kodaks and photographs in the window.

It was full of visitors waiting their turn to be served, and the Marquise, who was in no hurry, pretended to examine a book of local views, while at the same time she could see what was happening in the shop. They were both there, Monsieur Paul and his sister, he in his stiff shirt, an ugly pink this time, worse even than the blue, and the cheap grey coat, while the sister, like all women who served behind a counter, was in drab black, a shawl over her shoulders.

He must have seen her come into the shop, because almost at once he came forward from the counter, leaving the queue of visitors to the care of his sister, and was by her side, humble, polite, anxious to know in what manner he could serve her. There was no trace of familiarity, no look of knowledge in his eyes, and she took care to assure herself of this by staring directly at him. Then deliberately, bringing the children and Miss Clay into the conversation, asking Miss Clay to make her choice of the proofs which were to be sent to England, she kept him there by her side, treating him with condescension, with a sort of hauteur, even finding fault with certain of the proofs, which, so she told him, did not do the children justice, and which she could not possibly send to her husband, the Marquis. The photographer apologised. Most certainly the proofs mentioned did not do the children justice. He would be willing to come again to the hotel and try again, at no extra charge, of course. Perhaps on the terrace or in the gardens the effect would be better.

One or two people turned to look at the Marquise as she stood there. She could feel their eyes upon her, absorbing her beauty, and still in a tone of condescension, coldly, almost curtly, she told the photographer to show her various articles in his shop, which he hastened to do in his anxiety to please.

The other visitors were becoming restive, they shuffled their feet waiting for the sister to serve them, and she, hemmed about with customers, limped wretchedly from one end of the counter to the other, now and again raising her head, peering to see if her brother, who had so suddenly deserted her, would come to the rescue.

At last the Marquise relented. She had had her fill. The delicious furtive sense of excitement that had risen in her since her entrance to the shop died down and was appeased.

"One of these mornings I will let you know," she said to Monsieur Paul, "and then you can come out and photograph the children again. Meanwhile, let me pay what I owe. Miss Clay, attend to it, will you?"

And she strolled from the shop, not bidding him good morning, putting out her hands to the two children.

She did not change for déjeuner. She wore the same enchanting frock, and the hotel terrace, more crowded than ever because of the many visitors who had come on an excursion, seemed to her to buzz and hum with a murmur of conversation, directed at her and her beauty, and at the effect she made, sitting there at the table in the corner. The maître d'hôtel, the waiters, even the manager himself, were drawn towards her, obsequious, smiling, and she could hear her name pass from one to the other.

All things combined to her triumph: the proximity of people, the sell of food and wine and cigarettes, the scent of the gaudy flowers in their tubs, the feel of the hot sun beating down, the close sound of the splashing sea. When she rose at last with the children and went upstairs, she had a sense of happiness that she felt must only come to a prima donna after the clamour of long applause.

The children, with Miss Clay, went to their rooms to rest; and swiftly, hurriedly, the Marquise changed her frock and her shoes and tiptoed down the stairs and out of the hotel, across the burning sands to the path and the bracken headland.

He was waiting for her, as she expected, and neither of them made any reference to her visit in the morning, or to what brought her there on the cliff this afternoon. They made at once for the little clearing by the cliff's edge and sat down of one accord, and the Marquise, in a tone of banter, described the crowd at lunch, and the fearful bustle and fatigue of the terrace with so many people, and how delicious it was to get away from them all to the fresh clean air of the headland, above the sea.

He agreed with her humbly, watching her as she spoke of such mundane matters as though the wit of the world flowed in her speech, and then, exactly as on the previous day, he begged to take a few photographs of her, and she consented, and presently she lay back in the bracken and closed her eyes.

There was no sense of time to the long, languorous afternoon. Just as before, the dragonflies winged about her in the bracken, and the sun beat down upon her body, and with her sense of deep enjoyment at all that happened went the curiously satisfying knowledge that what she did was without emotion of any sort. Her mind and her affections were quite untouched. She might almost have been relaxing in a beauty parlour, back in

Paris, having the first telltale lines smoothed from her face and her hair shampooed, although these things brought only a lazy contentment and no pleasure.

Once again he departed, leaving her without a word, tactful and discreet, so that she could arrange herself in privacy. And once again, when she judged him out of sight, she rose to her feet and began the long walk back to the hotel.

Her good luck held and the weather did not break. Every afternoon, as soon as déjeuner was over and the children had gone to rest, the Marquise went for her promenade, returning about half-past four, in time for tea. Miss Clay, at first exclaiming at her energy, came to accept the walk as a matter of routine. If the Marquise chose to walk in the heat of the day, it was her own affair; certainly it seemed to do her good. She was more human towards her, Miss Clay, and less nagging to the children. The constant headaches and attacks of migraine were forgotten, and it seemed that the Marquise was really enjoying this simple seaside holiday alone with Miss Clay and the two little girls.

When a fortnight had passed, the Marquise discovered that the first delight and bliss of her experience were slowly fading. It was not that Monsieur Paul failed her in any way, but that she herself was becoming used to the daily ritual. Like an inoculation that "took" at the first with very great success, on constant repetition the effect lessened, dulled, and the Marquise found that to recapture her enjoyment she was obliged to treat the photographer no longer as a nonentity, or as she would a coiffeur who had set her hair, but as a person whose feelings she could wound. She would find fault with his appearance, complain that he wore his hair too long, that his clothes were cheap, ill-cut, or even that he ran his little shop in the town with inefficiency, that the material and paper he used for his prints were shoddy.

She would watch his face when she told him this, and she would see anxiety and pain come into his large eyes, pallor to his skin, a look of dejection fall upon his whole person as he realised how unworthy he was of her, how inferior in every way, and only when she saw him thus did the original excitement kindle in her again.

Deliberately she began to cut down the hours of the afternoon. She would arrive late at the rendezvous in the bracken and find him waiting for her with that same look of anxiety on his face, and if her mood was not sufficiently ripe for what should happen she would get through the business quickly, with an ill grace, and then dispatch him hastily on his return journey, picturing him limping back, tired and unhappy, to the shop in the little town.

She permitted him to take photographs of her still. This was all part of the experience, and she knew that it troubled him to do this, to see her to perfection, and so she delighted in taking advantage of it, and would sometimes tell him to come to the hotel during the morning, and then she would pose in the grounds, exquisitely dressed, the children beside her, Miss Clay an admiring witness, the visitors watching from their rooms or from the terrace.

The contrast of these mornings, when as an employee he limped back and forth at her bidding, moving the tripod first here, first there, while she gave him orders, with the sudden intimacy of the afternoons in the bracken under the hot sun, proved, during the third week, to be her only stimulation.

Finally, a day breaking when quite a cold breeze blew in from the sea, and she did not go to the rendezvous as usual but rested on her balcony reading a novel, the change in the routine came as a real relief.

The following day was fine and she decided to go to the headland, and for the first time since they had encountered one another in the cool dark cellar below the shop he upbraided her, his voice sharp with anxiety.

"I waited for you all yesterday afternoon," he said. "What happened?"

She stared at him in astonishment.

"It was an unpleasant day," she replied. "I preferred to read on my balcony in the hotel."

"I was afraid you might have been taken ill," he went on. "I very nearly called at the hotel to enquire for you. I hardly slept last night, I was so upset."

He followed her to the hiding place in the bracken, his eyes still anxious, lines of worry on his brow, and though in a sense it was a stimulation to the Marquise to witness his distress, at the same time it irritated her that he should so forget himself to find fault in her conduct. It was as though her coiffeur in Paris, or her masseur, expressed anger when she broke an appointment fixed for a certain day.

"If you think I feel myself bound to come here every afternoon, you are very much mistaken," she said. "I have plenty of other things to do."

At once he apologised, he was abject. He begged her to forgive him.

"You cannot understand what this means to me," he said. "Since I have known you, everything in my life is changed. I live only for these afternoons."

His subjection pleased her, whipping her to a renewal of interest, and pity came to her too, as he lay by her side, pity that this creature should be so utterly devoted, depending on her like a child. She touched his hair, feeling for a moment quite compassionate, almost maternal. Poor fellow, limping all this way because of her, and then sitting in the biting wind of yesterday, alone and wretched. She imagined the letter she would write to her friend Elise.

"I am very much afraid I have broken Paul's heart. He has taken this little *affaire des vacances au sérieux*. But what am I to do? After all, these things must have an end. I cannot possibly alter my life because of him. *Enfin*, he is a man, he will get over it." Elise would picture the beautiful blond American playboy climbing wearily into his Packard, setting off in despair to the unknown.

The photographer did not leave her today, when the afternoon session had ended. He sat up in the bracken and stared out towards the great rock jutting out into the sea.

"I have made up my mind about the future," he said quietly.

The Marquise sensed the drama in the air. Did he mean he was going to kill himself? How very terrible. He would wait, of course, until she had left the hotel and had returned home. She need never know.

"Tell me," she said gently.

"My sister will look after the shop," he said. "I will make it all over to her. She is very capable. For myself, I shall follow you, wherever you go, whether it is to Paris, or to the country. I shall be close at hand; whenever you want me, I shall be there."

The Marquise swallowed. Her heart went still.

"You can't possibly do that," she said. "How would you live?"

"I am not proud," he said. "I know, in the goodness of your heart, you would allow me something. My needs would be very small. But I know that it is impossible to live without you, therefore the only thing to do is to follow you, always. I will find a room close to your house in Paris, and in the country too. We will find ways and means of being together. When love is as strong as this there are no difficulties."

He spoke with his usual humility, but there was a force behind his words that was unexpected, and she knew that for him this was no false drama, ill-timed to the day, but true sincerity. He meant every word. He would in truth give up the shop, follow her to Paris, follow her also to the château in the country.

"You are mad," she said violently, sitting up, careless of her appearance and her dishevelled hair. "Once I have left here I am no longer free. I cannot possibly meet you anywhere, the danger of discovery would be too great. You realise my position? What it would mean to me?"

He nodded his head. His face was sad, but quite determined. "I have thought of everything," he answered, "but as you know, I am very discreet.

You need never be apprehensive on that score. It has occurred to me that it might be possible to obtain a place in your service as footman. It would not matter to me, the loss of personal dignity. I am not proud. But in such a capacity our life together could continue much as it does now. Your husband, the Marquis, must be a very busy man, often out during the day, and your children and the English miss no doubt go walking in the country in the afternoon. You see, everything would be very simple if we had the courage."

The Marquise was so shocked that she could not answer. She could not imagine anything more terrible, more disastrous, than that the photographer should take a place in the house as footman. Quite apart from his disability—she shuddered to think of him limping round the table in the great *salle à manger*—what misery she would suffer knowing that he was there, in the house, that he was waiting for her to go up to her room in the afternoon, and then, timidly, the knock upon the door, the hushed whisper. The degradation of this—this creature—there was really no other word for him—in the house, always waiting, always hoping.

"I am afraid," she said firmly, "that what you are suggesting is utterly impossible. Not only the idea of coming to my house as a servant, but of our ever being able to meet again once I return home. Your own common sense must tell you so. These afternoons have been—have been pleasant, but my holiday is very nearly over. In a few days' time my husband will be coming to fetch me and the children, and that finishes everything."

To show finality she got up, brushed her crumpled frock, combed her hair, powdered her nose, and, reaching for her bag, fumbled inside it for her note-case.

She drew out several ten-thousand-franc notes.

"This is for the shop," she said, "any little fittings it may require. And buy something for your sister. And remember, I shall always think of you with great tenderness."

To her consternation his face went dead white, then his mouth began to work violently and he rose to his feet.

"No, no," he said, "I will never take them. You are cruel, wicked, to suggest it." And suddenly he began to sob, burying his face in his hands, his shoulders heaving with emotion.

The Marquise watched him helplessly, uncertain whether to go or to stay. His sobs were so violent that she was afraid of hysteria, and she did not know what might happen. She was sorry for him, deeply sorry, but even more sorry for herself, because now, on parting, he cut such a ridiculous figure in her eyes. A man who gave way to emotion was pitiable. And it seemed to her that the clearing in the bracken took on a sordid, shameful appearance, which once had seemed so secret and so warm. His shirt, lying on a stem of bracken, looked like old linen spread by washerwomen in the sun to dry. Beside it lay his tie and the cheap trilby hat. It needed only orange peel and silver paper from a chocolate carton to complete the picture.

"Stop that noise," she said in sudden fury. "For God's sake pull yourself together."

The crying ceased. He took his hands away from his ravaged face. He stared at her, trembling, his brown eyes blind with pain. "I have been mistaken in you," he said. "I know you now for what you are. You are a wicked woman and you go about ruining the lives of innocent men like myself. I shall tell your husband everything."

The Marquise said nothing. He was unbalanced, mad. . . .

"Yes," said the photographer, still catching at his breath, "that is what I shall do. As soon as your husband comes to fetch you I will tell him everything. I will show him the photographs I have taken here on the headland. I will prove to him without a doubt that you are false to him, that you are bad. And he will believe me. He cannot help but believe me. What he does to me does not matter. I cannot suffer more than I suffer now. But your life, that will be finished, I promise you. He will know, the English miss will know, the manager of the hotel will know; I will tell everybody how you have been spending your afternoons."

He reached for his coat, he reached for his hat, he slung his camera around his shoulder, and panic seized the Marquise, rose from her heart to her throat. He would do all that he threatened to do; he would wait there in the hall of the hotel by the reception desk, he would wait for Edouard to come.

"Listen to me," she began, "we will think of something, we can perhaps come to some arrangement . . ."

But he ignored her. His face was set and pale. He stooped, by the opening at the cliff's edge, to pick up his stick, and as he did so the terrible impulse was born in her, and flooded her whole being, and would not be denied. Leaning forward, her hands outstretched, she pushed his stooping body. He did not utter a single cry. He fell, and was gone.

The Marquise sank back on her knees. She did not move. She waited. She felt the sweat trickle down her face, to her throat, to her body. Her hands were also wet. She waited there in the clearing, upon her knees, and presently, when she was cooler, she took her handkerchief and wiped away the sweat from her forehead, and her face, and her hands.

It seemed suddenly cold. She shivered. She stood up and her legs were firm; they did not give way, as she feared. She looked about her, over the bracken, and no one was in sight. As always, she was alone upon the headland. Five minutes passed, and then she forced herself to the brink of the cliff and looked down. The tide was in. The sea was washing the base of the cliff below. It surged, and swept the rocks, and sank, and surged again. There was no sign of his body on the cliff face, nor could there be, because the cliff was sheer. No sign of his body in the water, and had he fallen and floated it would have shown there, on the surface of the still blue sea. When he fell he must have sunk immediately.

The Marquise turned back from the opening. She gathered her things together. She tried to pull the flattened bracken to its original height, and so smooth out the signs of habitation, but the hiding place had been made so long that this was impossible. Perhaps it did not matter. Perhaps it would be taken for granted that people came out upon the cliff and took their ease.

Suddenly her knees began to tremble and she sat down. She waited a few moments, then glanced at her watch. She knew that it might be important to remember the time. A few minutes after half-past three. If she was asked, she could say, "Yes, I was out on the headland at about half-past three, but I heard nothing." That would be the truth. She would not be lying. It would be the truth.

She remembered with relief that today she had brought her mirror in her bag. She glanced at it fearfully. Her face was chalk-white, blotched and strange. She powdered carefully, gently; it seemed to make no difference. Miss Clay would notice something was wrong. She dabbed dry rouge on to her cheeks, but this stood out like the painted spots on a clown's face.

"There is only one thing to do," she thought, "and that is to go straight to the bathing cabin on the beach; and undress, and put on my swimming suit, and bathe. Then if I return to the hotel with my hair wet, and my face wet too, it will seem natural, and I shall have been swimming, and that also will be true."

She began to walk back along the cliff, but her legs were weak, as though she had been lying ill in bed for many days, and when she came to the beach at last she was trembling so much she thought she would fall. More than anything she longed to lie down on her bed, in the hotel bedroom, and close the shutters, even the windows, and hide there by herself in the darkness. Yet she must force herself to play the part she had decided.

She went to the bathing cabin and undressed. Already there were several people lying on the sands, reading or sleeping, the hour of siesta drawing to its close. She walked down to the water's edge, kicked off her rope-soled shoes, drew on her cap, and as she swam to and fro in the still, tepid water, and dipped her face, she wondered how many of the people on the beach noticed her, watched her, and afterwards might say, "But don't you remember, we saw a woman come down from the headland in the middle of the afternoon?"

She began to feel very cold, but she continued swimming, backwards and forwards, with stiff, mechanical strokes, until suddenly, seeing a little boy who was playing with a dog point out to sea, and the dog run in barking towards some dark object that might have been a piece of timber, nausea and terror combined to turn her faint, and she stumbled from the sea back to the bathing cabin and lay on the wooden floor, her face in her hands. It might be, she thought, that had she gone on swimming she would have touched him with her feet, as his body came floating in towards her on the water.

In four days' time the Marquis was due to arrive by car and pick up his wife, the governess, and the children, and drive them home. The Marquise put a call through to him at the château and asked if it would be possible for him to come sooner. Yes, the weather was still good, she said, but somehow she had become tired of the place. It was now getting too full of people, it was noisy, and the food had gone off. In fact she had turned against it. She longed to be back at home, she told her husband, amongst her own things, and the gardens would be looking lovely.

The Marquis regretted very much that she was bored, but surely she could stick it out for just the four days, he said. He had made all his arrangements, and he could not come sooner. He had to pass through Paris anyway for an important business meeting. He would promise to reach her by the morning of the Thursday, and then they could leave immediately after lunch.

"I had hoped," he said, "that you would want to stay on for the week end, so that I too could get some bathing. The rooms are held surely until the Monday?"

But no, she had told the manager, she said, that they would not require the rooms after Thursday, and he had already let them to someone else. The place was crowded. The charm of it had gone, she assured him. Edouard would not care for it at all, and at the week end it became quite insupportable. So would he make every effort to arrive in good time on the Thursday, and then they could leave after an early lunch?

The Marquise put down the receiver and went out to the balcony to the chaise longue. She took up a book and pretended to read, but in reality she was listening, waiting for the sound of footsteps, voices, at the entrance to the hotel, and presently for her telephone to ring, and it would be the manager asking her, with many apologies, if she would mind descending to his office. The fact was, the matter was delicate . . . but the police were with him. They had some idea that she could help them. The telephone did not ring. There were no voices. No footsteps. Life continued as before. The long hours dragged through the interminable day. Lunch on the terrace, the waiters bustling, obsequious, the tables filled with the usual faces or with new visitors to take the place of old, the children chattering, Miss Clay reminding them of their manners. And all the while the Marquise listened, waited . . .

She forced herself to eat, but the food she put in her mouth tasted of sawdust. Lunch over, she mounted to her room, and while the children rested she lay on the chaise longue on the balcony. They descended to the terrace again for tea, but when the children went to the beach for their second bathe of the day she did not go with them. She had a little chill, she told Miss Clay; she did not fancy the water. So she went on sitting there, on her balcony.

When she closed her eyes at night and tried to sleep, she felt his stooping shoulders against her hands once more, and the sensation that it had given her when she pushed them hard. The ease with which he fell and vanished, one moment there, and the next, nothing. No stumble, no cry.

In the daytime she used to strain her eyes towards the headland, in search of figures walking there amongst the bracken—would they be called "a cordon of police?" But the headland shimmered under the pitiless sun, and no one walked there in the bracken.

Twice Miss Clay suggested going down into the town in the mornings to make purchases, and each time the Marquise made an excuse.

"It's always so crowded," she said, "and so hot. I don't think it's good for the children. The gardens are more pleasant, the lawn at the back of the hotel is shady and quiet."

She herself did not leave the hotel. The thought of the beach brought back the pain in her belly, and the nausea. Nor did she walk.

"I shall be quite all right," she told Miss Clay, "when I have thrown off this tiresome chill."

She lay there on the balcony, turning over the pages of the magazines she had read a dozen times.

On the morning of the third day, just before déjeuner, the children came running on to the balcony, waving little windmill flags.

"Look, Maman," said Hélène, "mine is red, and Céleste's is blue. We are going to put them on our sand castles after tea."

"Where did you get them?" asked the Marquise.

"In the market place," said the child. "Miss Clay took us to the town this morning instead of playing in the garden. She wanted to pick up her snapshots that were ready today."

A feeling of shock went through the Marquise. She sat very still.

"Run along," she said, "and get ready for déjeuner."

She could hear the children chattering to Miss Clay in the bathroom. In a moment or two Miss Clay came in. She closed the door behind her. The Marquise forced herself to look up at the governess. Miss Clay's long, rather stupid face was grave and concerned.

"Such a dreadful thing has happened," she said, her voice low. "I don't want to speak of it in front of the children. I am sure you will be very distressed. It's poor Monsieur Paul."

"Monsieur Paul?" said the Marquise. Her voice was perfectly calm. But her tone had the right quality of interest.

"I went down to the shop to fetch my snapshots," said Miss Clay, "and I found it shut. The door was locked and the shutters were up. I thought it rather odd, and I went into the *pharmacie* next door and asked if they knew whether the shop was likely to be open after tea. They said no, Mademoiselle Paul was too upset, she was being looked after by relatives. I asked what had happened, and they told me there had been an accident, that poor Monsieur Paul's body had been found by some fishermen three miles up the coast, drowned."

Miss Clay had quite lost colour as she told her tale. She was obviously deeply shocked. The Marquise, at sight of her, gained courage.

"How perfectly terrible," she said. "Does anybody know when it happened?"

"I couldn't go into details at the *pharmacie* because of the children," said Miss Clay, "but I think they found the body yesterday. Terribly injured, they said. He must have hit some rocks before falling into the sea. It's so dreadful I can't bear to think of it. And his poor sister, whatever will she do without him?"

The Marquise put up her hand for silence and made a warning face. The children were coming into the room.

They went down to the terrace for déjeuner, and the Marquise ate better than she had done for two days. For some reason her appetite had returned. Why this should be so she could not tell. She wondered if it could possibly be that part of the burden of her secret was now lifted. He was dead. He had been found. These things were known. After déjeuner she told Miss Clay to ask the manager if he knew anything of the sad accident.

Miss Clay was to say that the Marquise was most concerned and grieved. While Miss Clay went about this business the Marquise took the children upstairs.

Presently the telephone rang. The sound that she had dreaded. Her heart missed a beat. She took off the receiver and listened.

It was the manager. He said Miss Clay had just been to him. He said it was most gracious of Madame la Marquise to show concern at the unfortunate accident that had befallen Monsieur Paul. He would have spoken of it when the accident was discovered yesterday, but he did not wish to distress the clientele. A drowning disaster was never very pleasant at a seaside resort, it made people feel uncomfortable. Yes, of course, the police had been called in directly the body was found. It was assumed that he had fallen from the cliffs somewhere along the coast. It seemed he was very fond of photographing the sea views. And of course, with his disability, he could easily slip. His sister had often warned him to be careful. It was very sad. He was such a good fellow. Everyone liked him. He had no enemies. And such an artist, too, in his way. Madame la Marquise had been pleased with the studies Monsieur Paul had done of herself and the children? The manager was so glad. He would make a point of letting Mademoiselle Paul know this, and also of the concern shown by Madame la Marquise. Yes, indeed, she would be deeply grateful for flowers, and for a note of sympathy. The poor woman was quite brokenhearted. No, the day of the funeral had not yet been decided . . .

When he had finished speaking, the Marquise called to Miss Clay and told her she must order a taxi and drive to the town seven miles inland, where the shops were larger, and where she seemed to remember there was an excellent florist. Miss Clay was to order flowers, lilies for choice, and to spare no expense, and the Marquise would write a note to go with them; and then if Miss Clay gave them to the manager when she returned he would see that they reached Mademoiselle Paul.

The Marquise wrote the note for Miss Clay to take with her to pin on the flowers. "In deepest sympathy at your great loss." She gave Miss Clay some money, and the governess went off to find a taxi.

Later the Marquise took the children to the beach.

"Is your chill better, Maman?" asked Céleste.

"Yes, chérie, now Maman can bathe again."

And she entered the warm yielding water with the children, and splashed with them.

Tomorrow Edouard would arrive, tomorrow Edouard would come in his car and drive them away, and the white dusty roads would lengthen the distance between her and the hotel. She would not see it any more, nor the headland, nor the town, and the holiday would be blotted out like something that had never been.

"When I die," thought the Marquise as she stared out across the sea, "I shall be punished. I don't fool myself. I am guilty of taking life. When I die, God will accuse me. Until then, I will be a good wife to Edouard, and a good mother to Céleste and Hélène. I will try to be a good woman from now. I will try and atone for what I have done by being kinder to everyone, to relations, friends, servants."

She slept well for the first time in three days.

Her husband arrived the next morning while she was still having her breakfast. She was so glad to see him that she sprang from her bed and flung her arms round his neck. The Marquis was touched at this reception.

"I believe my girl has missed me after all," he said.

"Missed you? But of course I've missed you. That's why I rang up. I wanted you to come so much."

"And you are quite determined to leave today after lunch?"

"Oh, yes, yes . . . I couldn't bear to stay. Our packing is done, there are only the last things to put in the suitcases."

He sat on the balcony drinking coffee, laughing with the children, while she dressed and stripped the room of her personal possessions. The room that had been hers for a whole month became bare once more, and quite impersonal. In a fever of hurry she cleared the dressing table, mantelpiece, the table by her bed. It was finished with. The *femme de chambre* would come in presently with clean sheets and make all fresh for the next visitor. And she, the Marquise, would have gone.

"Listen, Edouard," she said, "why must we stay for déjeuner? Wouldn't it be more fun to lunch somewhere on the way? There is always something a little dreary in lunching at a hotel when one has already paid the bill. Tipping, everything, has been done. I cannot bear a sense of anticlimax."

"Just as you like," he said. She had given him such a welcome that he was prepared to gratify every whim. Poor little girl. She had been really lonely without him. He must make up to her for it.

The Marquise was making up her mouth in front of the mirror in the bathroom when the telephone rang.

"Answer it, will you?" she called to her husband. "It is probably the concierge about the luggage."

The Marquis did so, and in a few moments he shouted through to his wife.

"It's for you, dear. It's a Mademoiselle Paul who has called to see you, and asks if she may thank you for her flowers before you go."

The Marquise did not answer at once, and when his wife came into the bedroom it seemed to him that the lipstick had not enhanced her appearance. It made her look almost haggard, older. How very strange. She must have changed the colour. It was not becoming.

"Well," he asked, "what shall I say? You probably don't want to be bothered with her now, whoever she is. Would you like me to go down and get rid of her?"

The Marquise seemed uncertain, troubled. "No," she said, "no, I think I had better see her. The fact is, it's a very tragic thing. She and her brother kept a little shop in the town—I had some photographs done of myself and the children—and then a dreadful thing happened, the brother was drowned. I thought it only right to send flowers."

"How thoughtful of you," said her husband, "a very kind gesture. But do you need to bother now? Why, we are ready to go."

"Tell her that," said his wife, "tell her that we are leaving almost immediately."

The Marquis turned to the telephone again, and after a word or two put his hand over the receiver and whispered to his wife.

"She is very insistent," he said. "She says she has some prints belonging to you that she wants to give to you personally."

A feeling of panic came over the Marquise. Prints? What prints?

"But everything is paid for," she whispered back. "I don't know what she can mean."

The Marquis shrugged his shoulders.

"Well, what am I to say? She sounds as if she is crying."

The Marquise went back into the bathroom, dabbed more powder on her nose.

"Tell her to come up," she said, "but repeat that we are leaving in five minutes. Meanwhile, you go down, take the children to the car. Take Miss Clay with you. I will see the woman alone."

When he had gone she looked about the room. Nothing remained but her gloves, her handbag. One last effort, and then the closing door, the *ascenseur*, the farewell bow to the manager, and freedom.

There was a knock at the door. The Marquise waited by the entrance to the balcony, her hands clasped in front of her.

"*Entrez*," she said.

Mademoiselle Paul opened the door. Her face was blotched and ravaged from weeping; her old-fashioned mourning dress was long, nearly touching the ground. She hesitated, then lurched forward, her limp grotesque, as though each movement must be agony.

"Madame la Marquise" she began, then her mouth worked, she began to cry.

"Please don't," said the Marquise gently. "I am so dreadfully sorry for what has happened."

Mademoiselle Paul took her handkerchief and blew her nose.

"He was all I had in the world," she said. "He was so good to me. What am I to do now? How am I to live?"

"You have relatives?"

"They are poor folk, Madame la Marquise. I cannot expect them to support me. Nor can I keep the shop alone, without my brother. I haven't the strength. My health has always been my trouble."

The Marquise was fumbling in her bag. She took out a twenty-thousand-franc note.

"I know this is not much," she said, "but perhaps it will help just a little. I am afraid my husband has not many contacts in this part of the country, but I will ask him, perhaps he will be able to make some suggestions."

Mademoiselle Paul took the notes. It was strange. She did not thank the Marquise. "This will keep me until the end of the month," she said. "It will help to pay the funeral expenses."

She opened her bag. She took out three prints.

"I have more, similar to these, back in the shop," she said. "It seemed to me that perhaps, going away suddenly as you are doing, you had forgotten all about them. I found them amongst my poor brother's other prints and negatives in the cellar, where he used to develop them."

She handed the prints to the Marquise. The Marquise went cold when she saw them. Yes, she had forgotten. Or rather, she had not been aware of their existence. They were three views of her taken in the bracken. Careless, abandoned, half-sleeping, with her head against his coat for a pillow, she had heard the click-click of the camera, and it had added a sort of zest to the afternoon. Some he had shown her. But not these.

She took the photographs and put them in her bag.

"You say you have others?" she asked, her voice without expression.

"Yes, Madame la Marquise."

She forced herself to meet the woman's eyes. They were swollen still with weeping, but the glint was unmistakable.

"What do you want me to do?" asked the Marquise.

Mademoiselle Paul looked about her in the hotel bedroom. Tissue paper strewn on the floor, odds and ends thrown into the wastepaper basket, the tumbled, unmade bed.

"I have lost my brother," she said, "my supporter, my reason for being alive. Madame la Marquise has had an enjoyable holiday and now returns home. I take it that Madame la Marquise would not desire her husband or her family to see these prints?"

"You are right," said the Marquise, "I do not even wish to see them myself."

"In which case," said Mademoiselle Paul, "twenty thousand francs is really very little return for a holiday that Madame la Marquise so much enjoyed."

The Marquise looked in her bag again. She had two *mille* notes and a few hundred francs.

"This is all I have," she said: "you are welcome to these as well."

Mademoiselle Paul blew her nose once more.

"I think it would be more satisfactory for both of us if we came to a more permanent arrangement," she said. "Now my poor brother has gone the future is very uncertain. I might not even wish to live in a neighbourhood that holds such sad memories. I cannot but ask myself how my brother met his death. The afternoon before he disappeared he went out to the headland and came back very distressed. I knew something had upset him, but I did not ask him what. Perhaps he had hoped to meet a friend, and the friend had not appeared. The next day he went again, and that night he did not return. The police were informed, and then three days later his body was found. I have said nothing of possible suicide to the police, but have accepted it, as they have done, as accidental. But my brother was a very sensitive soul, Madame la Marquise. Unhappy, he would have been capable of anything. If I make myself wretched thinking over these things, I might go to the police, I might suggest he did away with himself after an unhappy love affair. I might even give them leave to search through his effects for photographs."

In agony the Marquise heard her husband's footsteps outside the door.

"Are you coming, dearest?" he called, bursting it open and entering the room. "The luggage is all in, the children are clamouring to be off."

He said good morning to Mademoiselle Paul. She curtseyed.

"I will give you my address," said the Marquise, "both in Paris and in the country." She sought in her bag feverishly for cards. "I shall expect to hear from you in a few weeks' time."

"Possibly before that, Madame la Marqise," said Mademoiselle Paul. "If I leave here, and find myself in your neighbourhood, I would come and pay my humble respects to you and Miss, and the little children. I have friends not so very far away. I have friends in Paris, too. I have always wanted to see Paris."

The Marquise turned with a terrible bright smile to her husband.

"I have told Mademoiselle Paul," she said, "that if there is anything I can do for her at any time she has only to let me know."

"Of course," said her husband. "I am so sorry to hear of your tragedy. The manager here has been telling me all about it."

Mademoiselle Paul curtseyed again, looking from him back to the Marquise.

"He was all I had in the world, Monsieur le Marquis," she said. "Madame la Marquise knows what he meant to me. It is good to know that I may write to her, and that she will write to me, and when that happens I shall not feel alone and isolated. Life can be very hard for someone who is alone in the world. May I wish you a pleasant journey, Madame la Marquise, and happy memories of your holidays, and above all no regrets?"

Once more Mademoiselle Paul curtseyed, then turned and limped from the room.

"Poor woman," said the Marquis, "and what an appearance. I understand from the manager that the brother was crippled too?"

"Yes . . ." She fastened her handbag. Took her gloves. Reached for her dark glasses.

"Curious thing, but it often runs in families," said the Marquis as they walked along the corridor. He paused and rang the bell for the *ascenseur.* "You have never met Richard du Boulay, have you, an old friend of mine? He was crippled, much as this unfortunate little photographer seems to have been, but for all that, a charming, perfectly normal girl fell in love with him, and they got married. A son was born, and he turned out to be a hopeless clubfoot like his father. You can't fight that sort of thing. It's a taint in the blood that passes on."

They stepped into the *ascenseur* and the doors closed upon them.

"Sure you won't change your mind and stay for lunch? You look pale. We've got a long drive before us, you know."

"I'd rather go."

They were waiting in the hall to see her off. The manager, the receptionist, the concierge, the maître d'hôtel.

"Come again, Madame la Marquise. There will always be a welcome for you here. It has been such a pleasure looking after you. The hotel will not be the same once you have gone."

"Good-bye . . . Good-bye . . ."

The Marquise climbed into the car beside her husband. They turned out of the hotel grounds on to the road. Behind her lay the headland, the hot sands, and the sea. Before her lay the long straight road to home and safety. Safety . . . ?

ITALO CALVINO

THE ADVENTURES OF
A PHOTOGRAPHER

1955

*Calvino (1923–85), whose writings in shorter prose forms brought him interna-
tional recognition, was also a citizen of the world. Born in Havana, Cuba, and
raised in San Remo, Italy, he married his Argentinean wife in Paris and, after
their daughter was born, settled in Italy. Calvino worked for the distinguished
publishing house Einaudi, translating English works and producing his own often
experimental works in precise, visual prose; he asserted that "the world of drawing has always been closer to me than that of photography."[1] But this story of a
tragically alienated individual, whose limited sense of self subverts his desire for
companionship and love, also reflects the author's understanding of the camera and
the complex motives of some photographers. So does Calvino's sensitive analysis
of Roland Barthes, who, in his influential* Camera Lucida *(1980), had compli-
mented this story by referring to the author's use of the word* mask *to designate
"what makes a face into the product of a society and of its history" as well as the
phrase "true total photograph" to designate the rare picture that captures reality
as well as truth.[2]*

1. Calvino, "Cinema and the Novel," in *The Literature Machine: Essays*, trans.
Patrick Creagh (London: Secker & Warburg, 1987), p. 79. See also Franco Ricci,
"Painting with Words, Writing with Pictures," in *Calvino Revisited*, ed. Franco Ricci
(University of Toronto Italian Studies [2], Ottawa: Dovehouse Editions, 1989), pp.
189-206; Constance Pierce, "Calvino on Photography," *Review of Contemporary Fic-
tion* 6, no. 2 (Summer 1986): 130-37; and Calvino, *If on a Winter's Night*, trans.
William Weaver (New York: Harcourt Brace Jovanovich, 1981), pp. 37-38, 149, 255,
and 319.

2. See Barthes, *Camera Lucida: Reflections on Photography*, trans. Richard Howard
(New York: Farrar, Straus & Giroux, 1981), pp. 34 [cf. *Adventure*, p. 228] and 113 [cf.

Adventure, p. 235]; and see also Calvino, "In Memory of Roland Barthes," in *The Literature Machine*, pp. 300-306.

THE ADVENTURES OF
A PHOTOGRAPHER

W hen spring comes, the city's inhabitants, by the hundreds of thousands, go out on Sundays with leather cases over their shoulders. And they photograph one another. They come back as happy as hunters with bulging game bags; they spend days waiting, with sweet anxiety, to see the developed pictures (anxiety to which some add the subtle pleasure of alchemistic manipulations in the darkroom, forbidding any intrusion by members of the family, relishing the acid smell that is harsh to the nostrils). It is only when they have the photos before their eyes that they seem to take tangible possession of the day they spent, only then that the mountain stream, the movement of the child with his pail, the glint of the sun on the wife's legs take on the irrevocability of what has been and can no longer be doubted. Everything else can drown in the unreliable shadow of memory.

Seeing a good deal of his friends and colleagues, Antonino Paraggi, a nonphotographer, sensed a growing isolation. Every week he discovered that the conversations of those who praise the sensitivity of a filter or discourse on the number of DINs were swelled by the voice of yet another to whom he had confided until yesterday, convinced that they were shared, his sarcastic remarks about an activity that to him seemed so unexciting, so lacking in surprises.

Professionally, Antonino Paraggi occupied an executive position in the distribution department of a production firm, but his real passion was commenting to his friends on current events large and small, unraveling the thread of general causes from the tangle of details; in short, by mental attitude he was a philosopher, and he devoted all his thoroughness to grasping the significance of even the events most remote from his own experience. Now he felt that something in the essence of photographic man was eluding him, the secret appeal that made new adepts continue to join the ranks of the amateurs of the lens, some boasting of the progress of their technical and artistic skill, others, on the contrary, giving all the credit to the efficiency of the camera they had purchased, which was capable (according to them) of producing masterpieces even when operated by inept hands (as they declared their own to be, because wherever pride aimed at magnifying the virtues of mechanical devices, subjective talent accepted a proportionate humiliation). Antonino Paraggi understood that neither the one nor the other motive of satisfaction was decisive: the secret lay elsewhere.

It must be said that his examination of photography to discover the causes of a private dissatisfaction—as of someone who feels excluded from something—was to a certain extent a trick Antonino played on himself, to avoid having to consider another, more evident, process that was separating him from his friends. What was happening was this: his acquaintances, of his age, were all getting married, one after another, and starting families, while Antonino remained a bachelor. Yet between the two phenomena there was undoubtedly a connection, inasmuch as the passion for the lens often develops in a natural, virtually physiological way as a secondary effect of fatherhood. One of the first instincts of parents, after they have brought a child into the world, is to photograph it. Given the speed of growth, it becomes necessary to photograph the child often, because nothing is more fleeting and unmemorable than a six-month-old infant, soon deleted and replaced by one of eight months, and then one of a year; and all the perfection that, to the eyes of parents, a child of three may have reached cannot prevent its being destroyed by that of the four-year-old. The photograph album remains the only place where all these fleeting perfections are saved and juxtaposed, each aspiring to an incomparable absoluteness of its own. In the passion of new parents for framing their offspring in the sights to reduce them to the immobility of black-and-white or a full-color slide, the nonphotographer and non-procreator Antonino saw chiefly a phase in the race toward madness lurking in that black instrument. But his reflections on the iconography-family-madness nexus were summary and reticent: otherwise he would have realized that the person actually running the greatest risk was himself, the bachelor.

In the circle of Antonino's friends, it was customary to spend the weekend out of town, in a group, following a tradition that for many of them dated back to their student days and that had been extended to include their girl friends, then their wives and their children, as well as wet nurses and governesses, and in some cases in-laws and new acquaintances of both sexes. But since the continuity of their habits, their getting together, had never lapsed, Antonino could pretend that nothing had changed with the passage of the years and that they were still the band of young men and women of the old days, rather than a conglomerate of families in which he remained the only surviving bachelor.

More and more often, on these excursions to the sea or the mountains, when it came time for the family group or the multi-family picture, an outsider was asked to lend a hand, a passer-by perhaps, willing to press the button of the camera already focused and aimed in the desired direction. In these cases, Antonino couldn't refuse his services: he would take the camera from the hands of a father or a mother, who would then run to assume his or her place in the second row, sticking his head forward between two other heads, or crouching among the little ones; and Antonino, concentrating all his strength in the finger destined for this use, would press. The first times, an awkward stiffening of his arm would make the lens veer to capture the masts of ships or the spires of steeples, or to decapitate grandparents, uncles, and aunts. He was accused of doing this on purpose, reproached for making a joke in poor taste. It wasn't true: his intention was to lend the use of his finger as docile instrument of the collective wish, but also to exploit his temporary position of privilege to admonish both photographers and their subjects as to the significance of their actions. As soon as the pad of his finger reached the desired condition of detachment from the rest of his person and personality, he was free to communicate his theories in well-reasoned discourse, framing at the same time well-composed little groups. (A few accidental successes had sufficed to give him nonchalance and assurance with viewfinders and light meters.)

". . . Because once you've begun," he would preach, "there is no reason why you should stop. The line between the reality that is photographed because it seems beautiful to us and the reality that seems beautiful because it has been photographed is very narrow. If you take a picture of Pierluca because he's building a sand castle, there is no reason not to take his picture while he's crying because the castle has collapsed, and then while the nurse consoles him by helping him find a sea shell in the sand. The minute you start saying something, 'Ah, how beautiful! We must photograph it!' you are already close to the view of the person who thinks that everything that is not photographed is lost, as if it had never existed, and that therefore, in order really to live, you must photograph as much as you can, and to photograph as much as you can you must either live in the most photographable way possible, or else consider photographable every moment of your life. The first course leads to stupidity; the second to madness."

"You're the one who's mad and stupid," his friends would say to him, "and a pain in the ass, into the bargain."

"For the person who wants to capture everything that passes before his eyes," Antonino would explain, even if nobody was listening to him any more, "the only coherent way to act is to snap at least one picture a minute, from the instant he opens his eyes in the morning to when he goes to sleep.

This is the only way that the rolls of exposed film will represent a faithful diary of our days, with nothing left out. If I were to start taking pictures, I'd see this thing through, even if it meant losing my mind. But the rest of you still insist on making a choice. What sort of choice? A choice in the idyllic sense, apologetic, consolatory, at peace with nature, the fatherland, the family. Your choice isn't only photographic; it is a choice of life, which leads you to exclude dramatic conflicts, the knots of contradiction, the great tensions of will, passion, aversion. So you think you are saving yourselves from madness, but you are falling into mediocrity, into hebetude."

A girl named Bice, someone's ex-sister-in-law, and another named Lydia, someone else's ex-secretary, asked him to please to take a snapshot of them while they were playing ball among the waves. He consented, but since in the meanwhile he had worked out a theory in opposition to snapshots, he dutifully expressed it to the two friends:

"What drives you two girls to cut from the mobile continuum of your day these temporal slices, the thickness of a second? Tossing the ball back and forth, you are living in the present, but the moment the scansion of the frames is insinuated between your acts it is no longer the pleasure of the game that motivates you but, rather, that of seeing yourselves again in the future, of rediscovering yourselves in twenty years' time, on a piece of yellowed cardboard (yellowed emotionally, even if modern printing procedures will preserve it unchanged). The taste for the spontaneous, natural, lifelike snapshot kills spontaneity, drives away the present. Photographed reality immediately takes on a nostalgic character, of joy fled on the wings of time, a commemorative quality, even if the picture was taken the day before yesterday. And the life that you live in order to photograph it is already, at the outset, a commemoration of itself. To believe that the snapshot is more *true* than the posed portrait is a prejudice. . . ."

So saying, Antonino darted around the two girls in the water, to focus on the movements of their game and cut out of the picture the dazzling glints of the sun on the water. In a scuffle for the ball, Bice, flinging herself on the other girl, who was submerged, was snapped with her behind in closeup, flying over the waves. Antonino, so as not to lose this angle, had flung himself back in the water while holding up the camera, nearly drowning.

"They all came out well, and this one's stupendous," they commented a few days later, snatching the proofs from each other. They had arranged to meet at the photography shop. "You're good; you must take some more of us."

Antonino had reached the conclusion that it was necessary to return to posed subjects, in attitudes denoting their social position and their character, as in the nineteenth century. His antiphotographic polemic could be fought only from within the black box, setting one kind of photography against another.

"I'd like to have one of those old box cameras," he said to his girl friends, "the kind you put on a tripod. Do you think it's still possible to find one?"

"Hmm, maybe at some junk shop . . ."

"Let's go see."

The girls found it amusing to hunt for this curious object; together they ransacked flea markets, interrogated old street photographers, followed them to their lairs. In those cemeteries of objects no longer serviceable lay wooden columns, screens, backdrops with faded landscapes; everything that suggested an old photographer's studio, Antonino bought. In the end he managed to get hold of a box camera, with a bulb to squeeze. It seemed in perfect working order. Antonino also bought an assortment of plates. With the girls helping him, he set up the studio in a room of his apartment, all fitted out with old-fashioned equipment, except for two modern spotlights.

Now he was content. "This is where to start," he explained to the girls. "In the way our grandparents assumed a pose, in the convention that decided how groups were to be arranged, there was a social meaning, a custom, a taste, a culture. An official photograph, or one of a marriage or a family or a school group, conveyed how serious and important each role or institution was, but also how far they were all false or forced, authoritarian, hierarchical. This is the point: to make explicit the relationship with the world that each of us bears within himself, and which today we tend to hide, to make unconscious, believing that in this way it disappears, whereas . . ."

"Who do you want to have pose for you?"

"You two come tomorrow, and I'll begin by taking some pictures of you in the way I mean."

"Say, what's in the back of your mind?" Lydia asked, suddenly suspicious. Only now, as the studio was all set up, did she see that everything about it had a sinister, threatening air. "If you think we're going to come and be your models, you're dreaming!"

Bice giggled with her, but the next day she came back to Antonino's apartment, alone.

She was wearing a white linen dress with colored embroidery on the edges of the sleeves and pockets. Her hair was parted and gathered over her temples. She laughed, a bit slyly, bending her head to one side. As he let her in, Antonino studied her manner—a bit coy, a bit ironic—to discover what were the traits that defined her true character.

He made her sit in a big armchair, and stuck his head under the black cloth that came with his camera. It was one of those boxes whose rear wall was of glass, where the image is reflected as if already on the plate, ghostly, a bit milky, deprived of every link with space and time. To Antonino it was as if he had never seen Bice before. She had a docility in her somewhat heavy way of lowering her eyelids, of stretching her neck forward, that promised something hidden, as her smile seemed to hide behind the very act of smiling.

"There. Like that. No, head a bit farther; raise your eyes. No, lower them." Antonino was pursuing, within that box, something of Bice that all at once seemed most precious to him, absolute.

"Now you're casting a shadow; move into the light. No, it was better before."

There were many possible photographs of Bice and many Bices impossible to photograph, but what he was seeking was the unique photograph that would contain both the former and the latter.

"I can't get you," his voice emerged, stifled and complaining from beneath the black hood, "I can't get you any more; I can't manage to get you."

He freed himself from the cloth and straightened up again. He was going about it all wrong. That expression, that accent, that secret he seemed on the very point of capturing in her face, was something that drew him into the quicksands of moods, humors, psychology: he, too, was one of those who pursue life as it flees, a hunter of the unattainable, like the takers of snapshots.

He had to follow the opposite path: aim at a portrait completely on the surface, evident, unequivocal, that did not elude conventional appearance, the stereotype, the mask. The mask, being first of all a social, historical product, contains more truth than any image claiming to be "true"; it bears a quantity of meanings that will gradually be revealed. Wasn't this precisely Antonino's intention in setting up this fair booth of a studio?

He observed Bice. He should start with the exterior elements of her appearance. In Bice's way of dressing and fixing herself up—he thought—you could recognize the somewhat nostalgic, somewhat ironic intention, widespread in the mode of those years, to hark back to the fashions of thirty years earlier. The photograph should underline this intention: why hadn't he thought of that?

Antonino went to find a tennis racket; Bice should stand up in a three-quarter turn, the racket under her arm, her face in the pose of a sentimental postcard. To Antonino, from under the black drape, Bice's image—in its slimness and suitability to the pose, and in the unsuitable and almost incongruous aspects that the pose accentuated—seemed very interesting.

He made her change position several times, studying the geometry of legs and arms in relation to the racket and to some element in the background. (In the ideal postcard in his mind there would have been the net of the tennis court, but you couldn't demand too much, and Antonino made do with a Ping-Pong table.)

But he still didn't feel on safe ground: wasn't he perhaps trying to photograph memories—or, rather, vague echoes of recollection surfacing in the memory? Wasn't his refusal to live the present as a future memory, as the Sunday photographers did, leading him to attempt an equally unreal operation, namely to give a body to recollection, to substitute it for the present before his very eyes?

"Move! Don't stand there like a stick! Raise the racket, damn it! Pretend you're playing tennis!" All of a sudden he was furious. He had realized that only by exaggerating the poses could he achieve an objective alienness; only by feigning a movement arrested halfway could he give the impression of the unmoving, the nonliving.

Bice obediently followed his orders even when they became vague and contradictory, with a passivity that was also a way of declaring herself out of the game, and yet somehow insinuating, in this game that was not hers, the unpredictable moves of a mysterious match of her own. What Antonino now was expecting of Bice, telling her to put her legs and arms this way and that way, was not so much the simple performance of a plan as her response to the violence he was doing her with his demands, an unforeseeable aggressive reply to this violence that he was being driven more and more to wreak on her.

It was like a dream, Antonino thought, contemplating, from the darkness in which he was buried, that improbable tennis player filtered into the glass rectangle: like a dream when a presence coming from the depth of memory advances, is recognized, and then suddenly is transformed into something unexpected, something that even before the transformation is already frightening because there's no telling what it might be transformed into.

Did he want to photograph dreams? This suspicion struck him dumb, hidden in that ostrich refuge of his with the bulb in his hand, like an idiot; and meanwhile Bice, left to herself, continued a kind of grotesque dance, freezing in exaggerated tennis poses, backhand, drive, raising the racket high or lowering it to the ground as if the gaze coming from that glass eye were the ball she continued to slam back.

"Stop, what's this nonsense? This isn't what I had in mind." Antonino covered the camera with the cloth and began pacing up and down the room.

It was all the fault of that dress, with its tennis, prewar connotations. . . .

It had to be admitted that if she wore a street dress the kind of photograph he described couldn't be taken. A certain solemnity was needed, a certain pomp, like the official photos of queens. Only in evening dress would Bice become a photographic subject, with the décolleté that marks a distinct line between the white of the skin and the darkness of the fabric, accentuated by the glitter of jewels, a boundary between an essence of woman, almost atemporal and almost impersonal in her nakedness, and the other abstraction, social this time, the dress, symbol of an equally impersonal role, like the drapery of an allegorical statue.

He approached Bice, began to unbutton the dress at the neck and over the bosom, and slip it down over her shoulders. He had thought of certain nineteenth-century photographs of women in which from the white of the cardboard emerge the face, the neck, the line of the bared shoulders, while all the rest disappears into the whiteness.

This was the portrait outside of time and space that he now wanted; he wasn't quite sure how it was achieved, but he was determined to succeed. He set the spotlight on Bice, moved the camera closer, fiddled around the cloth adjusting the aperture of the lens. He looked into it. Bice was naked.

She had made the dress slip down to her feet; she wasn't wearing anything underneath it; she had taken a step forward—no, a step backward, which was as if her whole body were advancing in the picture; she stood erect, tall before the camera, calm, looking straight ahead, as if she were alone.

Antonino felt the sight of her enter his eyes and occupy the whole visual field, removing it from the flux of casual and fragmentary images, concentrating time and space in a finite form. And as if this visual surprise and the impression of the plate were two reflexes connected among themselves, he immediately pressed the bulb, loaded the camera again, snapped, put in another plate, snapped, and went on changing plates and snapping, mumbling, stifled by the cloth, "There, that's right now, yes, again, I'm getting you fine now, another."

He had run out of plates. He emerged from the cloth. He was pleased. Bice was before him, naked, as if waiting.

"Now you can dress," he said, euphoric, but already in a hurry. "Let's go out."

She looked at him, bewildered.

"I've got you now," he said.

Bice burst into tears.

Antonino realized that he had fallen in love with her that same day. They started living together, and he bought the most modern cameras, telescopic lens, the most advanced equipment; he installed a darkroom. He even had a set-up for photographing her when she was asleep at night. Bice would wake at the flash, annoyed; Antonino went on taking snapshots of her disentangling herself from sleep, of her becoming furious with him, of her trying in vain to find sleep again by plunging her face into the pillow, of her making up with him, of her recognizing as acts of love these photographic rapes.

In Antonino's darkroom, strung with films and proofs, Bice peered from every frame, as thousands of bees peer out from the honeycomb of a hive, but always the same bee: Bice in every attitude, at every angle, in every guise, Bice posed or caught unaware, an identity fragmented into a powder of images.

"But what's this obsession with Bice? Can't you photograph anything else?" was the question he heard constantly from his friends, and also from her.

"It isn't just a matter of Bice," he answered. "It's a question of method. Whatever person you decide to photograph, or whatever thing, you must go on photographing it always, exclusively, at every hour of the day and night. Photography has a meaning only if it exhausts all possible images."

But he didn't say what meant most to him: to catch Bice in the street when she didn't know he was watching her, to keep her in the range of hidden lenses, to photograph her not only without letting himself be seen but without seeing her, to surprise her as she was in the absence of his gaze, of any gaze. Not that he wanted to discover any particular thing; he wasn't a jealous man in the usual sense of the word. It was an invisible Bice that he wanted to possess, a Bice absolutely alone, a Bice whose presence presupposed the absence of him and everyone else.

Whether or not it could be defined as jealousy, it was, in any case, a passion difficult to put up with. And soon Bice left him.

Antonino sank into deep depression. He began to keep a diary—a photographic diary, of course. With the camera slung around his neck, shut up in the house, slumped in an armchair, he compulsively snapped pictures as he stared into the void. He was photographing the absence of Bice.

He collected the photographs in an album: you could see ashtrays brimming with cigarette butts, an unmade bed, a damp stain on the wall. He got the idea of composing a catalogue of everything in the world that resists photography, that is systematically omitted from the visual field not only by cameras but also by human beings. On every subject he spent days, using up whole rolls at intervals of hours, so as to follow the changes of light and shadow. One day he became obsessed with a completely empty corner of the room, containing a radiator pipe and nothing else: he was tempted to go on photographing that spot and only that till the end of his days.

The apartment was completely neglected; old newspapers, letters lay crumpled on the floor, and he photographed them. The photographs in the papers were photographed as well, and an indirect bond was established between his lens and that of distant news photographers. To produce those black spots the lenses of other cameras had been aimed at police assaults, charred automobiles, running athletes, ministers, defendants.

Antonino now felt a special pleasure in portraying domestic objects framed by a mosaic of telephotos, violent patches of ink on white sheets. From his immobility he was surprised to find he envied the life of the news photographer, who moves following the movements of crowds, bloodshed, tears, feasts, crime, the conventions of fashion, the falsity of official cere-monies; the news photographer, who documents the extremes of society, the richest and the poorest, the exceptional moments that are nevertheless produced at every moment and in every place.

Does this mean that only the exceptional condition has a meaning? Antonino asked himself. Is the news photographer the true antagonist of the Sunday photographer? Are their worlds mutually exclusive? Or does the one give meaning to the other?

Reflecting like this, he began to tear up the photographs with Bice or without Bice that had accumulated during the months of his passion, rip-ping to pieces the strips of proofs hung on the walls, snipping up the cel-luloid of the negatives, jabbing the slides, and piling the remains of this methodical destruction on newspapers spread out on the floor.

Perhaps true, total photography, he thought, is a pile of fragments of pri-vate images, against the creased background of massacres and coronations.

He folded the corners of the newspapers into a huge bundle to be thrown into the trash, but first he wanted to photograph it. He arranged the edges so that you could clearly see two halves of photographs from different newspapers that in the bundle happened, by chance, to fit together. In fact he reopened the package a little so that a bit of shiny pasteboard would stick out, the fragment of a torn enlargement. He turned on a spotlight; he wanted it to be possible to recognize in his photograph the half-crumpled and torn images, and at the same time to feel their unreality as casual, inky shadows, and also at the same time their concreteness as objects charged with meaning, the strength with which they clung to the attention that tried to drive them away.

To get all this into one photograph he had to acquire an extraordinary technical skill, but only then would Antonino quit taking pictures. Having exhausted every possibility, at the moment when he was coming full circle Antonino realized that photographing photographs was the only course that he had left—or, rather, the true course he had obscurely been seeking all this time.

EUGÈNE IONESCO

THE COLONEL'S PHOTOGRAPH

1955

———

Ionesco (1909–94), best known for his iconoclastic plays, recalled that his very first word was probably "Again," in response to the removal of a magic lantern image from the screen. The first sentences of his Memoirs *describe "how I'd had my photograph taken at the age of three" and how he long viewed himself as resembling his childhood photos, "eyes wide open, amazed by the very fact of existence," both its miraculous and evil aspects.[1] The image of a photograph—as well as dreams, remarks, and ideas—sparked various writings of the grown writer, who often turned short stories into plays and vice-versa.[2] Both this titular narrative for a collection of short stories and its much expanded dramatic version,* The Killer *(1957), despite their differences, share the quality of a surrealistic nightmare. Ionesco's archetypal characters dramatize their creator's lifelong yearning for an innocent world and his obsession with the human acceptance of evil, whether under the totalitarian regime in Romania, where he was born and received his higher education, or the more democratic one in France, where he spent most of his childhood and settled in 1939.[3]*

1. See Ionesco, *Present Past/Past Present* (1968), translated by Helen R. Lane (New York: Grove, 1971), p. 6; Claude Bonnefoy, *Conversations with Eugène Ionesco*, translated by Jan Dawson (London: Faber & Faber, 1970), p. 56; and Ionesco, "Why Do I Write? A Summing Up" in *The Two Faces of Ionesco*, edited by Rosette C. Lamont and Melvin J. Friedman (Troy, N.Y.: Whitston, 1978), p. 7. See also Gemma M. Galli, "Edifying the Reader: Ionesco's 'The Colonel's Photograph,'" *Modern Fiction Studies* 31, no. 4 (Winter 1985): 645–57.

2. See Ionesco, *Present Past/Past Present*, p. 177, which discusses a photograph of a Russian admiral as "the very face of tyranny," the kind all Frenchmen detest but, being psychologically uncomfortable, didn't fight.

3. See Ionesco, "Why Do I Write?" and "Towards a Dream Theatre" in *Two Faces*

of Ionesco, pp. 7-9, 245-46, which supply a provocative gloss on these ideas dramatized both in this story and in its stage version, *The Killer*, in *The Killer and Other
Plays* (New York: Grove, 1960), pp. 7-109. At the end of his life, Ionesco returned to
more visual interests, devoting his time to painting and exhibiting his canvases.

THE COLONEL'S PHOTOGRAPH

I had gone to visit the fine new district, with its white houses surrounded by bright little flower gardens. Trees lined the broad streets.
New, gleaming cars stood in front of the gates and in the garden
drives. The sky was cloudless, the light was blue. I took off my coat and
laid it over my arm.

"It's the rule round here," said my companion, a municipal architect,
"that the weather is always fine. So land is very expensive, the houses are
built of the best materials; the people in this district are all well-to-do,
cheerful, healthy and good-natured."

"Quite true. . . . Here, I notice, the trees are already in leaf—just enough
to let the light through and not enough to darken the housefronts—
whereas in all the rest of the town the sky is as grey as an old woman's hair,
and there's still frozen snow at the edge of the pavements and a cold wind
blowing. This morning I was shivering when I woke up. It's odd, one's
suddenly in the middle of spring; it's as if I were a thousand miles further
South. When you travel by air you get this feeling of having witnessed
the transfiguration of the world. And even so you have to go the airport
and fly for two hours or more to see the world transformed into a Côte
d'Azur, for instance. Whereas here I've scarcely even had a tram-ride. The
journey, which is no journey, takes place in the place itself, if you'll excuse that shocking little pun, which was quite unintentional," I said with
a forced and yet humorous smile. "How can you explain it? Is this a more
sheltered spot? Yet surely there are no hills round it to protect it against
the weather. Besides, hills don't repel the clouds or offer protection against
rain, as everybody knows. Are there warm and luminous currents of air
coming from below or above? We should have known of them. There's no
wind, although the air smells good. It's curious."

"It's quite simple, this is a little island," the city architect replied, "an
oasis, such as are to be found here and there in deserts, where you can
see amazing cities, covered with fresh roses and girdled with streams and
rivers, rise up in the midst of arid sands."

"Yes, that's true. You mean those cities that are also known as mirages," I said to show that I was not completely ignorant.

We walked for a while alongside a green park with an ornamental lake in the middle. Then there were more villas, large private houses, gardens and flowers. We covered nearly two miles in this way. Everything was perfectly calm and peaceful, too much so perhaps; it was almost disturbing.

"Why is nobody to be seen in the streets?" I asked. "We're the only people walking about. It's probably lunch time, and the inhabitants are all at home. But then why do we hear no laughter, no clinking of glasses? There's not a sound. The windows are all closed!"

We had just reached two recently abandoned building sites. The unfinished houses stood there, white amidst the greenery, waiting for the builders.

"It's rather charming!" I said. "If I had any money—unfortunately I earn very little—I would buy one of these plots; in a few days the house would be built, and I should no longer have to live among the down-and-outs, in that sordid district, with the snow or mud or dust of those gloomy streets and all those factories. It smells so good here," I said, taking a deep breath of the warm, heady air.

My companion frowned. "The police have stopped all building, which is quite unnecessary, for no one is buying plots. Even the inhabitants of the district want to leave it. They've nowhere else to go, otherwise they'd all have packed their bags. Perhaps, too, they're making it a point of honour not to run away. They prefer to stay in hiding in their fine houses. They only go out in cases of extreme urgency, in groups of ten or twelve. And even then the danger is not averted."

"You're joking! Why do you look so grave? You're casting a gloom over the whole landscape; are you trying to make my flesh creep?"

"I'm not joking, I assure you."

His words struck a chill into my heart; an inward darkness overwhelmed me. The dazzling landscape in which I had felt myself take root, which had immediately become part of me, or of which I had become a part, detached itself, became something quite outside me, a mere picture in a frame, an inanimate object. I felt alone, totally excluded, and the life had gone out of the light.

"Explain yourself!" I begged. "I'd been hoping to enjoy my day! I was so happy a few moments ago!"

We were just coming back to the ornamental pool.

"It's there," said the municipal architect, "it's in there that two or three of them are found every day drowned."

"Drowned?"

"Come and convince yourself that I'm not exaggerating."

I followed him. When we reached the edge of the pool I did indeed see the swollen body of an officer of the Engineering Corps floating on the water, and also that of a small boy of five or six, entangled in his hoop and clutching a little stick in his fist.

"There are actually three of them today," murmured my guide. "Over there," he pointed.

Strands of reddish hair, which for a second I have mistaken for some water-plant, had risen from the depths and were caught up on the marble rim of the pool.

"How dreadful! It's a woman, of course?"

"Obviously," he said, shrugging his shoulders, "this other's a man, and that's a child. We know nothing more about them."

"Perhaps she was the child's mother. . . . Poor things! Who has done this?"

"The murderer. It's always the same elusive person."

"But our lives are in danger, let's go away!" I exclaimed.

"You're quite safe with me. I'm the city architect, a municipal officer; he never attacks members of the administration. When I've retired, it'll be another story, but for the time being. . . ."

"Let's go away," I said.

We strode off hastily. I was impatient to leave this fine district. "The rich aren't always happy!" I thought. An indescribable anguish overcame me. I felt bruised and broken, and life was pointless. "What's the good of anything," I said to myself, "if this is what it leads to?"

"Surely you're hoping to arrest him before you retire?" I asked.

"It's not easy! . . . You can be sure we're doing all we can . . ." he answered gloomily. Then: "Not that way, you'll get lost, you keep going round in a circle and coming back to where you started from. . . ."

"Guide me. . . . Oh, the day had started so well. I shall always keep seeing those drowned bodies, the sight will never leave me!"

"I ought not to have shown you. . . ."

"Never mind, it's better to know everything, it's better to know everything. . . ."

In a few moments we had reached the limits of the district, and we stood at the end of the walk that runs alongside the outer Boulevard, where the cross-town trams stop. People were waiting there. The sky was dark. I was frozen. I put on my overcoat again and fastened my scarf round my neck. A fine rain was falling, a mixture of snow and water, and the pavement was wet.

"You're not going home right away?" asked the Superintendent (and that was how I discovered he was also a superintendent). "You've surely time for a drink. . . ."

The Superintendent seemed to have recovered his good spirits, unlike myself.

"There's a bistro there, just by the tram stop, it's close to the cemetery and you can buy wreaths there too."

"I've no wish to do so, you know . . ."

"Don't worry. If one thought about all the misfortunes of mankind one couldn't go on living. There are always children being murdered, old men starving, widows, orphans, people dying."

"Yes, Superintendent, but after having seen it at close quarters with my own eyes . . . I can't remain indifferent."

"You're too sensitive," my companion replied, clapping me heartily on the shoulder.

We went into the tavern.

"Let's try to comfort you! Two halves!" he ordered.

We sat down beside the window. The stout landlord, with his jacket off and his shirtsleeves rolled up, showing huge hairy arms, came to serve us.

"For you, I've got some real beer!"

I made as if to pay.

"No, no," said the Superintendent, "this is on me."

I was still deeply depressed.

"If you'd at least got his description!" I said.

"But we have. At least, the description of him when he's at work. His portrait is posted up on all the walls."

"How did you get it?"

"We found it on some of the drowned bodies. One or two of his victims, revived for a brief moment before they died, were even able to provide us with further details. We also know how he sets about it; indeed, everybody in the district knows that."

"But then why don't they take more care? All they need do is avoid him!"

"It's not so simple. I tell you, there are always two or three, every evening, who fall into his trap. But he himself never gets caught."

"I simply cannot understand."

To my surprise, the architect seemed quite amused at this.

"Look," he said, "it's right there at the tram stop that he functions. As the passengers alight to go to their homes, he comes up to them, dressed as a beggar. He whimpers, begs for alms, tries to arouse their pity. It's the old story: he's just out of hospital, he has no job, he's looking for work, he has nowhere to spend the night. That's not what does the trick. It's just an opening gambit. He sniffs around and picks on some kind soul. He starts up a conversation, clings to his victim like a limpet, tries to sell him bits and pieces which he produces from a basket—artificial flowers, scissors, dirty pictures, all sorts of things. Generally his offers are turned down, the victim hasn't time, is in a hurry. He goes on bargaining until they are close to the pool which you saw. Then, straight away, he plays his trump card. He offers to show his victim the Colonel's photograph. There's no resisting this. As the light, by now, is poor, the kind soul bends down to see better, and that seals his doom. While he's absorbed in gazing at the picture, the murderer gives him a push and he falls into the pool and is drowned. The job is done. The murderer merely has to look for his next victim."

"The extraordinary thing is that people should know this and yet let themselves be taken unawares."

"Why, it's a trap, you see. It's cunningly done. He's never been caught in the act."

Mechanically, I watched people alighting from the tram which had just arrived. I saw no beggar.

"You won't see him," said the Superintendent, guessing my thoughts, "he won't show himself, he knows that we're here."

"Perhaps you'd be wise to station a plain-clothes policeman there permanently."

"It's not possible. Our detectives are overworked, they've plenty of other jobs to do. Besides, they'd want to see the Colonel's photograph themselves. Five of them have already been drowned in that way. Oh, if we had proof, we'd know where to find him!"

I left my companion, after thanking him for taking me to visit the fine new district, and also for so kindly allowing himself to be interviewed about all these unpardonable crimes. Unfortunately, his instructive revelations will appear in no daily paper: I am not a journalist, I have never claimed to be one. The architect-Superintendent had given me all this information out of the kindness of his heart. It had filled me with anguish quite gratuitously. I went home in a state of indefinable unease.

Edouard was waiting for me in the everlastingly autumnal sitting-room, low-ceilinged and dark (the electricity is switched off during daylight). He was there sitting on the chest by the window, dressed in black, slender, with his pale mournful face and his burning eyes. He was probably still somewhat feverish. He noticed that I was depressed and asked me why. When I tried to tell him the story he stopped me after the first few words: he knew all about it, he told me in his quavering, almost childish voice, he was even surprised that I had not heard of it myself earlier. It was common knowledge throughout the city; that was why he had never talked about it. It was something people had heard about and accepted long ago. Deplorable, of course.

"Most deplorable!" I exclaimed.

I, in my turn, expressed surprise at not finding him more distressed. But perhaps I was being unfair to him, perhaps this was the cause of the pain that was consuming him, for he was tubercular. One can never see into people's hearts.

"Suppose we went for a short walk," he said. "I've been waiting for you for an hour. I'm freezing here. It's certainly warmer outside."

Although depressed and tired (I would rather have gone to bed) I agreed to go out with him.

He rose, put on his felt hat with its mourning ribbon and his iron-grey overcoat, and picked up his heavy, over-filled briefcase, which he dropped before he had even taken a step. It opened as it fell. We pounced on it, both at once. Some photographs had fallen out of one of the pockets, showing a colonel in full uniform, with a moustache, a very ordinary colonel, with quite a kindly sort of face. We laid the briefcase on the table so as to look through it more comfortably: we pulled out hundreds of photographs of the same sitter.

"What does this mean?" I asked, "it's the photograph, the notorious photograph of the Colonel! You had it there, you never told me about it!"

"I'm not forever looking into my briefcase," he retorted.

"But it's your own briefcase, you're never without it!"

"What difference does that make?"

"Well, let's take advantage of this opportunity; since we're at it, let's go on looking."

He thrust his white invalid's hand, with its bent fingers, into the other pocket of his huge black briefcase. He pulled out (how could there have been room for so much?) unimaginable quantities of artificial flowers, obscene pictures, sweets, moneyboxes, children's watches, pins, pens, cardboard boxes, and so on and so forth, a whole mass of junk, some cigarettes. ("Those belong to me," he said). There was no more room on the table.

"These are the monster's things!" I cried. "You have them there!"

"I had no idea."

"Empty it all out," I encouraged him. "Come on!"

He went on rummaging. Visiting cards appeared with the name and address of the criminal, his identity card complete with photograph, then, in a little box, index-cards with the names of all his victims and a private diary which we looked through, with his detailed confession, his schemes, his plan of action meticulously set out, his statement of faith, his doctrine.

"You've got all the proofs here. We can get him arrested."

"I didn't know," he stammered. "I didn't know. . . ."

"You could have saved so many human lives," I said reproachfully.

"I'm quite bewildered. I didn't know. I never know what I've got, I don't look into my briefcase."

"Shocking carelessness!" I said.

"I'm very sorry. I apologize for it!"

"But really, Edouard, these things can't have got there by themselves. You found them, or you were given them!"

I felt sorry for him. He was scarlet-faced, really ashamed.

He searched his memory. "Oh yes!" he exclaimed after a few moments. "It's come back to me now. The criminal had sent me his private diary, his notes, his cards, a long time ago, begging me to publish them in a literary magazine; it was before all these murders were done; I had quite forgotten all about it. I think he himself had not thought of committing them; it must only have occurred to him later to put his plans into practice; as for me, I had taken it all for idle fantasy, for mere science fiction. I'm sorry not to have given more thought to the matter, or seen the connection between these documents and what has happened."

"And yet the connection is that between intention and realization, neither more nor less, that's clear as daylight."

Next he pulled out of the briefcase a large envelope, which we opened; it was a map, on which were clearly marked all the spots where the murderer was to be, and his exact time-table, minute by minute.

"It's quite simple," I said. "We'll tell the police, and they'll merely have to pick him up. Let's make haste, the police headquarters will shut at night-fall. After that there's nobody there. He might change his plans overnight. Let's go and see the architect, let's show him the proofs."

"All right," said Edouard, without much enthusiasm.

We hurried out. In the corridor we collided with the concierge: "The very idea . . ." she exclaimed; the rest of her remark was lost as we flew by.

We slowed down to take breath when we reached the main avenue. On our right the ploughed fields stretched out as far as the eye could see. On our left rose the first houses of the town. Straight ahead of us, the sky was red with the glow of sunset. On either side, a few leafless trees. There were hardly any people.

We followed the tramlines (had the trams stopped running already?) which stretched far ahead to the horizon.

Three or four big military lorries, which had emerged from nowhere, suddenly blocked the road. They had parked beside the pavement, which at this point was lower than the road, making the latter seem inordinately high.

Edouard and I had to halt for a moment; fortunately, for this enabled me to discover that my friend was not carrying his briefcase: "What have you done with it, I thought you'd got it with you?" I asked him. The scatter-brain! He had left it at home, when we hurried off.

"It would be no use going to see the Superintendent without our proofs! Whatever were you thinking of? You're incredible! Run back and fetch it. I shall have to go on, I must at least go to Police Headquarters to warn the Superintendent in time, and get him to wait. Make haste and come back, try to catch me up as soon as you can. The Headquarters are at the end of the road. In a business like this I don't like being out by myself, it's not very pleasant, you realize."

Edouard disappeared. I was rather frightened. The pavement dipped even lower, so that steps had been built—four, to be precise—to provide pedestrians with access to the roadway. I was close to one of the big lorries (there were others in front of and behind it). This one was an open truck with rows of seats on which about forty young soldiers in dark uniforms were sitting close together. One of them had in his hand a big bunch of red carnations. He was using it as a fan.

A few policemen appeared to regulate the traffic, blowing their whistles. A good thing, too; this obstruction was delaying me. They were inordinately tall. One of them, stationed next to a tree, towered above it when he raised his truncheon.

Hat in hand, a little old man, quietly dressed and white-haired, looking even smaller by the policeman's side, asked him some simple questions very politely, too politely, humbly in fact. The policeman went on signalling and made some curt reply to the old gentleman (who might, given the difference in their ages, have been his father, although the difference in their heights was not in the old man's favour). The latter, deaf, or failing to understand, repeated his request. The policeman dismissed him with some insolent remark, turned his head, went on with his job, blew his whistle.

The officer's attitude shocked me. It was surely his *duty* to be polite to people: it must be set down somewhere in the regulations. "When I see his boss, the architect, I shall try not to forget to mention it!" I thought. We are far too polite, too timid with policemen, we have taught them bad habits, it's our own fault.

A second officer, as tall as the first, came up on the pavement quite close to me; he was obviously annoyed by the lorries, the traffic jam, and admittedly he had every right to be. Not bothering to step up on to the roadway he went up close to the lorry full of soldiers. Although his feet were on the level of mine his head was slightly higher than their heads. He rebuked them severely for holding up the traffic, although they were not to blame, least of all the young man with the bunch of red carnations, who incurred his special wrath.

"Have you nothing better to do than to play with that?" he asked him.

"I'm not doing any harm, officer," the soldier replied in a shy, gentle tone, "this isn't what's preventing the lorry from starting."

"How dare you? It jams the engine!" exclaimed the policeman, lashing out at the soldier, who never said a word. Then he tore the flowers from him and threw them away: they disappeared.

I was inwardly shocked to the core. In my opinion, a country's done for when the police has the upper hand over the army.

"Why are you interfering? Is it any of your business?" he said, turning to me.

And yet I had not expressed my thoughts aloud. They must have been easy to read.

"For one thing, what are you doing there?"

I took advantage of his question to explain my case and finally to ask for his advice and help.

"I've got all the proofs," I said, "you'll be able to lay hands on the murderer. I must go to Police Headquarters. It's quite a long way off. Can somebody go with me? I'm a friend of the Superintendent, the architect."

"It's not my branch. I'm in Traffic."

"All the same. . . ."

"It's not my job, d'you hear? I'm not interested in your story. Since you're a pal of the Chief's go and see him and leave me in peace. You know the way, so clear off, the road's all yours."

"All right, officer," I said, and in spite of myself I was as polite as the soldier, "all right, officer!"

The policeman turned to his colleague, stationed by the tree, and said in a harshly ironic tone: "Let the gentleman pass!"

The second policeman, whose face I could see through the branches, motioned me to hurry off. As I was passing close to him he spat out furiously: "I hate you!" although I surely had more right to say that to him.

I found myself alone in the middle of the road, with the lorries already far behind me. I was walking swiftly towards Police Headquarters. Night was drawing on, the winter wind was blowing keenly, and I was worried. Would Edouard catch up with me in time? And I felt furious with the police: all they're good for is to nag you and teach you good manners, but when you really need them, when you want protection . . . it's none of their business! They always let you down.

There were no more houses on my right; grey fields on either side. This road, or avenue, with its tramlines, seemed unending. I walked on and on: "Don't let it be too late, don't let it be too late!"

Suddenly he was there in front of me. Without a doubt, it was the murderer: all round us there was nothing but the darkening plain. The wind flung an old sheet of newspaper against the trunk of a leafless tree, and it stuck there. Behind the man, in the distance, several hundred yards away, the buildings of Police Headquarters were outlined against the setting sun, and close by was the tram stop: the tram-car could be seen arriving, and people got out of it, looking tiny in the distance. Help was out of the question, they were much too far off, they would not have heard me.

I stopped short, rooted to the spot. "Those beastly policemen," I thought, "they've deliberately left me alone with him; they want it to look as if we were settling a private quarrel!"

We were face to face, a couple of yards from one another. I gazed at him in watchful silence. He stared back at me, faintly sneering.

He was a man of middle age, slight and very short, ill-shaven, puny-looking, seemingly weaker than myself. He wore a shabby, dirty overcoat with torn pockets, and shoes with holes in them through which his toes showed. On his head he wore a shapeless, battered hat, one hand was in his pocket, the other was tightly clenched round a knife with a broad blade, that gave out a livid gleam. He stared at me with his one eye, a cold glare with the same steely glitter as the blade of his weapon.

I had never met so cruel a gaze, so ruthless (but why?), so ferocious. An implacable eye, a serpent's maybe or a tiger's, gratuitously murderous. No friendly or authoritative word, no argument could have weighed with him; all promise of future happiness, all the love in the world would fail to reach him; beauty would not have moved him nor irony put him to shame, nor could all the sages in the world have made him understand that crime is as futile as charity.

The tears of the saints would glide over that lidless eye, that steely gaze, without moistening it; armies of Christs would tread the path of Calvary in vain, for him.

Slowly I drew from my pocket my two pistols, and silently, for two seconds, aimed them at his motionless figure, then I lowered them, let my arms hang by my sides. I felt defenceless, desperate; for what use were bullets, or my own feeble strength, against the cold hatred and stubbornness, against the boundless energy of that absolute cruelty, devoid of reason as of mercy?

JULIO CORTÁZAR

BLOW-UP

1959

Cortázar (1914–84) followed what became a familiar cosmopolitan path for Latin American intellectuals. Born in Brussels of Argentine parents who returned to Buenos Aires after the First World War, he taught in secondary schools, wrote poems as well as plays, and worked as a translator of English and French literature. Cortázar declined a university professorship because of his opposition to the Péron regime yet remained active in Latin American socialist politics even after moving permanently in 1951 to France. Here he continued translating, writing, and, as one of many hobbies, taking photographs. Cortázar began to attract attention with his short stories, using multiple perspectives to explore the relationship between reality and its image, truth and fiction, the creator and his artifact, as in this narrative, which defies any definitive interpretation.[1] Indeed, the writer compared the short story to a photograph, resembling one limited frame of reality which the viewer-reader must expand to find answers to the questions raised by the narratives like this one; these questions inspired his friend Michelangelo Antonioni's film Blow-Up *(1966).[2] Cortázar subsequently provided the photographs for two of his own works and collaborated with well-known photographers on others.[3]*

1. See another Cortázar short story involving photography, "Apocalypse at Solentiname" [1976], in *A Change of Light and Other Stories* (New York: Knopf, 1980), pp. 119-27, which also uses a similarly complex perspective.

2. See Cortázar, "Algunos aspectos del cuento," in *Casa de Las Americas* 11, nos. 15-16 (November 1962–February 1963): 3-14, especially pp. 5-6, which Nicole Caso, thanks to Barbara Norwood, translated for the editor. For the most interesting discussions of the short story "Blow-Up" (whose original title was "Las babas del diablo" [The Devil's Drool] but changed when the work was first translated into English, doubtless to capitalize on the film's release), see Daniel R. Reedy, "The Symbolic

Reality of Cortázar's "Las babas del diablo," *Revista Hispanica Moderna* 36 (1970–71): 224–37, and the papers from an NEH seminar on the story in *Dieciocho: Hispanic Enlightenment, Aesthetics, and Literary Theory* 8, no. 2 (Fall 1985), one of which by Leonard A. Cheever—"Memory and Truth in Cortázar's 'Blow-Up,'" but later attributed to both Cheever and Leslie N. Thompson—was reprinted in *RE: Artes Liberales* 12, no. 1 (Fall 1985): 14–17. For a discussion of the story and the film it inspired, see Henry Fernandez, "From Cortázar to Antonioni: Study of an Adaptation," *Film Heritage* 4, no. 2 (Winter 1968–69): 26–30, called to the editor's attention by Richard Wendorf, and Terry J. Peavler, *"Blow Up:* A Reconsideration of Antonioni's Infidelity to Cortázar," *PMLA* 94, no. 5 (October 1979): 887–93. See also a relevant but much simpler short story by Luigi Pirandello, "With Other Eyes," *Esquire* 2 (July 1934): 54–55, reprinted in *Esquire* (October 1973): 312–14, in which the female protagonist keeps seeing different meanings in the photograph of her husband's first wife that she accidentally discovers.

3. See Cortázar: *Prosa del observatorio* (Barcelona: Editorial Lumen, 1972), with his photographs of the observatory of Jai Singh in Jaipur, Delhi, and *Around the Day in Eighty Worlds,* trans. Thomas Christensen (San Francisco: North Point Press, 1986), with photos by Lewis Carroll, Eugene Smith, and Cortázar (whose photographs on pp. 202–9 recall the disquieting photographs of dolls by Hans Bellmer [1902–75]). See also Cortázar: *Ultimo Round* (Mexico: Siglo XXI Editores, 1969); *Buenos Aires, Buenos Aires,* with photographs by Alicia D'Amico and Sara Facio (Buenos Aires: Editorial Sudamericana, 1968); "Estrictamente no profesional," in *Humanario,* by Sarah Facio, Alicia D'Amico, and Cortázar (Buenos Aires: La Azotea, 1976); and *Territorios,* with photographs by Alicia d'Amico (Mexico City: Siglo Ventiuno Editore, 1978); and an essay in *Paris: Essence of an Image,* by Alecio de Andrade (Geneva: RotoVision, [1981]).

BLOW-UP

I t'll never be known how this has to be told, in the first person or in the second, using the third person plural or continually inventing modes that will serve for nothing. If one might say: I will see the moon rose, or: we hurt me at the back of my eyes, and especially: you the blond woman was the clouds that race before my your his our yours their faces. What the hell.

Seated ready to tell it, if one might go to drink a bock over there, and the typewriter continue by itself (because I use the machine), that would be perfection. And that's not just a manner of speaking. Perfection, yes, because here is the aperture which must be counted also as a machine (of another sort, a Contax I.I.2) and it is possible that one machine may know more about another machine than I, you, she—the blond—and the clouds. But I have the dumb luck to know that if I go this Remington will sit turned to stone on top of the table with the air of being twice as quiet that mobile things have when they are not moving. So, I have to write. One of us all has to write, if this is going to get told. Better that it be me who am dead, for I'm less compromised than the rest; I who see only the clouds and can think without being distracted, write without being distracted (there goes another, with a grey edge) and remember without being distracted, I who am dead (and I'm alive, I'm not trying to fool anybody, you'll see when we get to the moment, because I have to begin some way and I've begun with this period, the last one back, the one at the beginning, which in the end is the best of the periods when you want to tell something).

All of a sudden I wonder why I have to tell this, but if one begins to wonder why he does all he does do, if one wonders why he accepts an invitation to lunch (now a pigeon's flying by and it seems to me a sparrow), or why when someone has told us a good joke immediately there starts up something like a tickling in the stomach and we are not at peace until we've gone into the office across the hall and told the joke over again; then it feels good immediately, one is fine, happy, and can get back to work. For I imagine that no one has explained this, that really the best thing is to put aside all decorum and tell it, because, after all's done, nobody is ashamed of breathing or of putting on his shoes; they're things that you do, and when something weird happens, when you find a spider in your shoe or if you take a breath and feel like a broken window, then you have to tell what's happening, tell it to the guys at the office or to the doctor. Oh, doctor, every time I take a breath . . . Always tell it, always get rid of that tickle in the stomach that bothers you.

And now that we're finally going to tell it, let's put things a little bit in order, we'd be walking down the staircase in this house as far as Sunday, November 7, just a month back. One goes down five floors and stands then in the Sunday in the sun one would not have suspected of Paris in November, with a large appetite to walk around, to see things, to take photos (because we were photographers, I'm a photographer). I know that the most difficult thing is going to be finding a way to tell it, and I'm not afraid of repeating myself. It's going to be difficult because nobody really knows who it is telling it, if I am I or what actually occurred or what I'm seeing (clouds, and once in a while a pigeon) or if, simply, I'm telling a truth which is only my truth, and then is the truth only for my stomach, for this impulse to go running out and to finish up in some manner with, this, whatever it is.

We're going to tell it slowly, what happens in the middle of what I'm writing is coming already. If they replace me, if, so soon, I don't know what to say, if the clouds stop coming and something else starts (because it's impossible that this keep coming, clouds passing continually and occasionally a pigeon), if something out of all this . . . And after the "if" what am I going to put if I'm going to close the sentence structure correctly? But if I begin to ask questions, I'll never tell anything, maybe to tell would be like an answer, at least for someone who's reading it.

Roberto Michel, French-Chilean, translator and in his spare time an amateur photographer, left number 11, rue Monsieur-le-Prince Sunday November 7 of the current year (now there're two small ones passing, with silver linings). He had spent three weeks working on the French version of a treatise on challenges and appeals by José Norberto Allende, professor at the University of Santiago. It's rare that there's wind in Paris, and even less seldom a wind like this that swirled around corners and rose up to whip at old wooden venetian blinds behind which astonished ladies commented variously on how unreliable the weather had been these last few years. But the sun was out also, riding the wind and friend of the cats, so there was nothing that would keep me from taking a walk along the docks of the Seine and taking photos of the Conservatoire and Sainte-Chapelle. It was hardly ten o'clock, and I figured that by eleven the light would be good, the best you can get in the fall; to kill some time I detoured around by the Isle Saint-Louis and started to walk along the quai d'Anjou, I stared for a bit at the hôtel de Lauzun, I recited bits from Apollinaire* which always get into my head whenever I pass in front of the hôtel de Lauzun (and at that I ought to be remembering the other poet, but Michel is an obstinate beggar), and when the wind stopped all at once and the sun came out at least twice as hard (I mean warmer, but really it's the same thing), I sat down on the parapet and felt terribly happy in the Sunday morning.

One of the many ways of contesting level-zero, and one of the best, is to take photographs, an activity in which one should start becoming an adept very early in life, teach it to children since it requires discipline, aesthetic education, a good eye and steady fingers. I'm not talking about waylaying the lie like any old reporter, snapping the stupid silhouette of the VIP leaving number 10 Downing Street, but in all ways when one is walking about with a camera, one has almost a duty to be attentive, to not lose that abrupt and happy rebound of sun's rays off an old stone, or the pigtails-flying run of a small girl going home with a loaf of bread or a bottle of milk. Michel knew that the photographer always worked as a permutation

---

*Guillaume Apollinaire (1880-1918), an influential avant-garde French writer.

of his personal way of seeing the world as other than the camera insidiously imposed upon it (now a large cloud is going by, almost black), but he lacked no confidence in himself, knowing that he had only to go without the Contax to recover the keynote of distraction, the sight without a frame around it, light without the diaphragm aperture or 1/250 sec. Right now (what a word, *now*, what a dumb lie) I was able to sit quietly on the railing overlooking the river watching the red and black motorboats passing below without it occurring to me to think photographically of the scenes, nothing more than letting myself go in the letting go of objects, running immobile in the stream of time. And then the wind was not blowing.

After, I wandered down the quai de Bourbon until getting to the end of the isle where the intimate square was (intimate because it was small, not that it was hidden, it offered its whole breast to the river and the sky), I enjoyed it, a lot. Nothing there but a couple and, of course, pigeons; maybe even some of those which are flying past now so that I'm seeing them. A leap up and I settled on the wall, and let myself turn about and be caught and fixed by the sun, giving it my face and ears and hands (I kept my gloves in my pocket). I had no desire to shoot pictures, and lit a cigarette to be doing something; I think it was that moment when the match was about to touch the tobacco that I saw the young boy for the first time.

What I'd thought was a couple seemed much more now a boy with his mother, although at the same time I realized that it was not a kid and his mother, and that it was a couple in the sense that we always allegate to couples when we see them leaning up against the parapets or embracing on the benches in the squares. As I had nothing else to do, I had more than enough time to wonder why the boy was so nervous, like a young colt or a hare, sticking his hands into his pockets, taking them out immediately, one after the other, running his fingers through his hair, changing his stance, and especially why was he afraid, well, you could guess that from every gesture, a fear suffocated by his shyness, an impulse to step backwards which he telegraphed, his body standing as if it were on the edge of flight, holding itself back in a final, pitiful decorum.

All this was so clear, ten feet away—and we were alone against the parapet at the tip of the island—that at the beginning the boy's fright didn't let me see the blond very well. Now, thinking back on it, I see her much better at that first second when I read her face (she'd turned around suddenly, swinging like a metal weathercock, and the eyes, the eyes were there), when I vaguely understood what might have been occurring to the boy and figured it would be worth the trouble to stay and watch (the wind was blowing their words away and they were speaking in a low murmur). I think that

I know how to look, if it's something I know, and also that every looking oozes with mendacity, because it's that which expels us furthest outside ourselves, without the least guarantee, whereas to smell, or (but Michel rambles on to himself easily enough, there's no need to let him harangue on this way). In any case, if the likely inaccuracy can be seen beforehand, it becomes possible again to look; perhaps it suffices to choose between looking and the reality looked it, to strip things of all their unnecessary clothing. And surely all that is difficult besides.

As for the boy I remember the image before his actual body (that will clear itself up later), while now I am sure that I remember the woman's body much better than the image. She was thin and willowy, two unfair words to describe what she was, and was wearing an almost-black fur coat, almost long, almost handsome. All the morning's wind (now it was hardly a breeze and it wasn't cold) had blown through her blond hair which pared away her white, bleak face—two unfair words—and put the world at her feet and horribly alone in front of her dark eyes, her eyes fell on things like two eagles, two leaps into nothingness, two puffs of green slime. I'm not describing anything, it's more a matter of trying to understand it. And I said two puffs of green slime.

Let's be fair, the boy was well enough dressed and was sporting yellow gloves which I would have sworn belonged to his older brother, a student of law or sociology; it was pleasant to see the fingers of the gloves sticking out of his jacket pocket. For a long time I didn't see his face, barely a profile, not stupid—a terrified bird, a Fra Filippo* angel, rice pudding with milk—and the back of an adolescent who wants to take up judo and has had a scuffle or two in defense of an idea or his sister. Turning fourteen, perhaps fifteen, one would guess that he was dressed and fed by his parents but without a nickel in his pocket, having to debate with his buddies before making up his mind to buy a coffee, a cognac, a pack of cigarettes. He'd walk through the streets thinking of the girls in his class, about how good it would be to go to the movies and see the latest film, or to buy novels or neckties or bottles of liquor with green and white labels on them. At home (it would be a re-spectable home, lunch at noon and romantic landscapes on the walls, with a dark entryway and a mahogany umbrella stand inside the door) there'd be the slow rain of time, for studying, for being mama's hope, for looking like dad, for writing to his aunt in Avignon. So that there was a lot of walk-

---

*Fra Filippo di Tomasso Lippi (1406–69) was a Carmelite monk and noted Florentine art-ist of the early Renaissance who was later featured in one of Robert Browning's best known dramatic monologues, "Fra Lippo Lippi" (1855).

ing the streets, the whole of the river for him (but without a nickel) and the mysterious city of fifteen-year-olds with its signs in doorways, its terrifying cats, a paper of fried potatoes for thirty francs, the pornographic magazine folded four ways, a solitude like the emptiness of his pockets, the eagerness for so much that was incomprehensible but illuminated by a total love, by the availability analogous to the wind and the streets.

This biography was of the boy and of any boy whatsoever, but this particular one now, you could see he was insular, surrounded solely by the blond's presence as she continued talking with him. (I'm tired of insisting, but two long ragged ones just went by. That morning I don't think I looked at the sky once, because what was happening with the boy and the woman appeared so soon I could do nothing but look at them and wait, look at them and . . .) To cut it short, the boy was agitated and one could guess without too much trouble what had just occurred a few minutes before, at most half-an-hour. The boy had come onto the tip of the island, seen the woman and thought her marvelous. The woman was waiting for that because she was there waiting for that, or maybe the boy arrived before her and she saw him from one of the balconies or from a car and got out to meet him, starting the conversation with whatever, from the beginning she was sure that he was going to be afraid and want to run off, and that, naturally, he'd stay, stiff and sullen, pretending experience and the pleasure of the adventure. The rest was easy because it was happening ten feet away from me, and anyone could have gauged the stages of the game, the derisive, competitive fencing; its major attraction was not that it was happening but in foreseeing its denouement. The boy would try to end it by pretending a date, an obligation, whatever, and would go stumbling off disconcerted, wishing he were walking with some assurance, but naked under the mocking glance which would follow him until he was out of sight. Or rather, he would stay there, fascinated or simply incapable of taking the initiative, and the woman would begin to touch his face gently, muss his hair, still talking to him voicelessly, and soon would take him by the arm to lead him off, unless he, with an uneasiness beginning to tinge the edge of desire, even his stake in the adventure, would rouse himself to put his arm around her waist and to kiss her. Any of this could have happened, though it did not, and perversely Michel waited, sitting on the railing, making the settings almost without looking at the camera, ready to take a picturesque shot of a corner of the island with an uncommon couple talking and looking at one another.

Strange how the scene (almost nothing: two figures there mismatched in their youth) was taking on a disquieting aura. I thought it was I imposing it, and that my photo, if I shot it, would reconstitute things in their true stupidity. I would have liked to know what he was thinking, a man in a grey hat sitting at the wheel of a car parked on the dock which led up to the footbridge, and whether he was reading the paper or asleep. I had just discovered him because people inside a parked car have a tendency to disappear, they get lost in that wretched, private cage stripped of the beauty that motion and danger give it. And nevertheless, the car had been there the whole time, forming part (or deforming that part) of the isle. A car: like saying a lighted streetlamp, a park bench. Never like saying wind, sunlight, those elements always new to the skin and the eyes, and also the boy and the woman, unique, put there to change the island, to show it to me in another way. Finally, it may have been that the man with the newspaper also became aware of what was happening and would, like me, feel that malicious sensation of waiting for everything to happen. Now the woman had swung around smoothly, putting the young boy between herself and the wall, I saw them almost in profile, and he was taller, though not much taller, and yet she dominated him, it seemed like she was hovering over him (her laugh, all at once, a whip of feathers), crushing him just by being there, smiling, one hand taking a stroll through the air. Why wait any longer? Aperture at sixteen, a sighting which would not include the horrible black car, but yes, that tree, necessary to break up too much grey space . . .

I raised the camera, pretended to study a focus which did not include them, and waited and watched closely, sure that I would finally catch the revealing expression, one that would sum it all up, life hat is rhythmed by movement but which a stiff image destroys, taking time in cross section, if we do not choose the essential imperceptible fraction of it. I did not have to wait long. The woman was getting on with the job of handcuffing the boy smoothly, stripping from him what was left of his freedom a hair at a time, in an incredibly slow and delicious torture. I imagined the possible endings (now a small fluffy cloud appears, almost alone in the sky), I saw their arrival at the house (a basement apartment probably, which she would have filled with large cushions and cats) and conjectured the boy's terror and his desperate decision to play it cool and to be led off pretending there was nothing new in it for him. Closing my eyes, if I did in fact close my eyes, I set the scene: the teasing kisses, the woman mildly repelling the hands which were trying to undress her, like in novels, on a bed that would have a lilac-colored comforter, on the other hand she taking off his clothes, plainly mother and son under a milky yellow light, and everything would end up as usual, perhaps, but maybe everything would go otherwise, and the initiation of the adolescent would not happen, she would not let it happen, after a long prologue wherein the awkwardnesses, the exasperating caresses, the running of hands over bodies would be resolved in who knows what, in a separate and solitary pleasure, in a petulant denial mixed with the art of tiring and disconcerting so much poor innocence. It might go like that, it might very well go like that; that woman was not looking for the boy as a lover, and at the same time she was dominating him toward some end impossible to understand if you do not imagine it as a cruel game, the desire to desire without satisfaction, to excite herself for someone else, someone who in no way could be that kid.

Michel is guilty of making literature, of indulging in fabricated unrealities. Nothing pleases him more than to imagine exceptions to the rule, individuals outside the species, not-always-repugnant monsters. But that woman invited speculation, perhaps giving clues enough for the fantasy to hit the bullseye. Before she left, and now that she would fill my imaginings for several days, for I'm given to ruminating, I decided not to lose a moment more. I got it all into the view-finder (with the tree, the railing, the eleven-o'clock sun) and took the shot. In time to realize that they both had noticed and stood there looking at me, the boy surprised and as though questioning, but she was irritated, her face and body flat-footedly hostile, feeling robbed, ignominiously recorded on a small chemical image.

I might be able to tell it in much greater detail but it's not worth the trouble. The woman said that no one had the right to take a picture without permission, and demanded that I hand her over the film. All this in a dry, clear voice with a good Parisian accent, which rose in color and tone with every phrase. For my part, it hardly mattered whether she got the roll of film or not, but anyone who knows me will tell you, if you want anything from me, ask nicely. With the result that I restricted myself to formulating the opinion that not only was photography in public places not prohibited, but it was looked upon with decided favor, both private and official. And while that was getting said, I noticed on the sly how the boy was falling back, sort of actively backing up though without moving, and all at once (it seemed almost incredible) he turned and broke into a run, the poor kid, thinking that he was walking off and in fact in full flight, running past the side of the car, disappearing like a gossamer filament of angel-spit in the morning air.

But filaments of angel-spittle are also called devil-spit, and Michel had to endure rather particular curses, to hear himself called meddler and imbecile, taking great pains meanwhile to smile and to abate with simple movements of his head such a hard sell. As I was beginning to get tired, I heard the car door slam. The man in the grey hat was there, looking at us. It was only at that point that I realized he was playing a part in the comedy.

He began to walk toward us, carrying in his hand the paper he had been pretending to read. What I remember best is the grimace that twisted his mouth askew, it covered his face with wrinkles, changed somewhat both in location and shape because his lips trembled and the grimace went from one side of his mouth to the other as though it were on wheels, independent and involuntary. But the rest stayed fixed, a flour-powdered clown or bloodless man, dull dry skin, eyes deepset, the nostrils black and prominently visible, blacker than the eyebrows or hair or the black necktie. Walking cautiously as though the pavement hurt his feet; I saw patent-leather shoes with such thin soles that he must have felt every roughness in the pavement. I don't know why I got down off the railing, nor very well why I decided to not give them the photo, to refuse that demand in which I guessed at their fear and cowardice. The clown and the woman consulted one another in silence: we made a perfect and unbearable triangle, something I felt compelled to break with a crack of a whip. I laughed in their faces and began to walk off, a little more slowly, I imagine, than the boy. At the level of the first houses, beside the iron footbridge, I turned around to look at them. They were not moving, but the man had dropped his newspaper; it seemed to me that the woman, her back to the parapet, ran her hands over the stone with the classical and absurd gesture of someone pursued looking for a way out.

What happened after that happened here, almost just now, in a room on the fifth floor. Several days went by before Michel developed the photos he'd taken on Sunday; his shots of the Conservatoire and of Sainte-Chapelle were all they should be. Then he found two or three proof-shots he'd forgotten, a poor attempt to catch a cat perched astonishingly on the roof of a rambling public urinal, and also the shot of the blond and the kid. The negative was so good that he made an enlargement; the enlargement was so good that he made one very much larger, almost the size of a poster. It did not occur to him (now one wonders and wonders) that only the shots of the Conservatoire were worth so much work. Of the whole series, the snapshot of the tip of the island was the only one which interested him; he tacked up the enlargement on one wall of the room, and the first day he spent some time looking at it and remembering, that gloomy operation of comparing the memory with the gone reality; a frozen memory, like any photo, where nothing is missing, not even, and especially, nothingness, the true solidifier of the scene. There was the woman, there was the boy, the tree rigid above their heads, the sky as sharp as the stone of the parapet, clouds and stones melded into a single substance and inseparable (now one with sharp edges is going by, like a thunderhead). The first two days I accepted what I had done, from the photo itself to the enlargement on the wall, and didn't even question that every once in a while I would interrupt my translation of José Norberto Allende's treatise to encounter once more the woman's face, the dark splotches on the railing. I'm such a jerk; it had never occurred to me that when we look at a photo from the front, the eyes reproduce exactly the position and the vision of the lens; it's these things that are taken for granted and it never occurs to anyone to think about them. From my chair, with the typewriter directly in front of me, I looked at the photo ten feet away, and then it occurred to me that I had hung it exactly at the point of view of the lens. It looked very good that way; no doubt, it was the best way to appreciate a photo, though the angle from the diagonal doubtless has its pleasures and might even divulge different aspects. Every few minutes, for example when I was unable to find the way to say in good French what José Norberto Allende was saying in very good Spanish, I raised my eyes and looked at the photo; sometimes the woman would catch my eye, sometimes the boy, sometimes the pavement where a dry leaf had fallen admirably situated to heighten a lateral section. Then I rested a bit from my labors, and I enclosed myself again happily in that morning in which the photo was drenched, I recalled ironically the angry picture of the woman demanding I give her the photograph, the boy's pathetic and ridiculous flight, the entrance on the scene of the man with the white face. Basically, I was satisfied with myself; my part had not been too brilliant, and since the French have been given the gift of the sharp response, I did not see very well why I'd chosen to leave without a complete demonstration of the rights, privileges and prerogatives of citizens. The important thing, the really important thing was having helped the kid to escape in time (this in case my theorizing was correct, which was not sufficiently proven, but the running away itself seemed to show it so). Out of plain meddling, I had given him the opportunity finally to take advantage of his fright to do something useful; now he would be regretting it, feeling his honor impaired, his manhood diminished. That was better than the attentions of a woman capable of looking as she had looked at him on that island. Michel is something of a puritan at times, he believes that one should not seduce someone from a position of strength. In the last analysis, taking that photo had been a good act.

Well, it wasn't because of the good act that I looked at it between paragraphs while I was working. At that moment I didn't know the reason, the reason I had tacked the enlargement onto the wall; maybe all fatal acts happen that way, and that is the condition of their fulfillment. I don't think the almost-furtive trembling of the leaves on the tree alarmed me, I was working on a sentence and rounded it out successfully. Habits are like immense herbariums, in the end an enlargement of 32 x 28 looks like a movie screen, where, on the tip of the island, a woman is speaking with a boy and a tree is shaking its dry leaves over their heads.

But her hands were just too much. I had just translated: "In that case, the second key resides in the intrinsic nature of difficulties which societies . . ." —when I saw the woman's hand beginning to stir slowly, finger by finger. There was nothing left of me, a phrase in French which I would never have to finish, a typewriter on the floor, a chair that squeaked and shook, fog. The kid had ducked his head like boxers do when they've done all they can and are waiting for the final blow to fall; he had turned up the collar of his overcoat and seemed more a prisoner than ever, the perfect victim helping promote the catastrophe. Now the woman was talking into his ear, and her hand opened again to lay itself against his cheekbone, to caress and caress it, burning it, taking her time. The kid was less startled than he was suspicious, once or twice he poked his head over the woman's shoulder and she continued talking, saying something that made him look back every few minutes toward that area where Michel knew the car was parked and the man in the grey hat, carefully eliminated from the photo but present in the boy's eyes (how doubt that now) in the words of the woman, in the woman's hands, in the vicarious presence of the woman. When I saw the man come up, stop near them and look at them, his hands in his pockets and a stance somewhere between disgusted and demanding, the master who is about to whistle in his dog after a frolic in the square, I understood, if that was to understand, what had to happen now, what had to have happened then, what would have to happen at that moment, among these people, just where I had poked my nose in to upset an established order, interfering innocently in that which had not happened, but which was now going to happen, now was going to be fulfilled. And what I had imagined earlier was much less horrible than the reality, that woman, who was not there by herself, she was not caressing or propositioning or encouraging for her own pleasure, to lead the angel away with his tousled hair and play the tease with his terror and his eager grace. The real boss was waiting there, smiling petulantly, already certain of the business; he was not the first to send a woman in the vanguard, to bring him the prisoners manacled with flowers. The rest of it would be so simple, the car, some house or another, drinks, stimulating engravings, tardy tears, the awakening in hell. And there was nothing I could do, this time I could do absolutely nothing. My strength had been a photograph, that, there, where they were taking their revenge on me, demonstrating clearly what was going to happen. The photo had been taken, the time had run out, gone; we were so far from one another, the abusive act had certainly already taken place, the tears already shed, and the rest conjecture and sorrow. All at once the order was inverted, they were alive, moving, they were deciding and had decided, they were going to their future; and I on this side, prisoner of another time, in a room on the fifth floor, to not know who they were, that woman, that man, and that boy, to be only the lens of my camera, something fixed, rigid, incapable of intervention. It was horrible, their mocking me, deciding it before my impotent eye, mocking me, for the boy again was looking at the flour-faced clown and I had to accept the fact that he was going to say yes, that the proposition carried money with it or a gimmick, and I couldn't yell for him to run, or even open the road to him again with a new photo, a small and almost meek intervention which would ruin the framework of drool and perfume. Everything was going to resolve itself right there, at that moment; there was like an immense silence which had nothing to do with physical silence. It was stretching it out, setting itself up. I think I screamed, I screamed terribly, and that at that exact second I realized that I was beginning to move toward them, four inches, a step, another step, the tree swung its branches rhythmically in the foreground, a place where the railing was tarnished emerged from the frame, the woman's face turned toward me as though surprised, was enlarging, and then I turned a bit, I mean that the camera turned a little, and without losing sight of the woman, I began to close in on the man who was looking at me with the black holes he had in place of eyes, surprised and angered both, he looked, wanting to nail me onto the air, and at that instant I happened to see something like a large bird outside the focus that was flying in a single swoop in front of the picture, and I leaned up against the wall of my room and was happy because the boy had just managed to escape, I saw him running off, in focus again, sprinting with his hair flying in the wind, learning finally to fly across the island, to arrive at the footbridge, return to the city. For the second time he'd escaped them, for the second time I was helping him to escape, returning him to his precarious paradise. Out of breath, I stood in front of them; no need to step closer, the game was played out. Of the woman you could see just maybe a shoulder and a bit of the hair, brutally cut off by the frame of the picture; but the man was directly center, his mouth half open, you could see a shaking black tongue, and he lifted his hands slowly, bringing them into the foreground, an instant still in perfect focus, and then all of him a lump that blotted out the island, the tree, and I shut my eyes, I didn't want to see any more, and I covered my face and broke into tears like an idiot.

Now there's a big white cloud, as on all these days, all this untellable time. What remains to be said is always a cloud, two clouds, or long hours of a sky perfectly clear, a very clean, clear rectangle tacked up with pins on the wall of my room. That was what I saw when I opened my eyes and dried them with my fingers: the clear sky, and then a cloud that drifted in from the left, passed gracefully and slowly across and disappeared on the right. And then another, and for a change sometimes, everything gets grey, all one enormous cloud, and suddenly the splotches of rain cracking down, for a long spell you can see it raining over the picture, like a spell of weeping reversed, and little by little, the frame becomes clear, perhaps the sun comes out, and again the clouds begin to come, two at a time, three at a time. And the pigeons once in a while, and a sparrow or two.

THE DAY OF
THE DYING RABBIT
1969

—

"The short story may be what I do best," declared Updike (1932–), whose polished style and perceptive domestic insights are perhaps more consistently evident in this genre than in his novels.[1] He is also a talented comic draftsman who has studied and written about art, including photography.[2] Updike uses a camera himself— more often when he was "at the peak of my taking-pics-of-the-kids phrase, a phase I guess most American men go through"[3] —and has used photography in a variety of ways throughout his writing. He devoted several early poems to the subject, accompanying some of them with family photographs in "Midpoint" (1969), written about the same time as this tender tale whose narrator is a professional photographer trying to recapture happy family moments.[4] Another photographer is the guest of honor at a chic New York party in Bech Is Back *(1982), which wittily reflects the rise in the commercial value of photographs and the consequent celebrity status of photographers.[5] Updike has subsequently written several essays on photography, including a foreword for a catalogue to accompany an exhibition of pictures by fifteen eminent photographers of their own family members; a description of the photograph he thought most memorable; an afterword to a reissue of Edward Steichen's* First Picture Book *(1930) for young readers; introductions to a book of Magnum photographs and literary portraits by Jill Krementz; and poems for an alphabet with photographic illustrations by one of his own children.[6]*

1. Updike, quoted in Robert M. Luscher, *John Updike: A Study of the Short Fiction* (New York: Twayne, 1993), p. 171.

2. Updike studied at the Ruskin School of Drawing and Fine Art at Oxford (1954–55) and has written a lot of art criticism. His most recent volume on the subject, *Just Looking: Essays on Art* (New York: Knopf, 1989), does not include a piece about pho-

tography, but a future volume of collected essays could conceivably be devoted to the subject, no doubt including many, if not all, of the pieces cited below in n. 6.

3. Updike, quoted from his letter to the editor, February 28, 1991. A celebrated writer since his college years, Updike has been photographed often, most frequently perhaps by Jill Krementz. See her remarks about Updike in *Something About the Author Autobiography Series*, vol. 8, p. 176; four of her portraits of him and his family, 1975 and 1979, included in *The Writer's Image: Literary Portraits*, with an introduction by Kurt Vonnegut (Boston: David Godine, 1980), npn., and three others in *The Writer's Desk* (New York: Random House, 1996), pp. ix, x, and xiii.

4. See Updike: "Midpoint," pp. 3–44, especially pp. 12–13, 23–37, and "Camera," p. 54, in *Midpoint and Other Poems* (New York: Knopf, 1969); "Exposure," p. 22, and "Meditation on a News Item," pp. 37–39, in *Telephone Poles and Other Poems* (New York: Knopf, 1963); "Snapshots" in *The Carpentered Hen and Other Tame Creatures* (New York: Harper & Brothers, 1958), pp. 59–60. See also Updike, "The Day of the Dying Rabbit," in *Museums and Women and Other Stories* (New York: Knopf, 1972), pp. 26–40—interestingly analyzed by Diane Culbertson, "Updike's 'The Day of the Dying Rabbit,'" *Studies in American Fiction* 7 (1979): 95–99; and Luscher, *John Updike*, pp. 94–95, 171—and "Ethiopia," in *Problems and Other Stories* (New York: Knopf, 1979), pp. 77–87.

5. See Updike, "White on White," from *Bech Is Back* (New York: Alfred A. Knopf, 1982), pp. 180–95. Updike has also drawn on photographs for action and imagery in other fiction: "From the Journal of a Leper," in *Problems and Other Stories* (New York: Knopf, 1979), pp. 184, 187; and in "Bech Panics," in *Bech: A Book* (New York: Knopf, 1970), pp. 99–132.

6. See Updike: "Just Family: Family Photographs by 15 American Photographers," unpub. MS, slightly revised as "All in the Family" in Rabb, *Literature and Photography*, pp. 521–28; "A State of Ecstasy" [about the image of a 'Dancing Wahine' celebrating Hawaii's statehood in *Life* (March 23, 1959): 25)], *Art and Antiques* (January 1990): 74–75; "First Things First," *Art and Antiques* (October 1991): 56–61, also published as "The Steichens' Book of First Things," an afterword to a reissue of Mary Steichen Calderone and Edward Steichen, *The First Picture Book: Everyday Things for Babies* (New York: Library Fellows of the Whitney Museum of American Art, 1991), originally published by Mary Steichen [then Martin], (New York: Harcourt Brace, 1930); introduction to *Heroes and Anti-Heroes: Magnum Images* (New York: Random House, 1991), pp. 10–23, and to Krementz, *The Writer's Desk*, pp. viii–xii; and *A Helpful Alphabet of Friendly Objects*, with photographs by David Updike (New York: Knopf, 1995).

THE DAY OF
THE DYING RABBIT

The shutter clicks, and what is captured is mostly accident—that happy foreground diagonal, the telling expression forever pinned in mid-flight between two plateaus of vacuity. Margaret and I didn't exactly intend to have six children. At first, we were trying until we got a boy. Then, after Jimmy arrived, it was half our trying to give him a brother so he wouldn't turn queer under all those sisters, and half our missing, the both of us, the way new babies are. You know how they are—delicate as film, wrapped in bunting instead of lead foil, but coiled with that same miraculous brimming whatever-it-is: *susceptibility*, let's say. That wobbly hot head. Those navy-blue eyes with the pupils set at f/2. The wrists hinged on silk and the soles of the feet as tender as the eyelids: film that fine-grained would show a doghouse roof from five miles up.

Also, I'm a photographer by trade and one trick of the trade is a lot of takes. In fact, all six kids have turned out pretty well, now that we've got the baby's feet to stop looking at each other and Deirdre fitted out with glasses. Having so many works smoothly enough in the city, where I go off to the studio and they go off to school, but on vacations things tend to jam. We rent the same four-room shack every August. When the cat dragged in as a love-present this mauled rabbit it had caught, it was minutes before I could get close enough even to *see*.

Henrietta—she's the second youngest, the last girl—screamed. There are screams like flashbulbs—just that cold. This one brought Linda out from her murder mystery and Cora up from her Beatles magazine, and they crowded into the corridor that goes with the bedrooms the landlord added to the shack to make it more rentable and that isn't wide enough for two pairs of shoulders. Off this corridor into the outdoors is a salt-pimpled aluminum screen door with a misadjusted pneumatic attachment that snaps like lightning the first two-thirds of its arc and then closes the last third slow as a clock, ticking. That's how the cat got in. It wasn't our cat exactly, just a tattered calico stray the children had been feeding salami scraps to out in the field between our yard and the freshwater pond. Deirdre had been helping Margaret with the dishes, and they piled into the corridor just ahead of me, in time to hear Linda let crash with a collection of those four-letter words that come out of her face more and more. The more pop out, the more angelic her face grows. She is thirteen, and in a few years I suppose it will be liquor and drugs, going in. I don't know where she gets the words, or how to stop them coming. Her cheeks are trimming down, her nose bones edging up, her mouth getting witty in the corners, and her eyes gathering depth; and I don't know how to stop that coming, either. Faces, when you look at them through a lens, are passageways for angels, sometimes whole clouds of them. Jimmy told me the other day—he's been reading books of records, mostly sports—about a man so fat he had been buried in a piano case for a casket, and he asked me what a casket was, and I told him, and a dozen angels overlapped in his face as he mentally matched up casket with fatness, and piano, and earth; and got the picture. Click.

After Linda's swearing, there was the sound of a slap and a second's silence while it developed who had been hit: Henrietta. Her crying clawed the corridor walls, and down among our legs the cat reconsidered its offer to negotiate and streaked back out the screen door, those last ticking inches, leaving the rabbit with us. Now I could see it: a half-grown rabbit huddled like a fur doorstop in the doorway to the bigger girls' room. No one dared touch it. We froze around it in a circle. Henrietta was still sobbing, and Cora's transistor was keeping the beat with static, like a heart stuffed with steel wool. Then God came down the hall from the smaller children's room.

Godfrey is the baby, the second boy. We were getting harder up for names, which was one reason we stopped. Another was, the club feet seemed a warning. He was slow to walk after they took the casts off, and at age four he marches along with an unstoppable sort of deliberate dignity, on these undeformed but somehow distinctly rectangular big feet. He pushed his way through our legs and without hesitation squatted and picked up the rabbit. Cora, the most squeamish of the children—the others are always putting worms down her back—squealed, and God twitched and flipped the bunny back to the floor; it hit neck first, and lay there looking bent. Linda punched Cora, and Henrietta jabbed God, but still none of the rest of us was willing to touch the rabbit, which might be dead this time, so we let God try again. We needed Jimmy. He and Deirdre have the natural touch—middle children tend to. But all month he's been out of the shack, out of our way, playing catch with himself, rowing in the pond, brooding on what it means to be a boy. He's ten. I've missed him. A father is like a dog—he needs a boy for a friend.

This time in God's arms, the rabbit made a sudden motion that felt ticklish, and got dropped again, but the sign of life was reassuring, and Deirdre pushed through at last, and all evening there we were, paying sick calls on this shoebox, whispering, while Deirdre and Henrietta alternately dribbled milk in a dropper, and God kept trying to turn it into a Steiff stuffed animal, and Cora kept screwing up her nerve to look the bunny in its left eye, which had been a little chewed, so it looked like isinglass. Jimmy came in from the pond after dark and stood at the foot of Deirdre's bed, watching her try to nurse the rabbit back to health with a dropper of stale milk. She was crooning and crying. No fuss; just the tears. The rabbit was lying panting on its right side, the bad eye up. Linda was on the next bed, reading her mystery, above it all. God was asleep. Jimmy's nostrils pinched in, and he turned his back on the whole business. He had got the picture. The rabbit was going to die. At the back of my brain I felt tired, damp, and cold.

What was it in the next twenty-four hours that slowly flooded me, that makes me want to get the day on some kind of film? I don't know exactly, so I must put everything in, however underexposed.

Linda and Cora were still awake when headlights boomed in the driveway—we're a city block from the nearest house and a half mile from the road—and the Pingrees came by. Ian works for an ad agency I've photographed some nudes shampooing in the shower for, and on vacation he lives in boat-neck shirts and cherry-red Bermudas and blue sunglasses, and grows a salt-and-pepper beard—a Verichrome fathead, and nearsighted at that. But his wife, Jenny, is nifty: low forehead, like a fox. Freckles. Thick red sun-dulled hair ironed flat down her back. Hips. And an angle about her legs, the way they're put together, slightly bowed but with the something big and bland and smooth and unimpeachable about the thighs that you usually find only in the fenders of new cars. Though she's very serious and liberal and agitated these days, I could look at her forever, she's such fun for the eyes. Which isn't the same as being photogenic. The few shots I've taken of her show a staring woman with baby fat, whereas some skinny snit who isn't even a name to me comes over in the magazines as my personal version of Eros. The camera does lie, all the time. It has to.

Margaret doesn't mind the Pingrees, which isn't the same as liking them, but in recent years she doesn't much admit to liking anybody; so it was midnight when they left, all of us giddy with drink and talk under the stars, that seem so presiding and reproachful when you're drunk, shouting goodbye in the driveway, and agreeing on tennis tomorrow. I remembered the rabbit. Deirdre, Linda, and Cora were asleep, Linda with the light still on and the mystery rising and falling on her chest, Cora floating above her, in the upper bunk bed. The rabbit was in the shoebox under a protective lean-to of cookout grilles, in case the cat came back. We moved a grille aside and lit a match, expecting the rabbit to be dead. Photograph by sulphur-glow: undertakers at work. But though the rabbit wasn't hopping, the whiskers were moving, back and forth no more than a millimeter or two at the tips, but enough to signify breathing, life, hope, what else? Eternal solicitude brooding above us, also holding a match, and burning Its fingers. Our detection of life, magnified by liquor, emboldened us to make love for the first time in, oh, days beyond counting. She's always tired, and says the Pill depresses her, and a kind of arms race of avoidance has grown up around her complaints. Moonlight muted by window screens. Great eyesockets beneath me, looking up. To the shack smells of mist and cedar and salt we added musk. Margaret slipped into sleep quick as a fish afterward, but for an uncertain length of time—the hours after midnight lose their numbers, if you don't remind them with a luminous dial—I lay there, the rabbit swollen huge and oppressive, blanketing all of us, a clenching of the nerves snatching me back from sleep by a whisker, the breathing and rustling all around me precarious, the rumbling and swaying of a ship that at any moment, the next or then the next, might hit an iceberg.

Morning. The rabbit took some milk, and his isinglass eye slightly widened. The children triumphantly crowed. Jubilant sun-sparkle on the sea beyond the sand beyond the pond. We rowed across, six in the rowboat and two in the kayak. The tides had been high in the night, delivering debris dropped between here and Portugal. Jimmy walked far down the beach, collecting light bulbs jettisoned from ships—they are vacuums and will float forever, if you let them. I had put the 135mm. telephoto on the Nikon and loaded in a roll of Plus-X and took some shots of the children (Cora's face, horrified and ecstatic, caught in the translucent wall of a breaker about to submerge her; Godfrey, his close-cut blond hair shiny as a helmet, a Tritonesque strand of kelp slung across his shoulders) but most of grass and sand and shadows, close-up, using the ultraviolet filter, trying to get, what may be ungettable, the way the shadow edges stagger from grain to grain on the sand, and the way some bent-over grass blades draw circles around themselves, to keep time away.

Jimmy brought the bulbs back and arranged them in order of size, and before I could get to him had methodically smashed two. All I could see was bleeding feet but I didn't mean to grab him so hard. The marks of my hand were still red on his arm a half hour later. Our fight depressed Henrietta; like a seismograph, she feels all violence as hers. God said he was hungry and Deirdre began to worry about the rabbit: there is this puffy look children's faces get that I associate with guilt but that can also signal grief. Deirdre and Jimmy took the kayak, to be there first, and Linda, who maybe thinks the exercise will improve her bosom, rowed the rest of us to our dock. We walked to the house, heads down. Our path is full of poison ivy, our scorched lawn full of flat thistles. In our absence, the rabbit, still lying on its side, had created a tidy little heap of pellet-like feces. The children were ecstatic; they had a dirty joke and a miracle all in one. The rabbit's recovery was assured. But the eye looked cloudier to me, and the arc of the whisker tips even more fractional.

Lunch: soup and sandwiches. In the sky, the clouding over from the west that often arrives around noon. The level of light moved down, and the hands of the year swept forward a month. It was autumn, every blade of grass shining. August has this tinny, shifty quality, the only month without a holiday to pin it down. Our tennis date was at two. You can picture for yourself Jenny Pingree in tennis whites: those rounded guileless thighs, and the bobbing, flying hair tied behind with a kerchief of blue gauze, and that humorless, utterly intent clumsiness—especially when catching the balls tossed to her as server—that we love in children, trained animals, and women who are normally graceful. She and I, thanks to my predatory net play, took Ian and Margaret, 6–3, and the next set was called at 4–4, when our hour on the court ran out. A moral triumph for Margaret, who played like the swinger of fifteen years ago, and passed me in the alley half a dozen times. Dazzling with sweat, she took the car and went shopping with the four children who had come along to the courts; Linda had stayed in the shack with another book, and Jimmy had walked to a neighboring house, where there was a boy his age. The Pingrees dropped me off at our mailbox. Since they were going back to the city Sunday, we had agreed on a beach picnic tonight. The mail consisted of forwarded bills, pencil-printed letters to the children from their friends on other islands or beside lakes, and *Life*. While walking down our dirt road I flicked through an overgorgeous photographic essay on Afghanistan. Hurrying blurred women in peacock-colored saris, mud palaces, rose dust, silver rivers high in the Hindu Kush. An entire valley—misted, forested earth—filled the center page spread. The *lenses* those people have! Nothing beautiful on earth is as selfless as a beautiful lens.

Entering the shack, I shouted out to Linda, "It's just me," thinking she would be afraid of rapists. I went into her room and looked in the shoebox. The eye was lustreless and the whiskers had stopped moving, even infinitesimally.

"I think the bunny's had it," I said.

"Don't make me look," she said, propped up in the lower bunk, keeping her eyes deep in a paperback titled *A Stitch in Time Kills Nine*. The cover showed a dressmaker's dummy pierced by a stiletto, and bleeding. "I couldn't *stand* it," she said.

"What should I do?" I asked her.

"Bury it." She might have been reading from the book. Her profile, I noticed, was becoming a cameo, with a lovely gentle bulge to the forehead, high like Margaret's. I hoped being intelligent wouldn't cramp her life.

"Deirdre will want to see it," I argued. "It's her baby."

"It will only make her *sad*," Linda said. "And dis*gust* me. Already it must be *full* of *ver*min."

Nothing goads me to courage like some woman's taking a high tone. Afraid to touch the rabbit's body while life was haunting it, I touched it now, and found it tepid, and lifted it from the box. The body, far from stiff, felt unhinged; its back or neck must have been broken since the moment the cat pounced. Blood had dried in the ear—an intricate tunnel leading brainwards, velvety at the tip, oddly muscular at the root. The eye not of isinglass was an opaque black bead. Linda was right; there was no need for Deirdre to see. I took the rabbit out beyond the prickly yard, into the field, and laid it beneath the least stunted swamp oak, where any child who wanted to be sure that I hadn't buried it alive could come and find it. I put a marsh marigold by its nose, in case it was resurrected and needed to eat, and paused above the composition—fur, flower, the arty shape of fallen oak leaves—with a self-congratulatory sensation that must have carried on my face back to the shack, for Margaret, in the kitchen loading the refrigerator, looked up at me and said, "Say. I don't mind your being partners with Jenny, but you don't have to toss the balls to her in that cute confiding way."

"The poor bitch can't catch them otherwise. You saw that."

"I saw more than I wanted to. I nearly threw up."

"That second set," I said, "your backhand was terrific. The Maggie-O of old."

Deirdre came down the hall from the bedrooms. Her eyes seemed enormous; I went to her and kneeled to hold her around the waist, and began, "Sweetie, I have some sad news."

"Linda told me," she said, and walked by me into the kitchen. "Mommy, can I make the cocoa?"

"You did everything you could," I called after her. "You were a wonderful nurse and made the bunny's last day very happy."

"I know," she called in answer. "Mommy, I *promise* I won't let the milk boil over this time."

Of the children, only Henrietta and Godfrey let me lead them to where the rabbit rested. Henrietta skittishly hung back and never came closer than ten yards. God marched close, gazed down sternly, and said, "Get up." Nothing happened, except the ordinary motions of the day: the gulls and stately geese beating home above the pond, the traffic roaring invisible along the highway. He squatted down, and I prevented him from picking up the rabbit, before I saw it was the flower he was after.

Jimmy, then, was the only one who cried. He came home a half hour after we had meant to set out rowing across the pond to the beach picnic, and rushed into the field toward the tree with the tallest silhouette and came back carrying on his cheeks stains he tried to hide by thumping God. "If *you* hadn't dropped him," he said. "You *baby*."

"It was nobody's fault," Margaret told him, impatiently cradling her basket of hot dogs and raw hamburger.

"I'm going to kill that cat," Jimmy said. He added, cleverly, an old grievance: "Other kids my age have BB guns."

"Oh, our big man," Cora said. He flew at her in a flurry of fists and sobs, and ran away and hid. At the dock I let Linda and Cora take the kayak, and the rest of us waited a good ten minutes with the rowboat before Jimmy ran down the path in the dusk, himself a silhouette, like the stunted trees and the dark bar of dunes between two sheets of reflected sunset. Ever notice how sunsets upside down look like stairs?

"Somehow," Margaret said to me, as we waited, "you've deliberately dramatized this." But nothing could fleck the happiness widening within me, to capture the dying light.

The Pingrees had brought swordfish and another, older couple—the man was perhaps an advertising client. Though he was tanned like a tobacco leaf and wore the smartest summer playclothes, a pleading uncertainty in his manner seemed to crave the support of advertisement. His wife had once been beautiful and held herself lightly, lithely at attention—a soldier in the war of self-preservation. With them came two teen-age boys clad in jeans and buttonless vests and hair so long their summer complexions had remained sallow. One was their son, the other his friend. We all collected driftwood—a wandering, lonely, prehistoric task that frightens me. Darkness descended too soon, as it does in the tropics, where the warmth leads us to expect an endless June evening from childhood. We made a game of popping champagne corks, the kids trying to catch them on the fly. Startling, how high they soared, in the open air. The two boys gathered around Linda, and I protectively eavesdropped, and was shamed by the innocence and long childish pauses of what I overheard: "Philadelphia . . . just been in the airport, on our way to my uncle's, he lives in Virginia . . . wonderful horses, super . . . it's not actually blue, just bluey-green, blue only I guess by comparison . . . was in France once, and went to the races . . . never been . . . I want to go." Margaret and Jenny, kneeling in the sand to cook, setting out paper plates on tables that were merely wide pieces of driftwood, seemed sisters. The woman of the strange couple tried to flirt with me, talking of foreign places: "Paris is so dead, suddenly . . . the girls fly over to London to buy their clothes, and then their mothers won't let them wear them . . . Malta . . . Istanbul . . . life . . . sincerity . . . the *people* . . . the poor Greeks . . . a friend absolutely assures me, the C.I.A. engineered . . . apparently used the NATO contingency plan." Another champagne cork sailed in the air, hesitated, and drifted down, Jimmy diving but missing, having misjudged. A remote light, a lightship, or the promontory of a continent hidden in daylight, materialized on the horizon, beyond the shushing of the surf. Margaret and Jenny served us. Hamburgers and swordfish full of woodsmoke. Celery and sand. God, sticky with things he had spilled upon himself, sucked his thumb and rubbed against Margaret's legs. Jimmy came to me, furious because the big boys wouldn't Indian-wrestle with him, only with Linda and Cora: "Showing off for their boyfriends . . . whacked me for no reason . . . just because I said 'sex bomb.' "

We sat in a ring, survivors, around the fire, the heart of a collapsing star, fed anew by paper plates. The man of the older couple, in whose breath the champagne had undergone an acrid chemical transformation, told me about his money—how as a youth just out of business school, in the depths of the Depression, he had made a million dollars in some deal involving Stalin and surplus wheat. He had liked Stalin, and Stalin had liked him. "The thing we must realize about your Communist is that he's just another kind of businessman." Across the fire I watched his wife, spurned by me, ardently gesturing with the teen-age boy who was not her son, and wondered how I would take their picture. Tri-X, wide-open, at 1/60; but the shadows would be lost, the subtle events within them, and the highlights would be vapid blobs. There is no adjustment, no darkroom trickery, equivalent to the elastic tolerance of our eyes as they travel.

As my new friend murmured on and on about his money, and the champagne warming in my hand released carbon dioxide to the air, exposures flickered in and out around the fire: glances, inklings, angels. Margaret gazing, the nick of a frown erect between her brows. Henrietta's face vertically compressing above an ear of corn she was devouring. The well-preserved woman's face a mask of bronze with cunningly welded seams, but her hand an exclamatory white as it touched her son's friend's arm in some conversational urgency lost in the crackle of driftwood. The halo of hair around Ian's knees, innocent as babies' pates. Jenny's hair an elongated flurry as she turned to speak to the older couple's son; his bearded face was a blur in the shadows, melancholy, the eyes seeming closed, like the Jesus on a faded, drooping veronica. I heard Jenny say, ". . . *must* destroy the system! We've forgotten how to *love!*" Deirdre's glasses, catching the light, leaped like moth wings toward the fire, escaping perspective. Beside me, the old man's face went silent, and suffered a deflation wherein nothing held firm but the reflected glitter of firelight on a tooth his grimace had absent-mindedly left exposed. Beyond him, on the edge of the light, Cora and Linda were revealed sitting together, their legs stretched out long before them, warming, their faces in shadow, sexless and solemn, as if attentive to the sensations of the revolution of the earth beneath them. Godfrey was asleep, his head pillowed on Margaret's thigh, his body suddenly wrenched by a dream sob, and a heavy succeeding sigh.

It was strange, after these fragmentary illuminations, to stumble through the unseen sand and grass, with our blankets and belongings, to the boats on the shore of the pond. Margaret and five children took the rowboat; I nominated Jimmy to come with me in the kayak. The night was starless. The pond, between the retreating campfire and the slowly nearing lights of our neighbors' houses, was black. I could scarcely see his silhouette as it struggled for the rhythm of the stroke: left, a little turn with the wrists, right, the little turn reversed, left. Our paddles occasionally clashed, or snagged on the weeds that clog this pond. But the kayak sits lightly, and soon we put the confused conversation of the rowers, and their wildly careening flashlight beam, behind. Silence widened around us. Steering the rudder with the foot pedals, I let Jimmy paddle alone, and stared upward until I had produced, in the hazed sky overhead, a single, unsteady star. It winked out. I returned to paddling and received an astonishing impression of phosphorescence: every stroke, right and left, called into visibility a rich arc of sparks, animalcula hailing our passage with bright shouts. The pond was more populous than China. My son and I were afloat on a firmament warmer than the heavens.

"Hey, Dad."

His voice broke the silence carefully; my benevolence engulfed him, my fellow-wanderer, my leader, my gentle, secretive future. "What, Jimmy?"

"I think we're about to hit something."

We stopped paddling, and a mass, gray etched on gray, higher than a man, glided swiftly toward us and struck the prow of the kayak. With this bump, and my awakening laugh, the day of the dying rabbit ended. Exulting in homogenous glory, I had steered us into the bank. We pushed off, and by the lights of our neighbors' houses navigated to the dock, and waited for the rowboat with its tangle of voices and impatience and things that would snag. The days since have been merely happy days. This day was singular in its, let's say, *gallantry:* between the cat's gallant intentions and my son's gallantly calm warning, the dying rabbit sank like film in the developing pan, and preserved us all.

GUY DAVENPORT

THE INVENTION OF PHOTOGRAPHY IN TOLEDO

1976/1979

―――――

Davenport (1927–), an essayist, poet, editor, librettist, translator of classical Greek, and occasional amateur photographer, is probably best known as a scholar and a teacher; indeed, he asserts that "all my writings are extensions of the class-room."[1] He turned to creative writing at age forty-three for the first time since undergraduate days. Davenport's short stories, even this one — a dream-like "improvisation," which was "written at one sitting, in less than an hour" at the request of an editor wanting "something imaginative and far-out"[2] — are often erudite "assemblages of history and necessary fiction."[3] As here, they are often accompanied by his own illustrations, sometimes based on real photographs.[4] Davenport clearly appreciates the power of photographs and has enjoyed the friendship of photographers, such as Ralph Eugene Meatyard, and writers who took pictures seriously, such as Thomas Merton and Jonathan Williams.[5] Davenport says the theme of this short story "would seem to be that photography is the most ambiguous of the arts while enjoying the reputation of being the last advance in realism."[6] He suggests the futility of ascribing reality to anything, whether a single word (like Toledo) or single images (like Niépce's famous self-erasing one of geese or an anonymous one in which Trotsky's head is replaced by Stalin's). And Davenport praises his invented historian of photography in this narrative for seeking more creative work, though such an endeavor is likely to be misunderstood by the world.

1. Davenport, "Guy Davenport" in *Contemporary Authors*, edited by Deborah A. Straub (Detroit: Gale Research, 1988), vol. 23, p. 115.

2. Davenport, in letters to the editor on June 3 and 14, 1994, explains that the original version of this piece, which he assumed few people would ever see, was composed directly on the typewriter for John Bernard Myers, the editor and publisher of *Parenthèse*, then a new, experimental magazine.

3. Davenport, "Guy Davenport," p. 113.

4. Davenport, in his "Acknowledgments" for *Da Vinci's Bicycle* (Baltimore: Johns Hopkins University Press), p. xi, states: "The drawings accompanying 'The Invention of Photography in Toledo' are derived from Edward S. Curtis (the Mohave girl), Nadar (Rossini), and a photograph of the young Van Gogh (c. 1866) in the possession of Pastor J. P. Scholte-van Houten, Lochem." The author adds, in the letters to the editor cited above, "That I translated the illustrations from photographs to pen-and-ink must mean something. . . . The ones I did choose, and drew in pen-and-ink make a kind of subtext. The drawing of these photos took about a hundred hours," in contrast to the one hour it took to write the piece. The original version, which appeared in *Parenthèse* 1-2, no. 3 (Spring 1976): 141-49, reproduces four photographs identified (unsequentially) on p. 196 as being by "Cecil Beaton [editor's note: probably the one representing Boxer], Berenice Abbott, Atget [editor's note: the Cart?], and Lazerge and Dallemagne"; yet, as Davenport notes in his letter of June 14, the Abrizio portrait is clearly signed on the lower right corner by Nadar, but, as he "had nothing to do with choosing these photos, I don't see any advantage to discussing them."

5. See Davenport: Introduction to Jonathan Williams, *An Ear in Bartram's Tree: Selected Poems 1957-1967* (Chapel Hill: University of North Carolina Press, 1969), reprinted New York: New Directions, 1972, and as "Jonathan Williams" in *The Geography of the Imagination: Forty Essays* (San Francisco: North Point Press, 1981); "Eudora Welty: Guy Davenport Celebrates a Writer and Photographer," *Aperture* 81 (1978): 48-59; Introduction to Jonathan Williams, *Elite/Elate: Selected Poems, 1971-75*, with a portfolio of photographs by Guy Mendes (Highlands, N.C.: Jargon Society, 1979); "Ralph Eugene Meatyard: Eight Photographs," *Kentucky Review* 2, no. 1 (February 1968): 33-36; "Reminiscence," in *Ralph Eugene Meatyard*, edited by James Baker Hall, *Aperture* 18, nos. 3 & 4 (1974): 127-31, [reissued as a book (Millerton, N.Y.: Aperture, 1974)], and reprinted as "Ralph Eugene Meatyard," in *Geography of the Imagination* (San Francisco: North Point Press, 1981); "Tom and Gene," Introduction to Ralph Eugene Meatyard, *Father Louie: Photographs of Thomas Merton* (New York: Timken, 1991). See also the Merton and Williams selections in Rabb, ed., *Literature and Photography*, pp. 449-57 and 511-14 respectively.

6. Davenport, letter to the editor, June 3, 1994.

THE INVENTION OF
PHOTOGRAPHY IN TOLEDO[1]

B itumen of Judea dissolves in oil of lavender in greater or lesser densities of saturation according to its exposure to light, and thus Joseph Nicéphore Niepce in the year of Thomas Jefferson's death photographed his barnyard at Chalon-sur Saône.[2] Hours of light streaming through a pinhole onto pewter soaked asphalt into lavender in mechanical imitation of light focussed on a retina by the lens of an eye.

The result, turned right side up, was pure de Chirico.[3]

Light, from a source so remote that its presence on a French farm is as alien as a plum tree blossoming upon the inert slag of the moon, projects a rhomboid of shadow, a cone of light. A wall. A barn. Geese walking back and forth across the barnyard erased themselves during the long exposure.

Foco Betún y Espliego,[4] the historian of photography, spends several pages sorting out the claims of Friedrich Wilhelm Herschel[5] and Nicéphore Niepce to the invention of photography and decides that the issue cannot be resolved without more evidence. Herschel, the discoverer of The George Star which Fourier the philosopher and Joel Barlow,[6] in his unfinished epic on the Erie Canal, called the planet Herschel, and which is now known as Uranus.

A small town safe in its whereabouts, Titus Livy said of Toledo.[7] It sits on a promontory at a convergence of rivers.

Has not a silver cornet band strutted down its streets in shakos and scarlet sashes, playing with brio and a kind of melancholy elation *Santa Ana's Retreat from Buena Vista?*[8] Swan Creek flows through its downtown into the blue Maumee, which flows into Lake Erie. It bore the name of Port Lawrence until Marcus Fulvius Nobilor erected the *fasces* and eagles of the SPQR in 193.[9] Originally a part of Michigan until Andrew Jackson gave his nod to Ohio's claim, the fierce violet of its stormy skies inspired El Greco to paint his famous view of the city.[10] It was in Toledo that the Visigoths joined the church and made Spain Catholic. And in 1897 Samuel L. (Golden Rule) Jones was elected mayor on the Independent ticket.[11] Its incredible sunsets began to appear in late Roman eclogues.

When the summer is green with grasshoppers and yellow with wasps, the shining Tagus slips under its arched bridges around the three sides of Toledo.[12] The house where photography was invented sits on a Roman base, its walls are Celtiberian, its windows Arab, but its rooms, for all their Moorish tiles, holy cards, and paralytic furniture from the age of Lope and the hidalgos, are bravely modern.[13]

Édouard Manet visited this house on his trip to Spain during which he almost starved owing to an inability to force a bite of Spanish cooking upon his Parisian palate. In fact, he called onto the field of honor a man who asked for a second helping of a dish that he found particularly revolting. Manet assumed that the man was offering him a deliberate insult.[14]

A radio that looks like a French cake with dials comes on at dusk when the powerhouse sends a thrill of electricity through all the wires of the city and small orange bulbs light up in pink glass shades and the radio sizzles *The March of the Toreadors*,[15] a talk by a priest on the oneness of our spiritual and political duties, a lecture by a Major Domo of Opus Dei[16] on the plague of heresies that besets the French, and a piano recital by Joaquin Turina,[17] playing furiously into a microphone in Madrid that looks like a Turkish medal worn only by field marshals who can claim collateral descent from the Prophet.[18]

There is a room off to the side of the house where photography was invented where you can look into a microscope and see cheesemites doing the act of nature if you are lucky. Some are of the opinion that this imperils one's soul, and others, more enlightened, maintain that it is educational.

—It is so French, you will hear.

—It is Darwinian, you will also hear.

—The Pope has given his blessing to photography. A maiden can send her photograph to her swain and thus spare herself the indecency of a personal encounter. You can go to the photographer's studio and choose a picture that most resembles your son who has gone to the front and have a likeness to put on his grave when the government sends his body home on the railway.[19]

El Caudillo has sat for his portrait many times.[20]

All the world loves a big gleaming jelly.

Napoleon as he was consummating his marriage to Joséphine was bitten in the butt by her faithful dog at, as he liked to relate to intimate friends, the worst possible moment.[21] Real life, said Remy de Gourmont,[22] makes miserable literature, and even Balzac[23] would not have known what to do with such an unmanageable a detail. It is simply appalling. But real life is all that photography has.

Betún y Espliego in the course of compiling his monumental history of photography sifted through thousands and thousands of tintypes and daguerreotypes to find the patterns of attention and curiosity into which this new art fell. He reproduces in his work a photograph of a man standing on a Berlin sidewalk with Einstein.[24] Einstein didn't know the man from Adam's off ox. The man had stopped Einstein and asked permission to be photographed beside him on a Berlin sidewalk.

—It is, Einstein conceded, a simple enough request.

A photograph of Lenin reading *Iskra*[25] at a Zürich café accidentally includes over to the left James and Nora Joyce[26] haggling with a taxi driver about the fare. A Philadelphia photographer made several plates of paleolithic horse fossils at the Museum of Natural History.[27] In one of the pictures two gentlemen stand in the background, spectators at the museum.

One wears a top hat and looks with neurotic intelligence at the camera. He is Edgar Allan Poe.[28] The other gentleman is cross-eyed and wears a beret. God knows who he is.

Butún y Espliego, at the time of his degree from the Sorbonne, explained in a lecture that for the first time in the history of art the accidental became the controlling iconography of a representation of the world.

There are no photographs of Van Gogh as a grown man except of the back of his head. This image occurs in a photograph of a man of some importance now forgotten. But we can identify the figure with its back to the camera as Van Gogh.[29]

There is a photograph of the ten-year-old Vincent. Picasso says that there is a strong resemblance to Rimbaud.[30] A classmate of Vincent's who survived to a great age remembers his hundred freckles across the cheeks and nose, and that the color of his curly hair was bright carrot. Note, says Betún y Espliego, how the accuracy of the photograph had in this instance to be supplemented by an old man's memory.

When the photograph was invented in Toledo the Indians came into town and sat for their portraits. It was the only interesting thing the white man had come up with in all these years.

A photograph of Socrates and his circle would simply look like an ugly old man with bushy eyebrows and the lips of a frog. The homespun texture of his wrinkled tunic would probably be the most eloquent part of the photograph, as the eyes would undoubtedly be lost in shadow. Which of the gangling, olive-skinned young Greeks around him is Plato? The one with pimples and sticky ringlets across his forehead?[31] Which is Xenophon?[32] Who is the woman stabbing a hex of two fingers at the camera?

Skepticism has no power whatever over the veracity of a photograph. It is fact and is accepted by all minds as evidence. The Soviets have gone through all their photographs of the revolution and erased Trotsky. They have put Stalin at Lenin's side even when he was a hundred miles away eating borshch.[33] Since the invention of the photograph we have ceased to dream in color.

On the door of the house in Toledo where photography was invented La Sociedad de la Historia Fotográfica placed a brass plate in 1934. Betún y Espliego made a speech. Ohio, he said, is a paradise on this earth. He alluded to the blue Susquehanna, to the sweet villages where, as Sarmiento said in his *Viajes*, there is more material progress and more culture than in all of Chile and Argentina combined.[34]

An exhibit of photography in historical perspective was mounted that year in the Louvre. The spectators saw photographs of Ibsen[35] walking in the frescade of a Milanese garden,[36] his hands behind his back, Corsican gypsies around a campfire, Orville Wright shaking hands with Wilbur Wright before they flipped a quarter to see who would make the world's first guided flight in a craft heavier than air,[37] Sir Marc Aurel Stein on the Great Wall of China,[38] Jesse James playing a Jew's harp,[39] T. E. Lawrence entering Damascus under the banners of Allah,[40] The Empress Eugenia saying her prayers,[41] Carnot and the Shah of Persia going aloft in a balloon,[42] La Duse reclined on a wicker chaise,[43] Ugo Ojetti and his mama,[44] ladies of fashion kneeling in the street as the Host passes (the Sicilian brass band looking strange beside priests in embroidered robes), Neapolitan convicts going down long stone stairs, emigrants filing through a Roman arch on their way to the boat train and Ellis Island, Allenby making a Turkish band play *The Crescent of Islam Moves Like a Scythe Across the Infidel* into a telephone held by a Sergeant Major of the Royal Welsh Dragoons,[45] Queen Victoria extending a finger to an Irish member of Parliament.

In 1912 Betún y Espliego abandoned his history of photography to devote his life to getting a clear picture of the Loch Ness Monster.[46] The last photograph we have from his hand is a group portrait of the Royal Scots Greys posed with His Imperial Majesty Nikolai II,[47] Colonel of the Regiment. It is an early example of color photography, and the Tsar's face is rusty orange, his beard kelp green. All the hues of the plaids are wrong, and the Elders of Edinburgh therefore refused to allow the picture to be exhibited in the Castle, though George V looked at it privately, and the Metropolitan of Moscow and Neva had one framed in silver and rubies for the high altar of SS. Boris and Gleb.

Betún y Espliego suffered awful loneliness in his vigil on the gray shores of Loch Ness. The bagpipes ruined his kidneys, the porridge his stomach. The religion of the locals seemed to be some revolting kind of speculative philosophy.

His wife Lucinda came to the edge of Scotland and shouted over the wall that he was to come home immediately to Madrid. Franco and the Falangistas were at the gates of Barcelona. Their children wept the large part of the time. She had not heard a string quartet in six months. Was this place, she shouted louder, the land of the Moors?

Wasps the meanwhile built several phalansteries in a china cabinet and the three corners of a ceiling in the house where photography was invented in Toledo. Young wasps practiced clapping and flip around the twenty-watt bulb of the electric light, and the queen of the colony droned in courtly splendor above the radio, the sound of which she took to be a fine summer storm.

There was no darker moment, a voice said from the radio, than when man fixed images of grandmothers and wars on paper with nitrate of silver, the pylons of Luxor and herds of buffalo, no profounder undoing of the spirit, so that the Spanish people must now see the savages of utmost Africa in all their immodesty, Protestant women in dresses that leave bare their ankles and elbows for all the world to see, zeppelins blooming into a cloud of fire, battlefields, refrigerators, and bicycles, leaving the unseen and invisible realities of devotion and meditation in that realm of the mind where the sleep of reason breeds monsters.

A little boy whose hair was a gorse of snarled rust and whose eyes were as blue as an October sky snuck one day as close as he dared to the caravan where Foco Betún y Espliego lived on constant lookout for the Loch Ness Monster. It was a morning when Betún had set up his camera on a tump of daisies and was under the black cloth, the sensitized plate ready in his hand, peering out through the lens at the waste waters that lay as still as a sodden carpet under a desolation of clouds.

—Och, said the bairn from a distance, ye're nae a ceevilized mon t'be sae enthralled by that trippid bonnet.

For response there was a swarthy hand waving him away from under the cloth.

—Rest ye easy, said the boy. I wadna coom closer for a great jool.

One day the boy brought the free-kirk minister, who had heard of photography, a French and frivolous art. He shouted his opinion that it would come to nothing. On another, he brought the laird of the manor and his two daughters. He charged a farthing a head for the service. Their parasols and curls danced in the wind, and the laird pronounced Betún an idiot.

—It's the munster lurks in the loch he's sae still aboot, the bairn explained to the laird.

On a spring day in 1913 the monster, *Nessiteras rhombopteryx*, a plesiosaurus with lots of teeth, saw Betún as clearly as his Jurassic vision allowed, an insect with five feet, black wings, and one large eye that caught the sun with a fierce flash. As a detail of the Out There, Betún held little interest, and until he came into the Here he would not eat him.

Betún's photograph shows a long wet nose and lifted lip, an expressionless reptilian eye, and a gleaming flipper. It was published in *La Prensa* upside down and in the London *Times* with a transposed caption identifying it as the Archduke Franz Ferdinand arriving in Sarajevo for a visit of state.[48]

The notes below consist of those by Davenport which accompanied the original 1976 publication of the story—some of which were worked into the 1979 text here . . . as indicated; the author's further comments in his letters of June 3 and 14, 1994, to the editor; and the editor's more pedestrian identifications. Davenport's original notes are indicated by quotation marks; his later comments by attribution as well.

1. "Our title derives from that of a book which the poet Robert Kelly read in a dream. Who wrote the book he does not remember, nor can he recall whether it is a book already published or one that will come out some years hence. Coveting the title, I purchased it from him as a gesture of homage to his genius."

2. Joseph Nicéphore Nièpce (1765-1833) is credited with being the father of photography owing to his discoveries of how to fix a camera image in c. 1826-27. Nièpce became partners with Louis Daguerre (1789-1851) in 1829 but died in 1833. Daguerre subsequently developed another way of fixing an image—the daguerreotype—which secured him credit as the inventor of photography in 1839.

3. Giorgio de Chirico (1888-1978), an Italian painter, was one of the founders of Surrealism.

4. Foco Betun y Espliego is a fictitious character whose name is the "Spanish for Focus Bitumen and Lavender." [Davenport's original note to what is now note 4 is inserted into the present fourth paragraph of the story.]

5. The two famous Herschels, father and son, have been conflated by Davenport, as in a dream. Frederick Wilhelm Herschel (1738-1822) was a German-born British astronomer who constructed a telescope which, in 1781, discovered a planet. Herschel's son, Sir John (1792-1871), also an astronomer, pioneered in celestial photography and researched photo-active chemicals. He successfully used hyposulfite of soda to fix his photographs, as did Daguerre and Henry Fox Talbot, whose process underlies present ones, and was the first to apply the terms "photography" and "positive" and "negative," which have been universally adopted.

6. Frederick Herschel named the planet he discovered Georgium Sidus—the George Star—in honor of King George III. But Charles Fourier (1772-1837), an influencial utopian French philosopher, and Joel Barlow (1754-1812), a worldly American poet-politician who became ambassador to France in 1811, called the planet Herschel; it is now known as Uranus.

7. Titus Livy (59 B.C.-A.D. 17), was a noted Roman historian who here is describing Toledo, Spain. Elsewhere, as the immediate context usually makes clear, Davenport is referring to Toledo, Ohio.

8. "Santa Ana's Retreat from Buena Vista" is the title of a march by Stephen Foster (1826-64), which refers to the defeat of Santa Ana, the famous Mexican military and political figure (1795-1876), by volunteer Texas forces led by Sam Houston in 1847. Foster is better known as a songwriter ("O Susannah," "Old Black Joe") for the then-popular black minstrel troupes.

9. Swan Creek, Maumee, Lake Erie, and Port Lawrence refer to areas in and around the American city of Toledo, Ohio. Marcus Fulvius Nobilor, a Roman consul (189 B.C.), was an enthusiast of Greek culture; SPQR, the abbreviation for *Senatus Populusque Romanus*—the Senate and People of Rome—was often affixed to public buildings in Rome.

10. Andrew Jackson (1767-1845) was the seventh president of the United States. El Greco (1541-1614),though born in Crete, became one of Spain's most notable and mystical painters after settling in c. 1577 in Toledo, where many of his works can still be seen.

11. Samuel L. Jones (1846-1904) was the mayor of Toledo, Ohio, and "quite a wonderful person," according to Davenport. The author also adds, "The idea for confusing the two Toledos probably comes from Brand Whitlock (who also wrote a life of "Golden Rule" Jones . . .), who, in his book about Belgium admired a handsome desk in the Spanish embassy. He was told that it came from Toledo. Whitlock murmured something about Old World craftsmanship, and was told that it came from 'your Toledo, in Ohio.' "

12. The Tagus is the longest river in Spain.

13. Lope de Vega (1562-1635) was a Spanish dramatic poet considered the founder of the country's national drama; hidalgos were members of the lower Spanish nobility.

14. Édouard Manet (1832-83) was the noted French painter who rebelled against convention and became a mentor to the Impressionists. In Davenport's original version of this piece, his note has another famous French impressionist painter, Claude Monet (1840-1926), making such a visit to Spain "during which he almost starved owing to an inability to force a bite of Spanish cooking upon his Parisian palate. In fact, a man who called for a second helping of a dish that Monet found particularly revolting he assumed to be offering him a deliberate insult and called him onto the field of honor." In fact, both artists visited Spain: Manet in 1865, Monet in 1904.

15. "The March of the Toreadors" is a famous march from the opera *Carmen* (1875) by the popular French composer Georges Bizet (1838-75).

16. Opus Dei is a conservative Catholic group, founded in Madrid in 1928, to spread among all levels of society the universal impetus to holiness in ordinary life.

17. Joaquin Turina (1882-1949) was a Spanish priest, conductor, and composer.

18. The Prophet refers to Mohammed (A.D. 570-632), the founder of Islam.

19. "The detail of buying a picture that most resembles your son," Davenport explains, "is from Gertrude Stein. She also reports hearing an old Spanish woman on portraits: "If it has a beard, it's Saint Joseph; if not, it's the virgin.""

20. El Caudillo, the Spanish word for "the head," refers to Francisco Franco (1892-1975), the soldier and dictator who overthrew the republican government in Spain during a civil war (1936-39) with the help of the Fascist governments of Germany and Italy; his followers were known as Falangistas.

21. Napoleon (1769-1821) was a brilliant general who became emperor of France and conqueror of most of continental Europe before finally being defeated in 1814; Josephine (1763-1814) was his consort. [Davenport's original note on Napoleon became a paragraph in his revised version.]

22. Remy de Gourmont (1858-1915) was a French poet, novelist, and scholarly critic.

23. Honoré de Balzac (1799-1850), a prolific French novelist of contemporary society, is considered the founder of fictional realism.

24. Albert Einstein (1879-1955) was a German-born physicist whose relativity theory revolutionized man's understanding of the universe.

25. Nikolai Lenin (1870-1924) was a Communist who assumed leadership of the Russian Revolution from 1917; he became premier, fended off counterrevolutionary attacks, and introduced many socialist reforms; *Iskra*, meaning "the spark," was his newspaper.

26. James Joyce (1882-1941) was the Irish-born writer whose groundbreaking novels such as *Ulysses* (1922) and *Finnegans Wake* (1939) are widely credited with introducing stream-of-consciousness techniques to fiction. He took refuge with his wife, Nora, in Zurich when the Germans invaded France in 1940, and died there soon afterward.

27. The photograph of Paleolithic horse fossils can be seen in Robert West Howard's *The Dawnseekers: The First History of American Paleontology* (New York: Harcourt Brace Jovanovich, 1975).

28. Edgar Allan Poe (1809-49), the noted American poet and short story writer, took an early interest in photography—as both a commentator and a frequent subject.

29. Vincent Van Gogh (1853-90) was a Dutch post-Impressionist painter whose tormented life, which ended in suicide, is as well known as his vivid paintings.

30. Arthur Rimbaud (1854-91) was a French writer whose verse anticipated both the symbolist and the surrealist poets.

31. Socrates (c. 469-399 B.C.) was a famous Greek philosopher whose concerns and teaching methods, using questions and answers, are still widely influential. Plato (c. 428-348 B.C.) was a disciple of Socrates, whose writings have proved equally influential.

32. Xenophon (c. 435-354 B.C.), another disciple of Socrates, became a noted historian, essayist, and military commander.

33. In his original text, Davenport has a note to the opening sentence ("Skepticism has no power . . .") saying that "Degas would not have a telephone in his house because, as he explained, there was no way of knowing who was calling." Leon Trotsky (1877-1940) was a leading figure in the 1917 Russian Revolution. After Lenin's death in 1924, he lost out to Stalin for control of the Communist Party; banished from Russia in 1929, he was assassinated in Mexico in 1940. Joseph Stalin (1879-1953), a Russian political leader, succeeded Lenin and, after eliminating any opposition, became virtual dictator of the U.S.S.R.

34. Domingo Faustino Sarmiento (1811-88) described Ohio, which he visited in 1847, in his *Viajes en Norte America;* Davenport reports that he also introduced American-style grammar into South America, and schoolchildren there still observe a day in his honor.

35. Henrik Ibsen (1828-1906) was Norway's most famous playwright, noted for his dramas of social and psychological problems.

36. After the mention of the Milanese garden, Davenport originally appended the following note [editor's note: number 7, which "follows" numbers 8 and 9]:

"O. Henry, Flaubert, and Charles Ives all declined to be photographed when they could get out of it."

37. The brothers Orville (1871–1948) and Wilbur Wright (1867–1912) were American aviation pioneers, making the first successful flight in a motor-powered airplane at Kitty Hawk, North Carolina, in 1903.

38. Sir Marc Aurel Stein (1862–1943) was a Hungarian-born British archaeologist and explorer who traced the caravan routes from China to the West.

39. Jesse James (1847–82) led a band of outlaws who robbed banks and trains from 1866 and was murdered by one of his gang, Robert Ford.

40. T. E. Lawrence (1888–1935) was an English archaeologist, soldier, and writer best known for his leadership of the Arab revolt against the Turks (1917–18), which he memorably described in *The Seven Pillars of Wisdom* (1926).

41. The Empress Eugenia (1826–1920) was empress of the French (1853–71).

42. Marie François Sadi Carnot (1937–94) was the president of France (1887–94); his Burgundian ancestors had been prominent during and after the French Revolution.

43. La Duse refers to Eleanora Duse (1859–1924), a famous Italian actress.

44. Ugo Ojetti (1871–1946) was an Italian art critic and writer of essays, novels, short stories, and plays.

45. Edmund Allenby (1861–1936) was the legendary British commander of the victorious Egyptian Expeditionary forces against the Turks, who entered Jerusalem in 1917. According to Davenport's original notes, some of the pictures mentioned in this photography exhibition—from Empress Eugenia through the emigrants—were taken by Count Giuseppe Primoli, the Proust of the camera, according to Lamberto Vitali in his *Un fotografico fin de siècle*.

46. "Photographs taken by Robert Rines after this story was written satisfy the British naturalist Sir Peter Scott that prehistoric saurians live in the peatblack waters of Loch Ness. The creatures are forty feet long, and distinctive holographs of them will have been shown at a conference of zoologists in Edinburgh on December tenth, 1975. Our guess that they are plesiosauri will by that time have been confirmed or shown to be wrong." Davenport later adds, "After years of worrying, I finally 'saw' what that photo of the Loch Ness monster is—it's a gull, one wing extended downward, the other up, looking for all the world like a dinosaur's neck and head."

47. Nikolai II or Nicholas (1868–1918), the last czar of Russia, was executed with his family by the Bolsheviks during the Russian Revolution.

48. Archduke Franz Ferdinand (1863–1914), the nephew of Emperor Franz Joseph of the Austro-Hungarian Empire, was assassinated at Sarajevo in August 1914, which triggered the start of the First World War.

VERONICA'S SHROUDS

1978

—————

Tournier (1924–), a prize-winning French author, shares the current widespread fascination with the cultural meanings of signs and images. But he remains less influential outside his own country, perhaps because of his adaptations of traditional narrative forms (such as the legend of St. Veronica's veil in this story),[1] symbolic characters, and layered meanings to dramatize his ideas about contemporary life and its representation in art.[2] Tournier has long been involved in photography in multiple ways. Taking photographs—especially self-portraits—has been an absorbing hobby since childhood, when his favorite toy was a Kodak caméra.[3] While becoming a writer, he initiated and hosted Chambre Noire *(1960–65), a television series about notable photographers, and from 1970 he was instrumental in setting up the first (and only) international photography festival, which is held annually in Arles.[4] Tournier often manifests his knowledge of photography in his writing, exploring its uses and, as here, its abuses in twentieth-century culture.[5] He also has devoted two collections of essays to the subject:* Des Clefs et des serrures *(1979) on selected photographs and* Le Crépuscule des masques *(1992) on selected photographers. In two of Tournier's novels,* The Ogre *(1970) and* The Golden Droplet *(1985), as well as in the short story below, his central characters' obsession with the camera, whether as active photographer or passive subject, irrevocably transforms their lives.[6]*

1. According to legend, Veronica, later canonized, wiped the face of Jesus as he passed by her in Jerusalem bearing his cross; the cloth she used reportedly retained the imprint of his features.

2. See Roger Shattuck, "Locating Michel Tournier," *The Innocent Eye: On Modern Literature and the Arts* (New York: Farrar, Straus & Giroux, 1984), pp. 205-18, which Martin Roberts called to the editor's attention.

3. See Tournier, "L'Estrange cas du Docteur Tournier" in *Le Crépuscule des masques* (Paris: Hobeke, 1992), [p. 9], and some self-portraits reproduced on pp. 13 and 16; another one is reproduced in Rabb, ed., *Literature and Photography*, p. 462. See also Tournier's portrait by Cartier-Bresson in *Photoportraits*, p. 159.

4. See Tournier, *Le Crépuscule des masques*, [p. 9], and Marianne Fulton, "Lucien Clergue," in *Lucien Clergue: Eros and Thanatos* (Boston: New York Graphic Society/ Eastman House [1985]), p. 26.

5. See David Bevan, "Tournier's Photographer: A Modern Bluebeard?" *Modern Language Studies* 15, no. 3 (Summer 1985): 66–71; and Emily Apter, "Fore-skin and After-Image: Photographic Fetishism in Tournier's Fiction," *L'Esprit Créateur* 29, no. 1 (Spring 1989): 72–82. See also Bill Jay, "The Photographer as Aggressor," in *Observations: Essays on Documentary Photography* [*Untitled* 35], edited by David Featherstone (Carmel, Calif.: Friends of Photography, 1984), pp. 7–23.

6. See the brief discussion of "Veronica's Shrouds" in West, *Soft Murder by the Camera Eye*, pp. 15–16. See also Tournier: *The Ogre*, translated by Barbara Bray (New York: Doubleday, 1972), especially pp. 103–7, and see also pp. 9–10, 85–86, 92–93, 100, 108–9, 112, 114, 123–24, and 236; "Amandine, or The Two Gardens," also from *The Fetishist*, translated by Barbara Wright (New York: Doubleday, 1984), p. 29, [subtitled "An Initiatory Story for Olivia Clergue," the daughter of the photographer Lucien Clergue]; and *The Golden Droplet*, translated by Barbara Wright (New York: Doubleday, 1987), pp. 4–8, 13–14, 22, 45–46, 49, 71–75, 81–83, 85, 88, 103–4, 112, 118, 133–34, 148, 153–58, and especially 159–68. This last scene is a thinly disguised portrait of the photographer Bernard Faucon (1950–), according to Martin Roberts in "Mutations of the Spectacle: Vitrines, Arcades, Mannequins," *French Cultural Studies* 2 (1991): 211–49, especially 236–45, and in conversation with the editor on August 27, 1992.

VERONICA'S SHROUDS

Every year, in July, the International Photography Festival, held in Arles, attracts a huge crowd of photographers, both amateur and professional. During the few days the Festival lasts, exhibitions proliferate at every street corner, interminable discussions take place on the café terraces, and in the evenings the distinguished guests show their work on an enormous white screen erected in the courtyard of the Archbishop's Palace, to the cheers or boos of a young, passionate, and uncompromising audience. The connoisseurs of the Who's Who of photography delight in recognizing, in the little squares and alleyways of the town, Ansel Adams and Ernst Haas, Jacques Lartigue and Fulvio Roiter, Robert Doisneau and Arthur Tress, Eva Rubinstein and Gisèle Freund. People point out Cartier-Bresson, hugging the walls because he believes he can't see when he himself is being seen, Jean-Loup Sieff, who is so handsome that you wish he would concentrate entirely on self-portraits, Brassaï, nocturnal, mysterious, never to be seen in the blazing Provençal sun without an old black umbrella.

"Brassaï, why the umbrella?"

"It's an obsession. It came over me the day I gave up smoking."

The first time I saw Hector and Veronica they must have been together, but I am to be excused if at the start I noticed only Hector. It was on one of those narrow strips of land that run along the Camargue, and separate the sea from the last brackish ponds on which flamingos come swooping down like great red and white streaks of light. Guided by one of the organizers of the Festival, a group of photographers had assembled on this marshy ground to photograph a nude. The model, superbly curvaceous in his nudity, either ran up and down in the surf, or lay flat on his stomach on the sand, or curled up in a foetal position, or waded in the stagnant waters of the pond, warding off seaweeds and salty ripples with his sturdy thighs.

Hector was the Mediterranean type; of medium height, with powerful muscles, a round, rather childish face overshadowed by a young bull's forehead festooned with a mop of black, curly hair. He took full advantage of his natural animality which was in perfect harmony with the simple, primitive things of this region: fresh water or stagnant ponds, russet grasses, bluish-grey sands, tree stumps whitened with age. He was indeed nude, though not absolutely, for he wore a kind of necklace, a leather thong threaded through a hole pierced in a huge tooth. This savage ornament actually emphasized his nudity, and he met the incessant volleys of the photographers with naïve complaisance, as the right and proper homage due to his splendid body.

We went back to Arles in half a dozen cars. Fate had decreed that I should sit next to a slim, lively little woman in whom intelligence and a kind of feverish charm took the place of beauty, and who ruthlessly made me share the weight and clutter of the photographic equipment she had lumbered herself with. In spite of this she seemed to be in a rather bad mood, and kept muttering severely critical remarks about the working session that morning, although I wasn't quite sure whether or nor her remarks were addressed to me.

"Not a single photo worth keeping. That beach! That Hector! So banal you could weep! Postcard stuff! Even though I had my forty-millimetre distagon. You can get some interesting distortions with that super-wide-angle lens. If only Hector had held his hand out towards it he would have had a gigantic hand with a small body and a sparrow's head behind it. Amusing. But after all, that's just originality on the cheap. Never mind. We can forget about the sea, and the sand, and the worm-eaten, prop-room tree trunks, but it would be nice to make something of that young Hector. Only it would take a lot of work. Work, and sacrifices . . .

At the end of that day, while I was taking a little walk in nocturnal Arles, I caught sight of the two of them — Hector and Veronica — on the terrace of the Vauxhall Hotel. She was talking. He was listening to her with an astonished expression. Was she talking about work and sacrifices? I walked slowly enough to hear him, even so, answer a question Veronica had asked him. He had pulled out of his shirt collar the necklace I had noticed that morning.

"Yes, it's a tooth," he was explaining. "A tiger's tooth. It comes from Bengal. The natives there are convinced that so long as they wear this fetish there's no risk of their being eaten by a tiger."

While he was speaking, Veronica observed him with a sombre, insistent gaze.

The Festival came to an end. I lost sight of Hector and Veronica, and I even more or less forgot them during the following winter.

A year later I was once again in Arles. So were they. I found Veronica unchanged. But Hector was unrecognizable. His rather childish, puppyish behaviour, his splendid animal swagger, his sunny, optimistic efflorescence, had all disappeared. As a result of goodness knew what change in his life style he had grown so much thinner that it was almost alarming. Veronica seemed to have communicated her own feverish rhythm to him, and she kept gazing possessively at him. She didn't refuse, however — quite the contrary — to comment on his metamorphosis.

"Last year, Hector was beautiful, but not really photogenic," she told me. "He was beautiful, and if they wanted to the photographers could make fairly faithful copies which would therefore also be beautiful — of both his body and his face. But like all copies, photos taken that way are obviously inferior to the original.

"Now, though, he has become *photogenic*. And what does photogenesis consist of? It implies the possibility of producing photos that *go beyond* the real object. In vulgar terms, the photogenic man surprises people who, although they know him, are seeing his photos for the first time: they are more beautiful than he is, they seem to be revealing a beauty which was previously hidden. But such photos do not *reveal* that beauty, they create it."

I learned later that they were living together in a modest farmhouse that Veronica had rented in the Camargue, not far from Méjannes. She invited me there.

It was one of those squat, thatched-roof cottages which you don't even notice in the Camargue landscape until you stumble up against the gate in their ring fence. I found it difficult to imagine the life they shared in these few, poorly-furnished rooms. Photography alone was in its element, there. The place was cluttered with electric spots, electronic flashes, reflectors, cameras, plus a developing and printing laboratory with a great wealth of chemicals in bottles, flasks, sealed cans, and individual quantities in plastic containers. One of the rooms, however, seemed to be reserved for Hector. But here, apart from a monastic table and a shower bath enclosed by a rubber curtain, there was a whole arsenal of equipment for the intensive culture of the muscles which spoke only of effort, work, and the unflagging repetition of the same movement made when painfully weighed down with iron or steel. There were rib stalls on one wall. Opposite, on racks, was a complete range of weight-lifting apparatus and a whole set of polished oak Indian clubs. The rest of the room was nothing but chest expanders, spring-grips, muscle-developers, a stomach-exercising board, a rowing machine, and bar-bells. The whole suggested both an operating theatre and a torture chamber.

"Last year, if you remember," Veronica explained, "Hector was still like a young, hard, ripe fruit. Very appetizing, but quite useless for photography. The light glided over his smooth, rounded forms but neither caught them nor played on them. Three hours of exercises every day have changed all that. I must tell you that since I took him in hand, all this gymnastic gear comes with us wherever we go. It's the normal complement of the photographic equipment I take everywhere with me. Whenever we travel, the station wagon is absolutely chock-a-block."

We went into another room. On a trestle table there was a pile of enlargements—a suite of variations on the same theme.

"There!" said Veronica, with a touch of exaltation in her voice. "There is the true, the only Hector! Look!"

Was it really Hector, that hollow mask, all cheekbones, chin, and sunken eyes, with a helmet of hair whose disciplined curls looked as if they had been varnished?

"One of the great laws of the photographic nude," Veronica went on, "is the paramount importance of the face. How many photos that we hoped were going to be magnificent—and which could have, and should have been magnificent—are spoiled by an imperfect face, or simply by a face that isn't in keeping with its body! Lucien Clergue, whose guests at Arles we all more or less are, has solved the problem by cutting off the heads of his nudes. But decapitation is obviously a radical procedure! Logically, it should kill the photo, whereas on the contrary, it gives it a more intense, a more secret life. You might almost think that all the soul that the head contained has flowed back from the severed head into the body represented, and that it manifests itself there by creating a host of little details that are full of life but not present in ordinary nudes: the pores in the skin, its down, contrasty grains, bristling goose flesh, and also the gentle density of the soft parts caressed and modelled by water and sun.

"This is great art. But I think it's only possible with the female body. The masculine nude wouldn't lend itself to this game of the head being as it were swallowed up by the body. Look at this picture. The head is the code to the body. What I mean is: the body itself, translated into a different system of signs. And at the same time it's the key to the body. Look at some of the mutilated statues in museum storehouses. A headless man becomes indecipherable. He can't see anything because he's lost his eyes. And he gives the visitor the unbearable feeling that it is he, the visitor, who has gone blind. Whereas a statue of a woman comes into its own, blossoms into a creature of flesh and blood far more when it has lost its head."

"Nevertheless," I observed, "no one could say that the face you have given Hector radiates intelligence and interest in the outside world."

"Of course it doesn't! An alert, inquisitive, extrovert face would be a catastrophe for the naked body. It would drain it of its substance. The body would become a negligible medium for the light that focuses on things, like a lighthouse which is itself immersed in darkness and only exists in order to illuminate the sky with its revolving light. The right face for a nude is an impassive, imperturbable face, concentrating on itself. Look at Rodin's *Thinker*. He's an animal who, with his face in his fists, is making a violent effort to extract some vague gleam of light from his miserable brain. The whole of his powerful body is penetrated and as it were transfigured by this effort, from the inward-turning feet up to the bull's neck, by way of the furniture remover's spine."

"Yes, I was thinking about statues' eyes, with their strange gaze which always seems to look straight through us without seeing us, as if, being made of stone, they could only perceive stone."

"Statues' eyes are sealed fountains," Veronica agreed.

There was a silence, during which we examined three proofs printed on extrahard paper. Hector's body, seen against a uniformly black background (how well I know those huge rolls of paper of all colours that photographers use to isolate their models, just like insects pinned up in an entomologist's box), his body silhouetted by the shadows and luminous areas of one single, violent source of light, looked frozen, stripped to the bone, dissected by a kind of autopsy or anatomical demonstration.

"It isn't exactly what they call 'life photography'," I said, joking in order to try to break the rather maleficent charm of these pictures.

" 'Life' isn't my strong point," Veronica admitted. "And remember what

Paul Valéry said: 'Truth is naked, but underneath the naked is the *écorché.*'
Now there are two schools of photography. Those who belong to the first
are always on the look-out for the surprising, the touching, the frightening image. They scour the towns and the countryside, the beaches and the
battlefields, trying to capture the evanescent scene, the furtive gesture, the
shining moment, all of which illustrate the heart-rending insignificance of
the human condition, which arose out of nothingness and is condemned
to return to nothingness. These, today, are called Brassaï, Cartier-Bresson,
Doisneau, William Klein. And there is the other movement, entirely derived from Edward Weston. This is the school of the deliberate, calculated,
immobile image that aims at capturing not the instant, but eternity. One
of these is Denis Brihat, whom you may have seen here with his beard and
his Hemingway glasses. He has gone off to live in the Luberon mountains,
east of Avignon, and for the last twenty years he has photographed nothing but plants. And do you know what his worst enemy is?"

"Tell me."

"The wind! The wind that makes flowers move."

"And he has chosen to live in the mistral country!"

"This school of the immobile has four private domains: portraits, nudes,
still lifes, and landscapes."

"So in the first school you have photographs 'taken from life', and in the
opposite school you have 'still lifes' — which is a strange term for a genre
consisting entirely of inanimate objects! But I sometimes feel that the first
category is badly named too, and we should rather talk about photographs
'taken from death'."

"That wouldn't bother me," Veronica conceded. "Death interests me —
it more than interests me. One of these days I shall inevitably go and take
photographs in the morgue. In a corpse — a real, raw corpse, not one that
has been prettified on its bed, its hands joined, ready to be sprinkled with
holy water without batting an eye — in such a corpse, yes, there is a truth . . .
how shall I put it? . . . a marmoreal truth. Have you noticed, with very
young children who don't want to be picked up, the way they are able to
make themselves heavier, to give themselves an extraordinary *dead weight?*
I've never carried dead person. If I tried to, I'm sure *I* should be crushed
to death."

"You frighten me!"

"Don't put on airs! There's nothing more ridiculous, in my opinion, than
the new form of prudery that is shocked by death and by the dead. The
dead are everywhere — starting with art. And just a minute! Do you know
exactly what Renaissance art is? There are several definitions of it. This

is the best one, in my opinion: it's the discovery of the corpse. Neither Antiquity nor the Middle Ages dissected corpses. Greek statuary, which is absolutely irreproachable from the anatomical point of view, is entirely based on the observation of the living body."

" 'Taken from life.' "

"Precisely. Praxiteles had watched athletes in action. For religious, moral, or whatever reasons, he had never cut up a corpse. We have to wait until the sixteenth century, and more precisely for the Fleming, Andreas Vesalius, for the true birth of anatomy. He was the first to dare to dissect corpses. After that, every artist went rushing off to the cemetery. And almost all the nudes of the time began to stink of the corpse. Not only are the manuscripts of Leonardo da Vinci and Benvenuto Cellini full of anatomical illustrations, but in the frequent appearance of very living nudes you can sense their obsession with the *écorché*. Benozzo Gozzoli's Saint Sebastian, Luca Signorelli's frescos in Orvieto Cathedral, seem to have escaped from some *danse macabre*."

"That's certainly a somewhat unexpected aspect of the Renaissance."

"When you compare it with the flourishing health of the Middle Ages, the Renaissance strikes you as being the era of the morbid and the anguished. It was the golden age of the Inquisition, with its witch-hunts, torture chambers and stakes."

I had put down the nude photos of Hector, which all of a sudden seemed like exhibits in the trial of a witch.

"Dear Veronica, if we were transported back to those days, don't you think there might have been a great risk of your ending up being burned at the stake?"

"Not necessarily," she replied, so quickly that I wondered whether she had already asked herself that question. "In those days there was a very simple way of dabbling in witchcraft without running the slightest risk."

"What was that?"

"By becoming a member of the court of the Holy Inquisition! When it comes to the stake, for all sorts of reasons I consider the best place is not *on it*, but to one side, in a dress circle box."

"To be able to see and take photographs."

I was getting ready to leave, but there was one last question I was dying to ask.

"Talking about seeing, I'd be disappointed to leave you without saying hallo to Hector."

I thought I noticed that while her face had lit up for a moment at my irony, it now tautened as if I had been guilty of an indiscretion.

"Hector?"

She looked at her watch.

"He'll be asleep, at this hour. He used to have such absurd habits, but now I make him do just the opposite—eat little and sleep a lot."

But she did smile as she added:

"That's the golden rule for health: He who sleeps forgets his hunger."

I was on my way to the door when she seemed to change her mind.

"But even so, you can see him. I know him. It will take more than that to wake him up."

I followed her to a little room, a kind of cell, at the end of a corridor. I thought at first that it had no windows, but then I noticed some drawn curtains which were much the same colour as the pale walls and ceiling. Everything was so white and so bare that it was like being inside an eggshell. Hector was asleep, lying flat on his stomach on a low, wide bed, in a position that reminded me of one of his poses in the Camargue the previous year. The temperature justified the fact that he had neither sheet nor covers over him. In the uniformly milky half-light, that mahogany-coloured flesh, frozen in an asymmetrical position—one knee bent, the opposite arm stretched out over the side of the bed—in which there was both total abandon and a passionate desire to sleep, to forget, to repudiate the things and the people of the outside world—even so, it was a fine sight.

Veronica gave him a possessive look, and then looked at me triumphantly. It was her creation—and undeniably a magnificent success—this golden, sculptural mass, cast into the depths of this ovoid cell.

Three days later I found her in the back room of a little bar in the Place du Forum, which was only frequented by gypsies and the inhabitants of la Roquette, the poorer part of the town. I found it difficult to believe, but it was a fact: Veronica had been drinking. Furthermore, it seemed that drink made her maudlin. We exchanged a few disenchanted remarks about the previous day's corrida, about the performance of Rossini's *Elisabetta, Regina d'Inghilterra* which was due to take place the next day at the Roman theatre, and about the Bill Brandt exhibition which had opened that afternoon. She answered in short, stiff sentences, her thoughts obviously elsewhere. There was an embarrassed silence. Then she suddenly made up her mind.

"Hector's gone," she said.

"Gone? Where?"

"If only I knew!"

"Didn't he say anything?"

"No, well, yes—he left a letter on the table. Here!"

She threw an opened envelope on to the table. Then she began to scowl, as if to give me plenty of time to read the letter. The writing was neat and tidy, rather schoolboyish. I was struck by the tender tone, attenuated and as if refined and spiritualized by the fact that he had addressed her as *vous.*

Veronica darling,

Do you know how many photos you have taken of my body during the thirteen months and eleven days we have been together? You weren't counting, of course. You photographed me without counting. But while I was letting myself be photographed, I *was* counting. Only natural, isn't it? You have stolen my image twenty-two thousand two hundred and thirty-nine times. Obviously, this has given me time for thought, and I have come to understand a lot of things. I was so naïve last summer that I acted as a model for everyone in the Camargue. That wasn't serious. With you, Veronica, it became serious. Photography that isn't serious doesn't affect the model. It glances off him without touching him. But serious photography creates a perpetual interchange between the model and the photographer. It becomes like the system of communicating vessels. I owe you a lot, Veronica darling. You have made another man of me. But you have also taken a lot from me. Twenty-two thousand two hundred and thirty-nine times, some part of myself has been stolen from me and put into your little image trap, as you call it. You have plucked me like a hen, like an angora rabbit. I've got thinner, tougher, become desiccated, not through any diet or exercises, but because of what has been taken from me, because of the daily removal of some of my substance. Do I need to say that none of this would have been possible if I had kept my tooth? But you're no fool, you had it taken away from me, my magic tooth . . . And now I am empty, exhausted, tormented. Those twenty-two thousand two hundred and thirty-nine bits of me that you have so jealously classified, labelled and dated—you can have them. All I have left is my skin and bones, and I intend to keep them. You won't have my hide, dear Veronica! Find someone else, now, whether man or woman, someone intact and virginal, who has an unimpaired capital/image. What *I* am going to do is try to rest; I mean, I'm going to try to make myself a new face and body after the terrible mess you've made of me. Don't think I hold it against you. On the contrary, I love you dearly—in exchange for the sort of love you had for me, a devouring love. But don't bother to try to look for me. You won't find me anywhere. Not even

in front of your nose, if by any chance we happen to meet, because I
have become diaphanous, translucid, transparent—invisible.

With love
Hector.

P.S. I've taken my tooth back.

"His tooth? What's all that about his tooth?"

"But you know very well," Veronica said impatiently. "That talisman he
wore round his neck on a leather thong. I had a hell of a job to get him to
take it off when I wanted to photograph him."

"Ah yes, the fetish tooth that the Bengalis believe protects them from
being eaten by tigresses."

"Tigresses? Why do you say tigresses, and not tigers?" she asked irri-
tably.

Obviously, I couldn't justify my use of the feminine. There was a silence,
heavy with hostility. But as I had started to compromise myself between
Hector and her, I decided to come out with what I thought.

"Last time we met," I began, "you spoke at length about the anatomists
of the Renaissance, and in particular about the Fleming, Andreas Vesalius.
Your remarks whetted my appetite, and I had the curiosity to go to the
public library to find out more about this person who was the veritable creator of anatomy. I discovered that he had lived a mysterious, adventurous,
dangerous life, full of ups and downs, which was entirely motivated, from
beginning to end, by one single passion—that of scientific discovery.

" 'Born in Brussels in December 1514, Vesalius wasted no time in becoming familiar with cemeteries, gibbets, hospices, torture chambers—in
short, with all the places where people die. He spent a good part of his
life under the shadow of the gallows. His vocation seems to have been that
of a necrophile, a vampire, a vulture. This would indeed have been horrible had the whole not been purified by the light of the intelligence. The
emperor Charles V—also a Fleming—made him his private physician and
took him to Madrid. It was here that scandal erupted. The rumour spread
that Visalius did not confine himself to the dissection of corpses . . . Certainly, the lifeless corpse reveals its anatomy. But it says nothing about its
physiology, and for good reason. It is the living body that has something
to say about physiology. An intrepid researcher, Vesalius arranged to have
prisoners handed over to him. They were stupefied with opium, and then
he cut them up. In short, after inventing anatomy, he created vivisection.
This was a trifle crude, even for an age not much given to molly-coddling.
Vesalius was tried, and condemned to death. Philip II just managed to save
his life. His sentence was commuted into the obligation to make a pilgrim-

age to the Holy Land. But it would appear that fate was definitely against him. On his way back from Jerusalem he was wrecked on the desert island of Zante, where he died of hunger and exposure in October 1564'."

Aroused from her gloomy reflections, Veronica had been listening with increasing interest.

"What a marvellous life, and how marvellously it ended!" she said.

"Yes, but don't you see that for Vesalius, corpses were only the last resort. He much preferred the living."

"No doubt," she agreed, "but on condition that he could cut them up."

I rarely have occasion to meet my photographer friends during the Parisian winter. I only just missed Veronica, though, at the opening of an exhibition at the Photogalerie in the rue Christine.

"She left no more than five minutes ago," I was told by Chériau, who knew her. "She was so sorry not to see you but she couldn't wait. Though she told me some fascinating things, you know—absolutely fascinating!"

I had nothing to be sorry about, though. Chériau is a veritable mine of information about all the gossip in the photographic world and I had only to keep my ears wide open to hear everything Veronica had told him, and a whole lot more.

"In the first place," he began, "she found her whipping-boy-cum-model and got him back—you know, that young Hector she picked up in Arles?"

I did know.

"Then, thanks to him, she launched out into a series of 'direct photographs'. That's what she calls shots taken without a camera, without a film, and without an enlarger. In short, the dream of most great photographers who consider the technical constraints of their profession to be an ignominious defect. The theory of this direct photography is as easy to formulate as it is difficult to put into practice. Veronica uses big sheets of photographic paper and quite simply starts by exposing them to the daylight. The only reaction of the sensitized paper thus exposed, without a developer, is that it begins to turn a very, very pale yellow. After this she immerses poor Hector in a developing bath (metol, sulphate of soda, hydroquinone and borax). Then, while he's still wet, she lays him down on the photographic paper, in one position or another. After that, all she has to do is wash down the paper with an acid fixative . . . and send the model off to take a shower. The result of all this is strange, flattened silhouettes, a flat projection of Hector's body rather like, as Veronica actually said in so many words, what remained on some walls in Hiroshima of the Japanese blown up and disintegrated by the atom bomb."

"And Hector? What does he have to say about all this?" I asked, thinking of his farewell letter, which in my mind suddenly took on the aspect of a tragic, pathetic appeal for help.

"That's just it! When our dear Veronica was telling me about the marvels of 'direct photography' she didn't realize that I knew the other side of the operation. Because I heard from another source—I have my spies, as you know—that poor Hector was suffering from generalized dermatitis and had had to go to hospital. What especially intrigued the doctors was that his lesions had obviously been caused by chemicals and resembled the professional skin diseases to be found in tanners, dry-salters and engravers. But whereas with such artisans they are localized on the hands and forearms, Hector had vast, toxic erythema on parts of the body—the back, for example—which are rarely exposed, and hence more vulnerable.

"To my mind," Chériau had wound up, "he'd be well advised to get himself out of the clutches of that witch; if he doesn't, she'll end up having his hide."

Having his hide . . . The very expression he'd used in his letter! And yet I was still far from suspecting how it was going to be illustrated a few months later.

And indeed, a few months later the Photography Festival inevitably brought me back to Arles. It had already started when I arrived, and it was from the press that I learned that an exhibition called *Veronica's Shrouds* was being held in the Chapel of the Knights of Malta in the Musée Réattu. The paper also carried an interview with the artist. Veronica explained that after a series of experiments with "direct photography" on paper, she had gone on to a more supple material that had greater possibilities—linen. The cloth was impregnated with silver bromide, to make it photo-sensitive, and then exposed to the light. Next it was used to enswathe the model as he came out of a developing bath still dripping wet; he was wrapped in it from head to foot: "like a corpse in a shroud", Veronica added. Finally the cloth was fixed, and then washed. If you painted the model with titanium dioxide or uranium nitrate, you could get some interesting mordanting effects. The imprint then took on bluish or golden gradations. In short, Veronica had concluded, traditional photography has been surpassed by these new creations. *Dermography* would be a more appropriate word.

You can well imagine that my first visit was to the Chapel of the Knights. The height of its ceiling makes the nave seem tiny, and as if sunk in a pit. As a result, it is difficult for the visitor not to feel suffocated, and this impression was heightened by the "shrouds" entirely covering the walls and floor. Everywhere, high up, low down, to the right, to the left, your gaze was overwhelmed by the black and gold spectre of a flattened, stretched, wound, unwound, corpse, reproduced in every position like an obsessive funereal frieze. It resembled a whole series of human skins that had been peeled off and then paraded, like so many barbaric trophies.

I was alone in this little chapel, which was beginning to feel like a morgue, and my anguish increased every time I discovered a detail that reminded me of Hector's face or body. I remembered, not without horror, the bloody and symmetrical imprints we used to obtain at school when we trapped a fly between two sheets of paper and crushed it with a blow of the fist.

I was on my way out when I found myself face to face with Veronica. I had only one question to ask her, and I couldn't keep it back for a single second.

"Veronica, where's Hector? What have you done with Hector?"

She gave me a mysterious smile, and with a vague gesture indicated the shrouds surrounding us on all sides.

"Hector? But he's . . . here. What I've done with him . . . is this. What more do you want?"

I was going to press the point when I noticed something that reduced me to permanent silence.

Round her neck she was wearing a leather thong threaded through the pierced tooth of a Bengal tiger.

RAYMOND CARVER

VIEWFINDER

1981

———

Carver (1938–88), who inspired the minimalist school of short story writing (still in vogue), is best known for his tales about the bleakness of blue-collar life. One of his French translators thought his authorial stance ironic until a photographic portrait compelled him to realize that "the man I was looking at . . . could never condescend to his characters."[1] Carver evidently shared his translator's belief in the ability of photographs to reveal people, which often features in his writing. Such images, even though verbal and fictional, help the reader fill in or make connections between the deliberate omissions, silences, and elliptical dialogue of his typically inarticulate, faceless, and even, as here, nameless characters, living in sparsely described settings on the edge of contemporary American society.[2] For in Carver's poems and stories, especially after revision (and, sometimes, expansion), the omissions are often more significant than the material included.[3] In this story, originally called "Hooks," the published title has figurative as well as literal resonance as the bizarre photographer, his instant pictures, and intuitive comments enable the narrator to vent his long-repressed pain.[4]

1. Francois Lascan, quoted in Tess Gallagher's introduction to *Carver Country: The World of Raymond Carver,* with photographs by Bob Adelman (New York: Scribner's, 1990), p. 10.

2. Many of Carver's stories involving the use of photography are reprinted—with or without revision—in more than one of his collections, but only the most accessible source has been cited here. For examples, see Carver:

Will You Please Be Quiet Please? (New York: McGraw-Hill, 1976): "Neighbors," p. 15; "The Meadow," p. 102; and "The Student's Wife," p. 120.

Furious Seasons and Other Stories (Santa Barbara, Calif.: Capra, 1977): "So Much Water So Close to Home," p. 52, and "Furious Seasons," p. 95.

What We Talk About When We Talk About Love (New York: Knopf, 1981): "Sacks," p. 44; "The Bath," p. 47; "After the Denim,", p. 69; and "Popular Mechanics," p. 123.
Fires: Essays, Poems, Stories (Santa Barbara, Calif.: Capra, 1983; New York: Vintage, 1984): "My Father's Life," including "Photograph of My Father in His Twenty-Second Year," p. 59 [reprinted widely elsewhere, such as in "Where He Was: Memories of My Father," in *Bill Burke Portraits* (New York: Ecco Press, 1987)]; "Wes Hardin: From a Photograph," pp. 108-9; and "Where Is Everyone," pp. 173-79.
Cathedral (New York: Vintage, 1984): "Cathedral," p. 14; "Preservation," p. 36; "The Compartment," p. 49; "Fever," pp. 164-65; and "A Small, Good Thing," p. 59.
Where Water Comes Together with Other Water (New York: Random House, 1985): "Radio Waves," p. 7.
Where I'm Calling From: New And Selected Stories (New York: Atlantic Monthly Press, 1988): "Blackbird Pie," p. 379.
A New Path to the Waterfall (New York: Atlantic Monthly Press, 1989): "Transformation," pp. 10-11; "The World Book Salesman," p. 20; "On an Old Photograph of My Son," pp. 86-88; and "After-Glow," p. 121.
No Heroics Please (New York: Vintage, 1992): "Furious Seasons" (rev.), pp 26, 28-29; and "Friendship" [following a photograph of Carver and the two literary friends which is discussed in the essay], pp. 216-18.

3. The final, more difficult, and more sinister text here eliminated many of the connectives and explanatory details and even the more conventional paragraphing of the original version, which was initially entitled "Hooks," first published as "The View Finder" in *Iowa Review* 9, no. 1 (Winter 1978): 50-52, and subsequently reprinted with the present, even more succinct, title. Thomas Barrow called this story to the editor's attention.

4. See Jay, "The Photographer as Aggressor," in *Observations*, pp. 7-23.

VIEWFINDER

A man without hands came to the door to sell me a photograph of my house. Except for the chrome hooks, he was an ordinary-looking man of fifty or so.
"How did you lose your hands?" I asked after he'd said what he wanted.
"That's another story," he said. "You want this picture or not?"
"Come in," I said. "I just made coffee."
I'd just made some Jell-O, too. But I didn't tell the man I did.
"I might use your toilet," the man with no hands said.
I wanted to see how he would hold a cup.
I knew how he held the camera. It was an old Polaroid, big and black. He had it fastened to leather straps that looped over his shoulders and went

around his back, and it was this that secured the camera to his chest. He would stand on the sidewalk in front of your house, locate your house in the viewfinder, push down the lever with one of his hooks, and out would pop your picture.

I'd been watching from the window, you see.

"Where did you say the toilet was?"

"Down there, turn right."

Bending, hunching, he let himself out of the straps. He put the camera on the sofa and straightened his jacket.

"You can look at this while I'm gone."

I took the picture from him.

There was a little rectangle of lawn, the driveway, the carport, front steps, bay window, and the window I'd been watching from in the kitchen.

So why would I want a photograph of this tragedy?

I looked a little closer and saw my head, *my head*, in there inside the kitchen window.

It made me think, seeing myself like that. I can tell you, it makes a man think.

I heard the toilet flush. He came down the hall, zipping and smiling, one hook holding his belt, the other tucking in his shirt.

"What do you think?" he said. "All right? Personally, I think it turned out fine. Don't I know what I'm doing? Let's face it, it takes a professional."

He plucked at his crotch.

"Here's coffee," I said.

He said, "You're alone, right?"

He looked at the living room. He shook his head.

"Hard, hard," he said.

He sat next to the camera, leaned back with a sight, and smiled as if he knew something he wasn't going to tell me.

"Drink your coffee," I said.

I was trying to think of something to say.

"Three kids were by here wanting to paint my address on the curb. They wanted a dollar to do it. You wouldn't know anything about that, would you?"

It was a long shot. But I watched him just the same.

He leaned forward importantly, the cup balanced between his hooks. He set it down on the table.

"I work alone," he said. "Always have, always will. What are you saying?" he said.

"I was trying to make a connection," I said.

I had a headache. I know coffee's no good for it, but sometimes Jell-O helps. I picked up the picture.

"I was in the kitchen," I said. "Usually I'm in the back."

"Happens all the time," he said. "So they just up and left you, right? Now you take me. I work alone. So what do you say? You want the picture?"

"I'll take it," I said.

I stood up and picked up the cups.

"Sure you will," he said. "Me, I keep a room downtown. It's okay. I take a bus out, and after I've worked the neighborhoods, I go to another downtown. You see what I'm saying? Hey, I had kids once. Just like you," he said.

I waited with the cups and watched him struggle up from the sofa.

He said, "They're what gave me this."

I took a good look at those hooks.

"Thanks for the coffee and the use of the toilet. I sympathize."

He raised and lowered his hooks.

"Show me," I said. "Show me how much. Take more pictures of me and my house."

"It won't work," the man said. "They're not coming back."

But I helped him get into his straps.

"I can give you a rate," he said. "Three for a dollar." He said, "If I go any lower, I don't come out."

We went outside. He adjusted the shutter. He told me where to stand, and we got down to it.

We moved around the house. Systematic. Sometimes I'd look sideways. Sometimes I'd look straight ahead.

"Good," he'd say. "That's good," he'd say, until we'd circled the house and were back in the front again. "That's twenty. That's enough."

"No," I said. "On the roof," I said.

"Jesus," he said. He checked up and down the block. "Sure," he said. "Now you're talking."

I said, "The whole kit and kaboodle. They cleared right out."

"Look at this!" the man said, and again he held up his hooks.

I went inside and got a chair. I put it up under the carport. But it didn't reach. So I got a crate and put the crate on top of the chair.

It was okay up there on the roof.

I stood up and looked around. I waved, and the man with no hands waved back with his hooks.

It was then I saw them, the rocks. It was like a little rock nest on the screen over the chimney hole. You know kids. You know how they lob them up, thinking to sink one down your chimney.

"Ready?" I called, and I got a rock, and I waited until he had me in his viewfinder.

"Okay!" he called.

I laid back my arm and I hollered, "Now!" I threw that son of a bitch as far as I could throw it.

"I don't know," I heard him shout. "I don't do motion shots."

"Again!" I screamed, and took up another rock.

CYNTHIA OZICK

SHOTS

1982

———

Ozick (1928–), best known for her writings about Jewish subjects, also often explores the universal problems of all creative people, particularly the conflicting relationship between life and art. In "Shots," photography—whose "eeriness" draws Ozick because of the way it "represents both mortality and immortality"[1]—becomes a metaphor for writing or any creative act that tries to restore memory, whether to understand history or escape from it. The heroine, a photographer, is ultimately compelled to choose the camera over her lover, or art over life, becoming in the process the unchanging but lifeless picture of a young girl that initiated her career.[2] Ozick, always sensitive to the photograph's ability to reveal things both seen and unseen "as an impenetrable commentary on reality," often uses camera images in her writing.[3] Photographs, usually real but sometimes imaginary, appear as important symbols in many of her short stories, like the ones in "Freud's Room," and as evocative objects in some of her finest critical essays, like the ones about Edith Wharton as well as Virginia and Leonard Woolf. This fascination with pictures may have resulted because, as Ozick admitted, she had spent "more time drowning in old photographs in biographies than in the text."[4]

1. Ozick, quoted from interview with Elaine M. Kauvar, *Contemporary Literature* 26 (1985): 396. See also Haim Chartok, "Ozick's Hoofprints," *Yiddish* 4, no. 4 (1987): 5-12 for the fullest discussion of "Shots"; and Jay, "The Photographer as Aggressor," in *Observations*, 7-23.

2. It is interesting to compare Ozick's story with Alberto Moravia's "The Swollen Face," in *The Fetishist and Other Stories*, translated by Angus Davidson (New York: Farrar, Straus & Giroux, 1964), pp. 252-58, in which the wife of a photographer regards his camera as a rival to their relationship.

3. Ozick, quoted in *Contemporary Literature*, p. 397.

4. See Ozick: "Freud's Room," the first of the two fragments that compose "From a Refugee's Notebook," another short story in *Levitation* (New York: Dutton, 1983), pp. 59-63; "Justice (Again) to Edith Wharton," pp. 9-12, 17, 26, and "Mrs. Virginia Woolf: A Madwoman and Her Nurse," pp. 35-36, 54, in *Art and Ardor* (New York: Knopf, 1983); and Ozick, quoted in Kauvar, *Contemporary Literature*, p. 397. All these works are discussed, together with other relevant writings by Ozick, in Kauvar's useful overview, "Courier for the Past: Cynthia Ozick and Photography" in *The World of Cynthia Ozick*, edited by Daniel Walden, in *Studies in American Jewish Literature* 6 (Fall 1987): 129-46.

SHOTS

I came to photography as I came to infatuation—with no special talent for it, and with no point of view. Taking pictures—when *I* take them, I mean—has nothing to do with art and less to do with reality. I'm blind to what intelligent people call "composition," I revile every emanation of "grain," and any drag through a gallery makes me want to die. As for the camera as *machine*—well, I know the hole I have to look through, and I know how to press down with my finger. The rest is thingamajig. What brought me to my ingenious profession was no idea of the Photograph as successor to the Painting, and no pleasure in darkrooms, or in any accumulation of clanking detritus.

Call it necrophilia. I have fallen in love with corpses. Dead faces draw me. I'm uninformed about the history of photography—1832, the daguerreotype, mercury vapor; what an annoyance that so blatant a thing as picture-taking is considered worth applying a history to!—except to understand how long a past the camera has, measured by a century-old length of a woman's skirt. People talk of inventing a time machine, as if it hadn't already been invented in the box and shutter. I have been ravished by the last century's faces, now motes in their graves—such lost eyes, and noses, and mouths, and earlobes, and dress-collars: my own eyes soak these up; I can never leave off looking at anything brown and brittle and old and decaying at the edges.

The autumn I was eleven I found the Brown Girl. She was under a mound of chestnut-littered leaves near five tall trash barrels in a corner of the yard behind the Home for the Elderly Female Ill. Though the old-lady inmates were kept confined to a high balcony above the browning grass of their bleak overgrown yard, occasionally I would see some witless half-bald refugee shuffling through a weed-sea with stockings rolled midway down a sinewy blue calf engraved by a knotted garter. They scared me to death, these sticks and twigs of brainless ancients, rattling their china teeth and howling at me in foreign tongues, rolling the bright gems of their mad old eyes inside their nearly visible crania. I used to imagine that if one of these fearful witches could just somehow get beyond the gate, she would spill off garters and fake teeth and rheumy eye-whites and bad smells and stupid matted old flesh, and begin to bloom all plump and glowing and ripe again: Shangri-La in reverse.

What gave me this imagining was the Brown Girl. Any one of these pitiful decaying sacks might once have been the Brown Girl. If only someone had shot a kind of halt-arrow through the young nipples of the Brown Girl at the crest of her years, if only she had been halted, arrested, stayed in her ripeness and savor!

The Brown Girl lived. She lay in a pile of albums dumped into the leaves. It seemed there were hundreds of her: a girl in a dress that dropped to the buttons of her shoes, with an arched bosom and a hint of bustle, and a face mysteriously shut: you never once saw her teeth, you never once saw the lips in anything like the hope of a smile; laughter was out of the question. A grave girl; a sepia girl; a girl as brown as the ground. She must have had her sorrows.

Gradually (to my eyes suddenly) I saw her age. It wasn't that the plain sad big-nosed face altered: no crinkles at the lids, no grooves digging out a distinct little parallelogram from nostril-sides to mouth-ends—or, if these were in sight, they weren't what I noticed. The face faded out—became not there. The woman turned to ghost. The ghost wore different clothes now, too familiar to gape at. The fingers were ringless. The eyes whitened off. Somehow for this melancholy spinster's sake the first role of the box camera was always being violated: not to put the sun behind your subject. A vast blurred drowning orb of sun flooded massively, habitually down from the upper right corner of her picture Whoever photographed, over years and years and years, meant to obliterate her. But I knew it was no sunbleach that conspired to efface her. What I was seeing—what I *had* seen— was time. And not time on the move, either, the illusion of stories and movies. What I had seen was time as stasis, time at the standstill, time at the fix; the time (though I hadn't yet reached it in school) of Keats's Grecian urn. The face faded out because death was coming: death the changer, the collapser, the witherer; death the bleacher, blancher, whitener.

The truth is, I'm looked on as a close-mouthed professional, serious about my trade, who intends to shut up and keep secrets when necessary. I repel all "technical" questions—if someone wants to discuss the make of my camera (it's Japanese), or my favorite lens, or some trick I might have in developing, or what grade of paper I like, I'll stare her down. Moonings on Minor White's theories I regard as absolutely demeaning. I have a grasp on what I am about, and it isn't any of that.

What it is, is the Brown Girl. I kept her. I kept her, I mean, in a pocket of my mind (and one of her pictures in the pocket of my blouse); I kept her because she was dead. What I expect you to take from this is that I *could* keep her *even though* she was dead. I wasn't infatuated by her (not that she was the wrong sex: infatuation, like any passion of recognition, neglects gender); she was too oppressed and brown and quiet for that. But it was she who gave me the miraculous hint: a hint derived from no science of mechanics or physics, a rapturous hint on the other side of art, beyond metaphor, deep in the wonderfully literal. What she made me see was that if she wasn't a girl any more, if she wasn't a woman any more, if she was very likely not even a member of the elderly female ill any more (by the time her photos fell among the leaves, how long had she been lying under them?), still I *had* her, actually and physically and with the certainty of simple truth. I could keep her, just as she used to be, because someone had once looked through the bunghole of a box and clicked off a lever. Whoever had desultorily drowned her in too much sun had anyhow given her a monument two inches wide and three inches long. What happened then was here now. I had it in the pocket of my blouse.

Know this—that now will become then, that huge will turn little—doesn't cure. I walk around the wet streets with a historian now, a tenured professor of South American history: he doesn't like to go home to his wife. Somehow it always rains when we meet, and it's Sam's big blue umbrella, with a wooden horse's head for a handle, that preoccupies me this instant. Which is strange: he hasn't owned it for a whole year. It was left in a yellow garish coffee shop on the night side of a street you couldn't trust, and when Sam went back, only ten minutes later, to retrieve it, of course it wasn't there.

At that time I didn't care about one thing in Sam's mind. I had to follow him, on assignment, all through a course of some public symposia he was chairing. We had—temporarily—the same employer. His college was setting up a glossy little booklet for the State Department to win South American friends with: I had to shoot Sam on the podium with Uruguayans, Sam on the podium with Brazilians, Sam on the podium with Peruvians, and so forth. It was a lackluster job—I had just come, not so long ago, from photographing an intergalactic physicist whose bravest hope was the invention of an alphabet to shoot into the kindergartens of the cosmos—so it was no trouble at all not to listen to the speeches while I shot the principals. Half the speeches were in Portuguese or Spanish, and if you wanted to you could put on earphones anywhere in the hall and hear a simultaneous translation. The translator sat at the squat end of the long symposium table up on the stage with Sam and the others, but kept his microphone oddly close to his lips, like a kiss, sweat sliding and gleaming along his neck—it seemed he was tormented by that bifurcated concentration. His suffering attracted me. He didn't count as one of the principals—the celebrity of the day (now it was night, the last of the dark raining afternoon) was the vice-consul of Chile—but I shot him anyhow, for my own reasons: I liked the look of that shining sweat on his bulging Adam's apple. I calculated my aim (I'm very fast at this), shot once, shot again, and was amazed to see blood spring out of a hole in his neck. The audience fell apart—it was like watching an anthill after you've kicked into it; there was a spaghetti of wires and police; the simultaneous translator was dead. It made you listen for the simultaneous silence of the principal speaker, but the Chilean vice-consul only swerved his syllables into shrieks, with his coat over his head; he was walked away in a tremor between two colleagues suddenly sprouting guns. A mob of detectives took away my film; it was all I could do to keep them from arresting my camera. I went straight to Sam—it was his show—to complain. "That's *film* in there, not bullets." "It's evidence now," Sam said. "Who wanted to do that?" I said. "God knows," Sam said; "they didn't do what they wanted anyhow," and offered six political possibilities, each of which made it seem worthwhile for someone to do away with the Chilean vice-consul. He found his umbrella under the table and steered me out. The rain had a merciless wind in it, and every glassy sweep of it sent fountains spitting upward from the pavement. We stood for a while under his umbrella (he gripping the horse's head hard enough to whiten his knuckles) and watched them carry the simultaneous translator out. He was alone on a stretcher; his duality was done, his job as surrogate consummated. I reflected how quickly vertical becomes horizontal. "You knew him," I said.

"Only in a public way. He's been part of all these meetings."

"So have I," I said.

"I've watched you watching me."

I resisted this. "That's professional watching. It's more like stalking. I always stalk a bit before I shoot."

"You talk like a terrorist," Sam said, and began a history of South American conspiracy, which group was aligned with whom, who gave asylum, who withheld it, who the Chilean vice-consul's intimates across several borders were, at this instant plotting vengeance. He had exactly the kind of mentality—cumulative, analytical—I least admired, but since he also had the only umbrella in sight, I stuck with him. He was more interested in political factionalism—he had to get everything sorted out, and his fascination seemed to be with the victims—than in his having just sat two feet from a murder. "My God," I said finally, "doesn't the power of inaccuracy impress you? It could've been you on that stretcher."

"I don't suppose *you* ever miss your target," he said.

"No," I said, "but I don't shoot to kill."

"Then you're not one of those who want to change the world," he said, and I could smell in this the odor of his melancholy. He was a melancholic and an egotist; this made me a bit more attentive. His umbrella, it appeared, was going to pilot him around for miles and miles; I went along as passenger. We turned at last into a coffee shop—this wasn't the place he lost the horse's head in—and then turned out again, heated up, ready for more weather. "Don't you ever go home?" I asked him.

"Don't you?"

"I live alone."

"I don't. I hate my life," he said.

"I don't blame you. You've stuffed it up with South American facts."

"Would you like North American facts better?"

"I can't take life in whole continents," I protested.

"The thing about taking it in continents is that you don't have to take it face by face."

"The faces are the best part."

"Some are the worst," Sam said.

I looked into his; he seemed a victim of factionalism himself, as if you become what you study. He had rather ferocious eyes, much too shiny, like something boiling in a pot—the ferocity made you think them black, but really they were pale and black ripe rippled hair and unblemished orderly teeth, not white but near-white. "Which faces are the worst?"

"Now I'll go home," he said.

The murder had cut short the series of symposia; the South Americans scattered, which was too bad—they were Sam's source of vitality. But it never occurred to either of us that we might not meet again officially, and often enough we did—he on a platform, myself with camera. Whether this meant that all the magazine people I knew—the ones who were commissioning my pictures—were all at once developing a fevered concern for South American affairs (more likely it was for terrorism) is a boring question. I know *I* wasn't. I never wanted to listen to Sam on the subjects he was expert in, and I never did. I only caught what I thought of as their "moans"—impure and simmering and winnowing and sad. The sounds that came through his microphone were always intensely public: he was, his audience maintained—loyalists, they trotted after him from speech to speech—a marvelous generalist. He could go from predicting the demand for bauxite to tracing migrations of Indian populations, all in a single stanza. He could connect disparate packets of contemporary information with a linking historic insight that took your breath away. He was a very, very good public lecturer; all his claque said so. He could manage to make anyone (or everyone but me) care about South America. Still, I had a little trick in my head as he declaimed and as I popped my flashbulbs, not always at him—more often at the distinguished sponsors of the event. I could tell they were distinguished from the way they dragged me up to the dais to photograph them—it showed how important they were. Sometimes they wanted to be photographed just before Sam began, and sometimes, with their arms around him, when he was just finished, themselves grinning into Sam's applause. All the while I kept the little trick going.

The little trick was this: whatever he said that was vast and public and South American, I would simultaneously translate (I hoped I wouldn't be gunned down for it) into everything private and personal and secret. This required me to listen shrewdly to the moan behind the words—I had to blot out the words for the sake of the tune. Sometimes the tune would be civil or sweet or almost jolly—especially if he happened to get a look at me before he ascended to his lectern—but mainly it would be narrow and drab and resigned. I knew he had a wife, but I was already thirty-six, and who didn't have a wife by then? I wasn't likely to run into them if they didn't. Bachelors wouldn't be where I had to go, particularly not in public halls gaping at the per capita income of the interior villages of the Andes, or the future of Venezuelan oil, or the fortunes of the last Paraguayan bean crop, or the differences between the centrist parties in Bolivia and Colombia, or whatever it was that kept Sam ladling away at his tedious stew. I drilled through all these sober-shelled facts into their echoing gloomy melodies: and the sorrowful sounds I unlocked from their casings—it was like breaking open a stone and finding the music of the earth's wild core boiling inside—came down to the wife, the wife, the wife. That was the tune Sam was moaning all the while: wife wife wife. He didn't like her. He wasn't happy with her. His whole life was wrong. He was a dead man. If I thought I'd seen a dead man when they took that poor fellow out on that stretcher, I was stupidly mistaken; *he* was ten times deader than that. If the terrorist who couldn't shoot straight had shot *him* instead, he couldn't be more riddled with gunshot than he was this minute—he was smoking with his own death.

In the yellow garish coffee shop he went on about his wife—he shouldn't be telling me all this, my God, what the hell did he think he was doing; he was a fool; he was a cliché; he was out of a cartoon or an awful play; he was an embarrassment to himself and to me. It was either a trance or a seizure. And then he forgot his umbrella, and ran back after it, and it was gone. It wouldn't have had, necessarily, to be a desperate thief who stole his horse's head that night; it might easily have been a nice middle-class person like ourselves. A nice middle-class person especially would have hated to be out in such a drenching without a shred of defense overhead — Sam charged on into gales of cold rain, and made me charge onward too: for the first time he had me by the hand. I wouldn't let him keep it, though — I had to bundle my camera under my coat.

"How long are we going to walk in this?" I said.

"We'll walk and walk."

"I've got to go home or I'll soak my equipment," I complained.

"I'm not going home."

"Don't you ever go home?"

"My whole life is wrong," he said.

We spilled ourselves into another coffee place and sat there till closing. My shoes were seeping and seeping. He explained Verity: "I admire her," he said. "I esteem her, you wouldn't believe how I esteem that woman. She's a beautiful mother. She's strong and she's bright and she's independent and there's nothing she can't do."

"Now tell her good points," I said.

"She can fix a car. She always fixes the car. Puts her head into the hood and fixes it. She builds furniture. We live in a madhouse of excess property — she built every stick of it. She saws like a madwoman. She *sews* like a madwoman — I don't mean just *clothes*. She sews her own clothes and the girls' clothes too. What I mean is she *sews* — bedspreads and curtains and upholstery, even *car* upholstery. And she's got a whole budding career of her own. I've made her sound like a bull, but she's really very delicate at whatever she does — she does plates, you know."

"License plates?"

"She's done *some* metalwork — her minor was metallurgy — but what I'm talking about is ceramics. Porcelain. She does painted platters and pots and pitchers and sells them to Bloomingdale's."

"She's terrific," I said.

"She's terrific," he agreed. "There's nothing she can't do."

"Cook?"

"My God, *cook*," he said. "French, Italian, Indian, whatever you want. And bakes. Pastries, the difficult stuff, crusts made of cloud. She's a domestic genius. We have this big harp — hell, it was busted, a skeleton in a junk shop, so she bought it cheap and repaired it—she plays it like an angel. You think you're in heaven inside that hell. She plays the piano, too—classics, ragtime, rock. She's got a pretty nice singing voice. She's good at basketball —she practically never misses a shot. Don't ask me again if I admire her."

I asked him again if he admired her.

"I'm on my knees," he groaned. "She's a goddamn goddess. She's powerful and autonomous and a goddamn genius. Christ," he said, "I hate my life."

"If I had someone like that at home," I said, "I'd never be out in the rain."

"She could abolish the weather if she wanted to, only she doesn't want to. She has a terrific will."

I thought this over and was surprised by my sincerity: "You ought to go home," I told him.

"Let's walk."

After that we met more or less on purpose. The South American fad wore off—there was a let-up in guerrilla activity down there—and it got harder to find him in public halls, so I went up to his college now and then and sat in on his classes, and afterward, rain or shine, but mostly rain, we walked. He told me about his daughters—one of them was nearly as terrific as Verity herself—and we walked with our arms hooked. "Is something happening here?" I inquired. "Nothing will ever happen here," he said. We had a friend in common, the editor who'd assigned me to photographing that intergalactic physicist I've mentioned; it turned out we were asked, Sam with Verity, myself as usual, to the editor's party, in honor of the editor's ascension. There were some things the editor hadn't done which added immensely to his glory; and because of all the things he hadn't done they were making him vice-chancellor of Sam's college. I did justice to those illustrious gaps and omissions: I took the host, now majestic, and his wife, their children, their gerbil, their maid. I shot them embedded in their guests. I dropped all those pictures behind me like autumn leaves. I hadn't brought my usual Japanese spy, you see; I'd carried along a tacky Polaroid instead—instant development, a detective story without a detective, ah, I disliked that idea, but the evening needed its jester. I aimed and shot, aimed and shot, handing out portraits deciduously. Verity had her eye on all this promiscuity; she was blond and capacious and maybe capricious; she seemed without harm and without mercy.

"You're the one who shot the simultaneous translator," she said.

"Judicial evidence," I replied.

"Now let me," she said, "ask you something about your trade. In photography, do you consistently get what you expect?"

I said: "It's the same as life."

Verity expressed herself: "The viewfinder, the viewfinder!"

"I always look through that first," I admitted.

"And then do you get what you see? I mean can you predict exactly, or are you always surprised by what comes out?"

"I can never predict," I told her, "but I'm never surprised."

"That's fatalism," Verity said. Her voice was an iron arrow; she put her forefinger into my cheek as humbly as a bride. "Talk about shots, here's a parting one. You take a shot at Sam, no expectations. He's not like life. He's safe. He's *good.*"

He was safe and he was good: Sam the man of virtue. She knew everything exactly, even when everything was nothing she knew it exactly, she was without any fear at all; jealousy wasn't in her picture; she was more virtuous than he was, she was big, she had her great engine, she was her own cargo. And you see what it is with infatuation: it comes on you as quick as a knife. It's a bullet in the neck. It gets you from the outside. One moment you're in your prime of health, the next you're in anguish. Until then—until I had the chance to see for myself how clear and proud his wife was—Sam was an entertainment, not so entertaining after all. Verity was the Cupid of the thing, Verity's confidence the iron arrow that dragged me down. She had her big foot on her sour catch. I saw in her glow, in her sureness, in her pride, in her tall ship's prow of certitude, the plausibility of everything she knew: he'd have to go home in the end.

But the end's always at the end; in the meantime there's the meantime.

How to give over these middle parts? I couldn't see what I looked like, from then on, to Sam: all the same I had my automatic intelligence—light acting on a treated film. I was treated enough; Verity had daubed me. Since I was soaked in her solution, infatuation took, with me, a mechanical form—if you didn't know how mechanical it was, you would have imagined it was sly. I could listen now to everything Sam said. Without warning, I could *follow* him; I discovered myself in the act of wanting more. I woke up one morning in a fit of curiosity about the quantity of anthracite exports on the Brazilian littoral. I rooted in hard-to-find volumes of Bolívar's addresses. I penetrated the duskier hells of the public library and boned up on every banana republic within reach. It was astounding: all at once, and for no reason—I mean for *the* reason—Sam interested me. It was like walking on the lining of his brain.

On the South American issue he was dense as a statue. He had never noticed that I hadn't paid attention to his subject before; he didn't notice that I was attentive now. His premise was that everyone alive without exception was all the time infatuated with the former Spanish Empire. On *my* subject, though, Sam was trying; it was because of Verity; she had made him ambitious to improve himself with me.

"Verity saw at that party," he said, "that you had the kind of camera that gets you the picture right away."

"Not exactly right away. You have to wait a minute," I corrected.

"Why don't you use a camera like that all the time? It's magic. It's like a miracle."

"Practical reasons of the trade. The farther you are from having what you think you want, the more likely you are to get it. It's just that you have to wait. You really have to *wait*. What's important is the waiting."

Sam didn't get it. "But it's *chemistry*. The image is already on the film. It's the same image one minute later or two months later."

"You're too miracle-minded even for a historian," I admonished him. "It's not like that at all. If you have a change of heart between shooting your picture and taking it out of the developer, the picture changes too." I wanted to explain to him how, between the exposure and the solution, history comes into being, but telling that would make me bleed, like a bullet in the neck, so I said instead, "Photography is *literal*. It gets what's *there*."

Meanwhile the rain is raining on Sam and me. We meet in daylight now, and invent our own occasions. We hold hands, we hook arms, we walk through the park. There is a mole on his knuckle which has attached itself to my breathing; my lungs grasp all the air they can. I want to lay my tears on the hairs of his fingers. Because of the rain, the daylight is more like twilight; in this perpetual half of dusk, the sidewalks a kind of blackened purple, like fallen plums, we talk about the past and the future of the South American continent. Verity is in her house. I leave my camera behind too. Our faces are rivers, we walk without an umbrella, the leaves splash. When I can't find Sam on my own, I telephone Verity; she stops the motor of her sewing machine and promises to give him the message when he returns. He comes flying out to meet me, straight from his Committee on Inter-American Conditions; I'm practically a colleague now, and a pleasure to talk to about Ecuadorian peonage. He tells me he's never had a mistress and never will; his wife is too remarkable. I ask him whether he's ever walked in a summer rain this way with anyone else. He admits he has; he admits it hasn't lasted. "The rain hasn't lasted? Or the feeling?" He forgets to answer. I remember that *he* is only interested; it's I who feel. We talk some more about the native religions still hiding out in the pampas; we talk about the Jewish gauchos in nineteenth-century Argentina. He takes it all for granted. He doesn't realize how hard I've had to study. A big leaf like a pitcher overturns itself all over our heads, and we make a joke about Ponce de Léon and the Fountain of Youth. I ask him then if he'll let me take his picture in the park, under a dripping linden tree, in a dangerous path, so that I can keep him forever, in case it doesn't last.

I see that he doesn't understand. He doesn't understand: unlike me, he's not under any special spell, he's not in thrall to any cult. That's the rub always—infatuation's unilateral or it doesn't count as real. I think he loves me—he may even be "in love"—but he's not caught like me. He'd never trace my life over as I've traced over his brain waves. He asks me why I want to shoot him under the linden tree. I tell him the truth I took from his wife: virtue ravishes me. I want to keep its portrait. I am silent about the orphaned moment we're living in now, how it will leave us. I feel, I feel our pathos. We are virtue's orphans. The tree's green shoots are fleeting; all green corrupts to brown. Sam denies that he's a man of virtue. It's only his guilt about Verity; she's too terrific to betray.

He consents to having his picture taken in the sopping park if I agree to go home with him afterward.

I say in my amazement, "I can't go home with you. She's *there*."

"She's always there."

"Then how can I go home with you?"

"You have to *see*. It's all been too obscure. I want you to know what I know."

"I know it, you've told me. You've told and told."

"You have to get the smell of it. Where I am and how I live. Otherwise you won't believe in it. You won't know it," he insists. "Such cozy endurances."

"You endure them," I said.

"Yesterday," he said, "she brought home a box of old clothes from the Salvation Army. From a thrift shop. From an old people's home, who knows where she got it from. Pile of rags. She's going to sew them into God's bright ribbons. A patchwork quilt. She'll spin straw into gold, you'll see."

"She's terrific."

"She's a terrific wife," he says.

We walk to my place, pick up my camera—I stop to grab my light meter for the rain's sake—and walk crosstown to the park again. I shoot Sam, the man of virtue, under the dripping linden tree. Although I am using my regular equipment, it seems to me the picture's finished on the spot. It's as if I roll it out and fix it then and there. Sam has got his back against the bark, and all the little wet leaves lick down over his bumpy hair. He resembles a Greek runner resting. His face is dappled by all those heart-shaped leaves, and I know that all the rest of my life I'll regret not having shot him in the open, in a field. But my wish for now is to speckle him and see him darkle under the rainy shade of a tree. It comes to me that my desire—oh, my desire! it stings me in the neck—is just now not even for Sam's face: it's for the transitoriness of these thin vulnerable leaves, with their piteous veins turned upward toward a faintness of liverish light.

We walk the thirty-one blocks, in the quickening rain, to his place. It's only a four-room apartment, but Verity's made a palace of it. Everything plain is converted into a sweetness, a furriness, a thickness of excess. She weaves, she knits. She's an immense spider building out of her craw. The floors are piled with rugs she's woven, the chairs with throws she's knit. She's cemented up a handy little fireplace without a flue; it really works, and on a principle she invented herself. She's carpentered all the bookcases— I catch the titles of the four books Sam's written; he's a dignitary and a scholar, after all—and overhead there wafts and dazzles the royal chandelier she found in the gutter and refurbished. Each prism slid through her polishing and perfecting fingers. Verity resurrects. Verity's terrific—you can't avoid thinking it. She's got her big shoulders mounted over her sewing machine in the corner of the living room, hemming brown squares. "It's weird, you wouldn't believe it," she says, "*all* the stuff in this box they gave me is brown. It's good rich fabric, though—a whole load of clothes from dead nuns. You know what happened? A convent dissolved, the young nuns broke their vows and ran to get married."

"That's *your* story," Sam says.

Verity calls her daughter—only one of the girls is at home, the other is away at college. Clearly this one isn't the daughter that's so much like Verity. She has a solemn hard flank of cheek, and no conversation. She carries out a plate of sliced honey cake and three cups of tea; then she hides herself in her bedroom. A radio is in there; gilded waves of Bach tremble out of it. I look around for Verity's harp.

"Hey, let's dress you up," Verity says out of her teacup; she's already downed a quantity of cake. "There's stuff in that box that would just fit you. You've got a waist like our girls. I wish *I* had a waist like that." I protest; I tell her it's too silly. Sam smolders with his sour satisfaction, and she churns her palms inside the box like a pair of oars. She pulls out a long skirt, and a blouse called a bodice, and another blouse to wear under that, with long sleeves. Sam pokes my spine and nudges me into the girl's bedroom, where there's a tall mirror screwed into the back of the door. I look at myself.

"Period piece!" says Verity.

I'm all in brown, as brown as leaves. The huge high harp, not gold as

I imagined it but ivory, is along the wall behind me. I believe everything Sam has told about the conquistadore. I believe everything he's told about Verity. He's a camera who never lies. His wet hair is black as olives. He belongs to his wife, who's terrific. She's put a nun's bonnet on herself. She has an old-fashioned sense of fun—the words come to me out of, I think, Louisa May Alcott: she likes costume and dress-up. Soon she will have us guessing riddles and playing charades. They are a virtuous and wholesome family. The daughter, though her look is bone, is fond of Bach; no junk music in such a household. They are sweeter than the whole world outside. When Sam is absent the mother and her daughter climb like kittens into a knitted muff.

I shoot Verity wearing the nun's bonnet.

"Look at *you!*" she cries.

I return to the mirror to see. I am grave; I have no smile. My face is mysteriously shut. I'm suffering. Lovesick and dreamsick, I'm dreaming of my desire. I am already thirty-six years old, tomorrow I will be forty-eight years old, and a crafty parallelogram begins to frame the space between my nose and mouth. My features are very distinct—I will live for years and years before they slide out of the mirror. I'm the Brown Girl in the pocket of my blouse. I reek of history. If, this minute, I could glide into a chemical solution, as if in a gondola, splashed all over and streaming with wet silver, would the mirror seize and fix me, like a photographic plate? I watch Sam's eyes, poached and pale and mottled with furious old civilizations, steaming hatred for his wife. I trip over the long drapery of my nun's hem. All the same I catch up my camera without dropping it—my ambassador of desire, my secret house with its single shutter, my chaste aperture, my dead infant, husband of my bosom. Their two heads, hers light, his black, negatives of each other, are caught side by side in their daughter's mirror. I shoot into their heads, the white harp behind. Now they are exposed. Now they will stick forever.

SOURCES AND CREDITS

Bing, Xin (aka Ping Hsin). [Xie Wanying]. "The Photograph" (c. 1933). In *The Photograph*. Translated by Jeff Book. Beijing: Panda Books, 1992. Reprinted by permission of the Chinese Literature Press.

Calvino, Italo. "Adventures of a Photographer" (1955). In *Difficult Loves*. Translated by William Weaver, Archibald Colquhoun, and Peggy Wright. San Diego: Harcourt Brace Jovanovich, 1984. Originally an adaptation of "La Follia del mirino," which appeared in *Il Contemporaneo* (April 30, 1955): 12. The story is included in the 1970 edition of *Gli Amori Difficili* (Turin: Einaudi, 1970), but not in the 1958 edition. Copyright 1955 by Guilio Einaudi, editore, Turino. English translation copyright 1983 by Harcourt Brace & Company, reprinted by permission of Harcourt Brace & Company.

Carver, Raymond. "View Finder," *Iowa Review* 9, no. 1 (Winter 1978): 50-52. Reprinted with revisions as "Viewfinder" in *What We Talk About When We Talk About Love*, New York: Alfred A. Knopf, 1981; in *A Reader of New American Fiction*, edited by Robert Fromberg and Rebecca Best, Peoria, Ill.: I-74 Press, 1981; and in *See* 1, no. 1 (Autumn 1994): 14-15. Copyright 1981 by Raymond Carver. Reprinted by permission of Alfred A. Knopf, Inc.

Cortázar, Julio. "Blow-Up," 1959. In *End of the Game and Other Stories*. Translated by Paul Blackburn. New York: Pantheon, 1967. Reprinted in *Blow Up and Other Stories*, New York: Pantheon 1985, pp. 114-31. Originally published as "Las babas del diablo" in *Las Armas Secretas*, Buenos Aires:

Editorial Sudamerica, 1959. Copyright 1967 by Random House, Inc. Reprinted by permission of Pantheon Books, a division of Random House, Inc.

Davenport, Guy. "The Invention of Photography in Toledo," *Parenthèse* 3 (1976): 141–49. Revised version [used here] in *Da Vinci's Bicycle: Ten Stories*. Baltimore: Johns Hopkins University Press, 1979. Reprinted by permission of the publisher.

Doyle, Sir Arthur Conan. "A Scandal in Bohemia," *Strand Magazine* 2 (July 1891): 61–75. Reprinted in *The Complete Sherlock Holmes*, New York: Doubleday [1960, 1970], and widely elsewhere.

Du Maurier, Daphne. "The Little Photographer." In *The Apple Tree: A Short Novel and Some Stories*, London: Gollancz, 1952; and *Kiss Me Again, Stranger: A Collection of Eight Stories Long and Short*, New York: Doubleday, 1953. Copyright 1953. Reprinted in *The Birds and Other Stories*, London: Pan, 1977, and Arrow, 1992. Used by permission of Doubleday, a division of Bantam Doubleday Dell Publishing Group, Inc.

Faulkner, William. "Evangeline" (1925). In *The Uncollected Stories of William Faulkner*, edited by Joseph Blotner. New York: Random House, 1979. Copyright 1979 by William Faulkner. Reprinted by permission of Random House, Inc.

Hardy, Thomas. "An Imaginative Woman" [1893], *Pall Mall Magazine* 2, no. 12 (April 1894): 951–69. Reprinted in *Wessex Tales*, London: Osgood McIlvaine; New York: Harper & Brothers [1896]; then as the opening story in *Life's Little Ironies*, London: Macmillan, 1912.

Hornung, E. W. "A Spoilt Negative," *Belgravia* 65 (March 1888): 76–89.

Ionesco, Eugène. "The Colonel's Photograph." In *The Colonel's Photograph*, translated by Jean Stewart. New York: Grove, 1969. Originally published as "La Photo du Colonel," in *[La Nouvelle] Nouvelle Revue Française* 4 (November 1, 1955): 890–904. Copyright © by Editions Gallimard. Translation copyright © 1967 by Faber and Faber Limited. Reprinted by permission of Georges Borchardt.

Kipling, Rudyard. "At the End of the Passage," *Sunday Herald* [Boston] (July 20, 1890): 23. Reprinted in *Lippincott's Magazine* 46 (August 1890): 246–60; in *Life's Handicap; Being Stories of Mine Own People*, London, New York: Macmillan, 1892, and later; in *Mine Own People*, New York: Lovell, 1891, with an introduction by Henry James; and in W. Somerset Maugham, *Maugham's Choice of Kipling's Best*, Garden City, N.Y.: Doubleday, 1953.

Mann, Thomas. "Gladius Dei" (1902). In *Stories of Three Decades*, translated by H. T. Lowe Porter. New York: Alfred A. Knopf, 1979. Copyright 1936 by Alfred A. Knopf, Inc. Reprinted by permission of the publisher.

Ozick, Cynthia. "Shots." In *Levitation: Five Fictions*. New York: Alfred A. Knopf, 1982. Copyright © 1982 by Cynthia Ozick. Reprinted by permission of Alfred A. Knopf.

Tournier, Michel. "Veronica's Shrouds." In *The Fetishist*, translated by Barbara Wright. London: Collins, 1983; New York: Doubleday, 1984. Originally published as "Les Suaires de Veronique," *Le Coq de Bruyèr*, Paris: Gallimard, 1978. Copyright © 1983 by Doubleday, a division of Bantam Doubleday Dell Publishing Group, Inc., and William Collins Sons & Company, Ltd. Used by permission of Doubleday, a division of Bantam Doubleday Dell Publishing Group, Inc.

Updike, John. "The Day of the Dying Rabbit," *New Yorker* 45 (August 30, 1969): 22–26. Reprinted in *Museums and Woman and Other Stories*, New York, Alfred A. Knopf, 1972. Copyright © 1972 by John Updike. Reprinted by permission of Alfred A. Knopf, Inc.